3 0250 01354 6382

D0221144

F
851
C 68
1983
v. 1

DICTIONARY OF SPANISH PLACE NAMES

OF THE NORTHWEST COAST OF AMERICA

VOLUME I CALIFORNIA

BY

RENÉ COULET DU GARD

Editions des Deux Mondes

ABOUT THE AUTHOR

René Coulet du Gard was born in Algeria of French parents. He came to t
United States in 1952. He earned his Ph.D. at the Université de Besançon, Franc

He is the author of 35 books and received several literary awards among th
the PRIX DE LA FONDATION DE LA LANGUE FRANCAISE, and the PRIX D'HI
TOIRE awarded to him by the illustrious Académie Française; also the GRAND PR
DU ROMAN D'AVENTURES, by the Société des Arts et Lettres d'Algérie, and PR
DE LA MEDAILLE d'OR (Gold medal award) by the famous Académie Internation
de Lutèce, Paris, France.

René Coulet du Gard, is professor of French Language and Literature at t
University of Delaware. In 1977 the French Government honored him with the ti
and privileges of "Officier des Palmes Académiques".

ISBN: 0-939586-01-0

All rights reserved
Copyright 1983 by Editions des Deux Mondes
This book may not be reproduced in whole or in part,
by mimeograph or other means, without permission.

BY THE SAME AUTHOR

Poémes pour dire... Grassin, Paris, 1964

Feux Follets, poèmes, Ed. du Sphinx, 1969 (Seconde Edition,1970).

L'Anthologie des Poètes et Prosateurs Francophones de l'Amérique Septentrionale, vol. I and II, Ed. des Deux Mondes, 1970-1971.

L'Arithmosophie de Gérard de Nerval, Essai, Ed. des Deux Mondes 1972 (Médaille d'Argent Académie Internationale de Lutèce, Paris).

Reine, Novel. Ed. de la Revue Moderne, Paris, 1974. (Médaille d'Or, Académie Internationale de Lutèce, Paris).

The Handbook of French Place Names in the U.S.A., Ed. des Deux Mondes, U.S.A., 1974. Second edition, 1976.

L'Oiseau de Feu, poèmes de Yar Slavutych, traduit et adapté de l'Ukrainien par René Coulet du Gard, Ed. Slavuta, Canada, 1976.

La France Contemporaine de 1900 à 1976, Ed. Slavuta, Canada, 1976.

French Place Names in the U.S.A., published by the Cultural Services of the French Embassy, Washington, 1976.

Le Fruit défendu, poèmes historiques, Ed. Chantecler, 1976. Illustrations by Régine Coulet du Gard.

Pleure pas P'tit Bonhomme, Ed. du Vent, 1977.

Le prisonnier, roman, Ed. CEL, 1978.

Les fruits verts, short stories, Ed. Naaman, Canada, 1979.

La course et la piraterie en Méditérranéé, 1980, Ed. France-Empire, Paris.

Handbook of American Counties, Parishes and Independent Cities, Editions des Deux Mondes, 1980.

ACKNOWLEDGEMENTS

We would like to acknowledge the generous help of the mayors and municipal managers, the archivists and historians of the State of California who helped us with our project. A special mention of gratitude to Ms. Donna Swartz who helped us with our compilation and secretarial work.

TABLE OF CONTENTS

INTRODUCTION

Since the beginnings of civilization human beings have developed an inextinguishable thirst for the unknown . . . sometimes with fear, often with hope, and their eyes looking with wonder at the immensity of the oceans before them, they have dared to venture toward far away mysterious lands. To this unquenchable thirst to know more was added an immeasurable imagination that very often drove the adventurers, these indefatigable explorers of all times, to accomplish the boldest feats. We witness, then, a true maritime epic, for it was necessary to conquer first the oceans before reaching the "lost and unknown horizons". A handful of seamen, scattered themselves over the surface of the globe, in the beginning with shyness, then with an extraordinary boldness. The first discoveries, filled with legends, reinforced the lords' desires to lay hands on the fabulous treasures described by the navigators, who had heard stories about their existence. The Christian Kings dreamed of two things: to conquer these lands filled with wonders and to convert the savages who inhabited them to the Christian faith.

In the XVth century Spain ranked first among nations in the extent of its voyages and discoveries. In 1492, six years before Vasco da Gama reached India, Christopher Columbus had discovered and claimed the Bahama Islands, Cuba and Hispaniola for Ferdinand II and Isabela I of Spain. Columbus made four voyages to America in which he discovered the Greater Antilles, many of the lesser islands, and the mainland coasts of modern Venezuela, Central America and modern Panama.

Several Spanish voyagers had traced the South American Main from the Brazilian shoulder to the Isthmus of Panama. Americo Vespucci of Florence sailing under the Portuguese flag, had followed the continent southward to Patagonia.

The rulers of Spain and Portugal, by the Treaty of Tordesillas (1494), partitioned the non-Christian world between them by an imaginary line in the Atlantic 370 leagues west of the Cape Verde Islands. Spain could claim everything to the west of the line, Portugal everything to the east. In 1519 Ferdinand Magellan's circumnavigation of the earth proved that it was round.

By 1512 Spain had completed the occupation of the larger West Indian Islands. In 1513 Vasco Nunez de Balboa made his famous march to the Pacific. Balboa was judically murdered by Pedrarias Davila who turned his attention to Central America and founded Nicaragua. Diego Velazquez, explored the Maya Civilization of Yucatan. In 1519 Hernan Cortes fought the Aztec confederation of Mexico; later on Guatemala and part of Yucatan were conquered. Mexico yielded great quantity of gold and silver and the Spaniards thought that the North was even richer. Explorations northward by land (Alvar Nunez, Cabeza de Vaca, Hernando de Soto, and Francisco Vasquez Coronado) and by sea (Juan Rodriguez Cabrillo) brought a great deal of geographical knowledge but not the fabulous treasures they were expecting.

In 1531 the Pizarro brothers invaded the Inca Empire from Panama and proceeded with its conquest. By-products of the Inca conquest were the seizure of northern Chile by Pedro de Valdivia and the descent of the entire Amazon by Francisco de Orellana.

By 1550 the Spanish Empire in America was basically formed. The Spanish sovereigns created the "Casa de Contratacion" (the house of Trade) to regulate commerce between Spain and the New World. Their purpose was to make the trade monopolistic and thus pour the maximum amount of bullion into the royal treasury. But Spain did not succeed because it failed to provide necessary manufactured goods for its colonies. Foreign competitors appeared, and smuggling grew.

i

The viceregal system started in 1535 when Antonio de Mendoza was sent to govern New Spain (Mexico). In 1542 a second viceroy was named and two more viceroyalties: Granada (1739) and Rio de la Plata (1776) were formed. The problem early faced and never solved by the Spanish colonial regime was that of the Indians. According to the "encomienda" Indian groups were entrusted to Spanish proprietors who were to care for their welfare in exchange for rights to tribute and labour. The Spanish proprietors abused and enslaved them. Spanish Dominican friars were the first to condemn the "encomienda" (royal land grant, with Indian inhabitants) and work for its abolition. When Dominican zeal declined, the Jesuit order became the major Indian protector and led in missionary activity until its expulsion from the Spanish Empire in 1767. California had received scant attention from Europeans for more than three centuries after its first sighting in 1542 by the Spanish navigator Juan Rodriguez Cabrillo.

In 1565 Urdaneta made the first trip eastward across the Pacific, opening a northern route, which was used by the Manila traders for more than two centuries. In 1584, Francisco de Gali, coming from the west, reached the coast in $37^\circ 30'$, possibly $57^\circ 30'$, but he did not land. By a similar route Cermenon was wrecked in 1595 at Drake Bay, just above the present San Francisco. In 1602-03 Sebastian Vizcaino sailed the Southern California coast. He anchored at Monterey without landing at the old San Francisco under Point Reyes. Thence he went as high as 42°, where he named a "Cabo Blanco de San Sebastian". His associate Aguilar possibly reached 43° at another "Cabo Blanco", where there seemed to be the mouth of a great river. During his visit Vizcaino named: San Diego, Santa Catalina Island, Santa Barbara and Monterey Bay.

Despite these early explorations, however, California was left to its relatively primitive Indians. Pressure for settlement came from missionaries anxious to convert the Indians and from the intrusion of Russian and British trades, primarily in search of sea-otter pelts. In 1769 the Spanish viceroy dispatched land and sea expeditions from Baja California, and the Franciscan friar Junipero Serra established the first mission at San Diego. Gaspar de Portola set up a military outpost in 1770 at Monterey. It is really after 1773 that colonization of California began with the opening of an overland supply route across the southwestern deserts. The development of early California rests mostly on the twenty one missions established by Junipero Serra and his successors.

The period which deals with California and the Pacific Northwest Coast between 1773 and 1851 is rich in Spanish onomastics, and the first part of this publication will be devoted exclusively to the "Spanish Place Names in California". As the explorations of the Northwest Pacific Coast continued, Spanish onomastic history was well represented. We will try to revive the glorious past of Spain in these regions through its toponymic heritage.

The names of illustrious Spanish navigators, pilots and explorers will mark the period of the land discoveries from California to Alaska. Our first endeavor is to rediscover Spanish place names that existed at one time and that disappeared by chance or by the political ambition of another nation jealous of Spanish heritage. One has the right to question: Why, if Spain was so powerful in the XVIth century and so ambitious in the XVIIIth century to pursue her destiny in North American explorations and colonizations, why didn't she keep the fruit of her discoveries? Very often true credit was not given to the Spanish explorers or adventurers who visited unknown countries. More than once discoveries were not registered, the maps not chartered, or chartered with years of delay, not published, etc., at least these will explain the continuous quarrels between Spain and Great Britain concerning their voyages along the Northern Pacific Coast. To add to this onomastic conflict, the U.S., Great Britain, and Canada in many instances renamed former Spanish place names, although often these toponyms bear traces of the Spanish origin in the translation or mention the former Spanish naming. The quest for a "Northwest Passage" was certainly the strongest ingredient which led Russia, France, England and Spain to the northern lands. The legendary adventures of

Juan de Fuca, the real explorations of those who followed are depicted in this "onomastic excursion" and there, we see how history, legend, politics, tóponymy blend together to give life as a whole.

We will show the role played by the real actors of the "Northwest Coast" a cast as colorful as it is varied. Bering, Heceta, Cook, La Pérouse, Quadra, Maurelle, Meares, Vancouver, Gray . . . in short a cast of a hundred names. We will follow them in their daily combat and we will witness their hope, their joy, their disappointment, their surprise, their faith, their humour (good and bad), their enterprising mind, their respect for the first inhabitants, their gallantry and their greed; their treachery, their nostalgia for the motherland and those who were left far away, in short we will study this humanity and share their daily life.

We will find out that Spanish toponyms of the northwest coast are rich in religious expressions. The "Saints" dominate the scene, since faith was the greatest factor of the Spanish Conquest wherever it went; the descriptive toponyms are as abundant as the illustrious people; Indian names were translated (many times erroneously) into Spanish, then into English, to come back often in a new Spanish form that was scarcely recognizable. Very often the onomastic science surrendered to the victor of the moment, a human phenomenon encountered particularly in North America. The political forces that eventually governed North America determined the naming of former Spanish discoveries, however, the Spanish imprint remained in regions they had long occupied and the following American States are the richest in Spanish nomenclature: California, Texas, New Mexico, Florida, Arizona, Utah, Nevada, Oklahoma, even the states of Alaska, Oregon and Washington, with their neighbor British Columbia have kept a great number of Spanish toponyms. What is the reason for this? Recognition of the courage of these heroes whose past seems to vanish little by little into the night of time and oblivion created by a human race that adopts the will of the strongest and last occupant?

The westward march belongs to the American epic as well as the legends of Daniel Boone, Davy Crockett, Francis Marion that are part of the American history. Spanish exploration of the Pacific Northwest should be shown in its reality in order to reinforce the meaning of human ideals that reach sometimes to the sublime.

We hope this handbook will receive the same warm encouragements which were expressed by the readers of our previous: *Handbook of French Place Names in the U.S.A.*, and the *Handbook of American Counties, Parishes and Independent Cities*. We are confident that the *Dictionary of Spanish Place Names of the Northwest Coast of America*, will continue with your help to be the success of our endless journey through the field of onomastics.

ABALONE POINT   Los Angeles

Sp. "sea snail" Located southeast of San Pedro Bay, it was so named because of the abundance of the great sea snails called "abalone", whose iridescent shells once covered the beaches of California. This sea snail once formed a useful part of the food supply of the Indians.

ACAMPO   San Joaquin

Sp. "common pasture" Used here in the sense of "camp". It commemorates colony of wood choppers which was located here at the time of the completion of Southern Pacific Railroad's San Joaquin Valley Line circa 1876.

ACOLITA   Imperial

Origin unrevealed. Feminine form of acolyte or assistant.

ADELANTO   San Bernardino

"progress or advance" Possibly applied by forward-looking community builder of which California had many. The post office was established in 1917.

ADOBE

The name is common in about 30 features in the state. From the Spanish, for the sun-aked bricks introduced to Spain by the Arabs.

AGUA

A common generic geographical term of Spanish origin meaning "water". It appears frequently with the modifying adjectives "caliente" (hot or warm), fria (cold), buena (good), tibia (tepid), mansa (quiet), dulce (sweet), hedionda (stinking), amargosa (bitter), escondida (hidden) mala (bad), puerca (muddy).

AGUA ALTA CANYON   Riverside

Spanish words meaning "high water canyon"

AGUA CALIENTE CANYON   Sonoma Co.

From a land grant of May 7, 1836; regranted July 13, 1840.

AGUA CALIENTE CREEK   Alameda

Spanish "hot water" from a land grant of October 13, 1836.

AGUA CALLIENTE CREEK; Canada Caliente   San Diego

The name appears officially in the Valle de San Jose y Agua Caliente land grant of June 4, 1840.

AGUAS FRIAS   Butte and Glenn

Land grant of November 9, 1844 to Salvadore Osio. It means "cold waters".

AGUA FRIO CREEK   Mariposa

From Agua Fria Mine. Mining camp of 50's shown on map of mines a short distance west of Mariposa on tributary to Mariposa Creek.

AGUA GRANDE CANYON   Monterey

"Great Water Canyon"

AGUA HEDIONDA CREEK   San Diego

First viewed by Portola-Crespi expedition on July 17, 1769. Called area San Simon Lipnica. "Foul, stinking water". Land grant of August 10, 1842.

AGUA MANSA RANCHO   Riverside

Part of Jurupa Rancho obtained in 1841. Lorenzo Trujillo's New Mexican colony. The settlement established on the rancho was called "San Salvador". Colloquial meaning "quiet water".

AGUAS NIEVES   Butte

Mexican land grants, December 22, 1844.

AGUA PUERCA Y LAS TRANCAS RANCHO   Santa Cruz

Area granted October 31, 1843 to Ramon Rodriguez and Francisco Alviso. Colloquial name stems from east and west boundaries of grant: Cañada de Agua Puerca (glen of dirty water) and Cañada de las Trancas (glen of cudgels).

AGUA TIBIA   San Diego

Community meaning tepid water was projected as one of South California's boom towns of 80's but never developed farther than promotion stage. Absurd stories because of poor translation have been given. A writer mixed up the Spanish word "tibia" (tepid, lukewarm) with the latin "tibia" (the bone of the lower leg), thus the "shinbone water". In another case the absurd translation of "flute water" was given.

AGUA TIBIA MOUNTAINS   San Diego

It is located in the Cleveland National Forest of San Diego County; it is also a part of the Peninsular Range south of the Santa Ana Mountains. Agua Tibia means in Spanish "tepid water".

AGUAJE DEL CENTINELA   Los Angeles

Land grant of September 14, 1844. Spanish meaning "Spring of the Sentinel".

AGUAJITO CANYON   Monterey

Spanish dimunitive of "aguaje" (watering place, spring, reservoir". Land grant of August 13, 1835.

ALAMEDA   Alameda

Name first occurs in a report of exploration of region made by Sergt. Pedro Amador in 1795. Name probably first applied to Arroyo de la Alameda which was borrowed from alamos (poplars). The name means "grove of poplars" and was chosen for the city by popular vote in 1853. It was formerly the property of the Peralta family. It became an island in 1902 when a canal was dug between the Oakland estuary and San Leandro Bay.

ALAMEDA COUNTY

County seat is Oakland. The county was created March 25, 1853, chap. 41. It has an area of 733 sq. mi. from parts of Contra Costa and Santa Clara counties. The first whites to see this region were the explorers of Ortega expedition (1769) and the Anza party (1776). Mission San Jose, the initial settlement, was founded in 1797.

ARROYO DE LA ALAMEDA RANCHO

Western Alameda County granted 1842 to Jesus Vallejo. Name means "stream of the grove of poplar trees".

LOS ALAMITOS   Los Angeles

Stems from Los Alamitos Rancho "little poplars" or "little Cottonwoods". It was a beet-sugar factory in 1896.

ALAMITOS BAY   Los Angeles

It is part of the Nieto grant.

ALAMO

The Spanish word for cottonwood or poplar tree is often found as a place name particularly in desert areas where poplars were landmarks. The generic alamo appears often with modifying adjectives: Alamo Mocho (trimmed cottonwood), Alamo Rancho, Alamo River, Alamo Solo (lonely), Alamo Pintado (painted), Alamorio (alamo Rio).

ALAMO   Contra Costa

Community located on original San Ramon Rancho and named because of many alamos or poplars commonly called Fremon cottonwood. It was settled in 1852 and the name appears officially in the Statutes of 1854.

ALAMO CREEK   Contra Costa

Named for the "cottonwoods" that at a time lined up the stream.

ALAMO RIDGE   Costra Costa
   Named for the cottonwoods

LOS ALAMOS   Santa Barbara
   One site of Los Alamos Rancho that was practically devoid of alamos. Town laid out by John S. Bell
   in 1876 who purchased land from Jose de la Guerra in 1867.

ALCALDE   Fresno
   Spanish "important gentry" acted as inferior magistrates who had never studied law and were bribed
   in order to win cases. The office originated in Spain was established in Mexico and California.

ALCATRAZ ISLAND   San Francisco
   On August 12, 1775 Juan Manuel de Ayala commanded the "San Carlos" and entered San Francisco
   Bay. He named it Isla de los Alcatraces (pelican island); now it is Yerba Buena Island. It was Beechey
   who in 1826 transferred the name as Alcatraz Island to the present site. On it was built in 1854 the
   first Pacific Coast lighthouse. A federal penitentiary was built and was used from 1934 to 1953.

ALHAMBRA   Los Angeles
   Named from Washington Irving's book *The Alhambra* by the owners Benjamin D. Wilson and J. D.
   Shorb. Originally it was a farming community, now it is a residential settlement of 65,000 inhabitants.
   The city was founded in 1874.

ALHAMBRA CREEK
ALHAMBRA VALLEY   Contra Costa
   The original name appears under Canada del Hambre (Valley of hunger), Paraje de Ambre "Hambre"
   (Place of Hunger), and Arroyo del Hambre (Creek of hunger). It was recorded officially on a land
   grant May 8, 1842 under the name of Canada del Hambre y las Bolsas de Hambre.

ALCODONES   Imperial
   Spanish "cotton plants" for cotton grown in region on both sides of the border said one source; how-
   ever, it was for a Yuman tribe, the Achedomas whose name was certainly corrupted in "Algodones".
   Wilke's Map of 1841 used the present spelling.

ALGOSO   Kern
   First known as weed patch because weeds grew there in profusion. Spanish "weedy". It was named
   in 1922 "Algoso" to avoid confusion with the existing Weed Patch located in the south.

ALISAL CREEK   Monterey
   Spanish for "alder or sycamore grove". Land grant dated December 19, 1833. Alders grow preferably
   by streams or ponds and thus early travelers gave the tree's name to geographic sites.

ALISAL CREEK   Santa Barbara
   "Alder or sycamore grove" Land grant of June 26, 1834.

ALISOS RANCHO (Cañada de los)   Orange
   Area of two leagues southern Orange county granted June 18, 1841 to Jose Serrano. Spanish for "the
   glen of the alders or sycamores".

ALMADEN   Santa Clara
   From the Spanish "almadén" (mine). The name New Almaden was given after the rich quick silver
   mine of Spain by Andres Castillero who identified a quicksilver deposit in 1845.

ALMONTE   Marin
   Until 1912 this place was known as Mill Valley Junction. To avoid confusion with Mill Valley it was
   changed to the present Almonte, meaning in Spanish "to the mountain, up the mountain."

ALTA
   Spanish for "high or upper". It appears often as a true specific geographical term as we can see with
   the following:

ALTA   Placer

Spanish "high". Name given by Central Pacific Railroad because of its elevation of 3,800 feet. Founding of community was celebrated July 21, 1866 with railroad excursion from Sacramento.

ALTA CALIFORNIA

José de Galvez gave orders to Portola and Serra to explore Alta California (1769) and to establish the first missions with settlements. In 1804 California was divided into Antigua (Baja-lower) Nueva (Alta-Upper). The first governor in charge with the affairs of Alta California was José Joaquin de Arrillaga (1750-1814).

ALTACANYADA   Los Angeles

From "alta" and "cañada" (high valley).

ALTA LOMA   San Bernardino

Spanish "high hill". Better Spanish usage would have been Loma Alta. The name was applied in 1912 to a station of the Pacific Electric Railway Company.

ALTA MEADOW   Sequoia National Park

Named in 1876 by Wallace T. Witt and N. B. Witt who camped at the meadow.

ALTAMONT   Alameda

Alta from the Spanish "high" and mont from the French "mount". This locality is the highest point in Altamont pass, a defile through Mt. Diable range named by the Central Pacific in 1869.

ALTA PEAK   Tulare

Spanish for "high". It was named after Alta Meadow, which in turn was named in 1876 by W. B. Wallace and Tom and N. B. Witt. The peak was first known as Tharps Peak for Hale Tharp a mountaineer. The only remaining of the name Tharp is a part of the peak known as Tharp's Rock.

ALTAVILLE   Calaveras

Alta from Spanish "high" and Ville from French "village". Well known for number and quality of its gold placers and quartz veins. Variously known as Forks-of-the-Roads, Low Divide, Cherokee Flat. The present name was adopted in 1857.

ALTA VISTA   Sonoma

From the Spanish "high view"

ALTOS, LOS   Santa Clara

Origin unrevealed. From Spanish "highlands" Post Office established in 1908.

ALTURAS   Modoc

From Spanish "the heights". The locality was first known as Dorris' Bridge after owner of Ranch on which it was located. County seat of Modoc county. Its name was adopted in 1876.

ALVARADO   Alameda

Honors Juan Bautista Alvarado, Governor of California 1836-1842 during Mexican regime. It was previously named New Haven and had been founded in 1851 by Henry C. Smith. In March 1853 it became the seat of Alameda County. Two of its founders, the brothers Bernardino and Juan Bautista were with the expedition of 1769. Francisco Xavier (1756-1831) the third brother married a daughter of the Amador family, and his two daughters married Pio Pico and Gabriel Morago. San Jose was named "Pueblo de Alvarado", as well as a town of Alameda County, to honor Governor Alvarado, one of the descendants of the illustrious family.

ALVISO   Santa Clara
    Honors Ignacio Alviso patriarch of Alviso family in California who came from Sonora, Mexico with Juan Bautista de Anza in 1775. He was granted in 1838 Rincon de los Esteros Ranchos on which the community is situated. Important shipping point for the entire lower San Francisco Bay region. Alviso served as administrator of mission 1840-43, became judge in 1847, and died in 1848. The town was laid out in 1849. The Post Office was listed in 1862. The Santa Clara Mission was first established at this site in 1777 but was moved on higher ground in the present city of Santa Clara in 1779. The locality was known as the "Embarcadero de Santa Clara" (landing place of Santa Clara).

AMADOR   Amador
    Honors Jose María Amador son of Sgt. Pedro Amador who came to California with expedition of Portola Serra in 1769. Amador Creek and Amador County take names from this community. It was once the home of the Maidu and was explored first by John Sutter (1846) and Charles Weber (1848). In 1848 Amador, with some Indians established a mining camp near the site of the present city. The county was created and named May 11, 1854 and the post office listed in 1867. It has a population of 11,821 (1970).

AMADOR COUNTY
    Named for José María Amador (1794-1883), a rancher from the leading California family. Created March 16, 1864 chap. 180. Area: 723 sq. mi.

AMARGOSA   Kern
    Spanish meaning Bitter. The name applied when the Pacific Coast Borax Co. moved its operation to the vicinity from Death Valley. About 1938 the station was renamed Boron, that being one of the elements in razorite ores produced by borax company. The stream (Amargosa River) was recorded by the Spaniards- "Amargosa - the bitter-water of the desert".

AMARGOSA CREEK   Los Angeles
    It is named for the bitterness of its water.

ANACAPA ISLAND   Ventura
    Onomatopoeic Spanish rendering of Chumash Indian Place Name meaning of which is dubious. The Portola expedition in January 1770 called the westernmost island Falsa Vela "false sail" because it looked like a ship, and the two others "Las Mesitas" (small table hills). Years later Juan Perez named the group of islands Islotes de Santo Tomas. The name was corrupted and was submitted to the following changes: Anajup, Enceapah, Enecapa, Encapa, Anacape (1852) and Anacapa (1854); derived from the Chumash Indian "Anyapah". The real meaning is not known.

ANDRADE   Imperial
    Named for Don Guillermo Andrade who puchased large tract of land for colonization purposes about delta of Colorado River. Town began in 1907 when flood control work on Colorado necessitated employment in vicinity of much Mexican labor.

ANGELES NATIONAL FOREST   Los Angeles
    A reserve of 643,656 acres under the name of San Gabriel Timberland Reserve. It was the first National Forest in the state (1892). The present name was given by proclamation of President Theodore Roosevelt in 1908.

ANGEL ISLAND   San Francisco Bay
    In August 1775 Ayala anchored the "San Carlos" there. He named it "Isla de los Angeles". In 1826 Beechey anglicized it.

ANIMAS   Santa Clara
    "Las Animas" (the souls) refers to All Souls' Day. The land grant dated November 28, 1808 and August 7, 1835 was also known as Carnadero and La Brea. Gabriel Moraga went in a punishing expedition against the marauding Amajabas who had murdered a certain number of Christian natives. After having burried the dead, Gabriel Moraga named the spot "Las Animas Benditas" (The Blessed Souls) 1819.

ANO NUEVO POINT   San Mateo

It was named by Sebastian Vizcaino, a Spanish sea explorer who passed it along coast on January 3, 1603 and named it for "New Year". On May 27, 1842 the name was used for the land grant Punta del Año Nuevo. Some American maps of the 1850's have the translation, New Years Point.

ANTELOPE CREEK   Tehama

Was originally named "El Rio de los Berrendos" (The river of the antelopes) because those animals would use this site as a drinking place.

ANZA   Riverside

Named after Juan Bautista de Anza (1735-1788), greatest of all land explorers. He led two expeditions from Sonora to Monterey and San Francisco in 1774 and 1775-76. In the latter expedition he covered 1,500 miles. He stands fourth as one of the most competent of Spanish conquerors who settled California. Anza became later Governor of New Mexico (1777-88).

ANZA DESERT STATE PARK   San Diego

Named after the famous explorer Juan Bautista de Anza; established in 1933. It is the largest state park with 470,000 acres. The Park is also designated as: "Anza-Borrego Desert" named also for the bighorn sheep (borrego).

LAKE ANZA   Alameda

Named after Juan Bautista de Anza in 1939.

ANZAR LAKE   San Benito

Named for Juan Anzar, grantee of the land grant Aromites y Agua Caliente, October 12, 1835. Also in honor of José Antonio Anzar, Mexican born Franciscan missionary who came to California in 1831 and remained until 1854. From 1843 to 1854 he was President General of the northern missions.

APTOS CREEK   Santa Cruz

Name applied to provisional land grant September 4, 1831. Spanish rendering of the name of Costanoan village or its chief.

APACHE CANYON   Ventura

Named after the Apache warlike Indian tribe.

ARANA GULCH   Santa Cruz

It is named after José Arana grantee of the land grant Potrero y Rincon de San Pedro Regalado, August 15, 1842.

ARENA POINT   Mendocino

It has been known by more names than any other landmark on the northwest coast of America. 1. Cabo de Fortunas 1543, 2. Tierra de Blanquisales - 18th century charts, 3., Punta de Barrancas 1770, 4. Punta Delgade 1775, 5. Captain George Vancouver gave present name meaning sand point when he stopped on November 10, 1792 (Barro de Arena).

ARGUELLO POINT   Santa Barbara

Honors José Dario Arguello founder of Arguello family in California. He married Ignacia Moraga, niece of Joaquin Moraga founder of San Francisco. Named by Captain George Vancouver November 9, 1792 when Arguello was "commandante" at Monterey.

ARMADA   Riverside

Spanish word for "squadron or fleet". The only relationship with the Spaniards is its euphony; there is no Spanish historical origin known.

ARMONA   Kings

Possibly two origins: 1) Named after Matias de Armona who served as governor of California when Portola was on the sacred expedition 1769-70; 2) Possibly coined name from RAMONA applied to a station of the Goshen-Huron branch line in the 1880's.

AROMAS   San Benito

Locality's name means aromas or perfumes derives from Aromitas y Agua Caliente Rancho area of three leagues granted 1835 to Juan M. Ansar.

ARRASTRE SPRINGS   San Bernardino

Spring in Avawatz Mountains located near old arrastre mining mill. It was employed by Spanish miners during early stages of gold mining operations in region about 1860.

ARROYO

Spanish word for watercourse, creek bed. It has become a generic term in southwestern United States and replaces often the word "creek" or "canyon". More than 150 waterways are now called arroyos. Many have been hybridized such as Big Arroyo (Tulare County) once called Jenny Lind Creek; Dry Arroyo (Solano County); Surprise Arroyo (Fresno); there are also some tautologies: Arroyo Grande Creek (San Luis Obispo County). Arroyo Seco Creek (Monterey).

ARROYO GRANDE   San Luis Obispo

Derived from Arroyo Grande "big stream" which runs through ranch first under supervision of fathers of San Luis Obispo Mission about 1780 supplied mission with corn, beans, potatoes, etc. The land grant dated April 25, 1842. The name of the town dates from 1867-1868. Also Arroyo Creek and Arroyo Valley.

ASILOMAR   Monterey

Coined from the Spanish Asilo meaning refuge and Mar meaning sea. It applied to religious and educational conference center originally established here by the Y.W.C.A. in 1913. The Post Office listed in 1915.

ASUNCION   San Luis Obispo

Spanish refers to Ascension of Virgin Mary and is mentioned as a place name, La Assumpcion by Font on March 4, 1776. The name was applied to a land grant June 18, 1845.

ATASCADERO   San Luis Obispo

From Atascadero rancho meaning boggy ground. Ground area granted 1842 to Trifon Garcia.

AUMENTOS ROCK   Monterey

José Maria Armenta was grantee of the Punta land grant, May 13, 1833. The name Armenta, certainly corrupted in Aumentos was applied to the rock near Point Pinos.

AUSAYMAS   Santa Clara and San Benito

It was a land grant also known as Cañada de los Osos, or Ausaymas y San Felipe, dated November 21, 1833 and February 6, 1836.

AVENA   San Joaquin

Spanish meaning "oats". It was a railroad station when the line from Stockton to Merced was built in the early 1890's. Named for fields of wild oats which were numerous in the region.

AVENAL   Kings

Spanish meaning "oatfield". The creek gave the name to the community. For a while it was named Avendale. The Geographic Board adopted Avenal on May 15, 1908.

AVILA   San Luis Obispo

The town was laid out in 1867 and named in memory of Miguel Avila by his sons. He was Corporal at Mission San Luis Obispo and was the grantee of Rancho San Miguelito April 8, 1839.

AVISADERO POINT   San Francisco

It is assumed that this word which sounds Spanish is not; it is possible that it comes from "avistar" (to descry at a distance), or perhaps from "avisar" (to inform, to advise); it names the tip of Hunters Point, which was known at a time as Punta Avisadera, then Avisada. The present spelling dates from 1873.

AZUL

Spanish meaning blue. It is preserved in names of several valleys, hills, mountains and sierras perhaps because the ceanothus was observed blooming in spring. We witness several hybridization for instance: Azule Mountains, Azule Springs, (Santa Clara Co.)

EL BAILARIN   Santa Barbara

Spanish meaning the dancer. This site located one league from Carpintaria was named for a nimble-footed Indian who used to dance in front of the weary travelers in order to cheer them up. Father Crespi called this place "El Pueblo del Bailarin" (the town of the dancer).

BAILE DE LAS INDIAS (Rancheria del)   Santa Barbara

Spanish meaning village of the dance of the Indian women. So-named because Costanso witnessed a dance by Indian women, which was not customary because Indian women were not permitted to dance in public. In fact as a rule they are not to take part of any dancing, unless the chief lets them join in the festivities. This place was five leagues from Point Pedernales.

BAJA CALIFORNIA

This was the section between Tijuana to Cape San Lucas discovered by Fortún Jiménez while serving under Cortes (1533). Ulloa visited also the area (1539-40) and stated that it was not an island but a peninsula. (See Alta California). Baja California remained part of Mexico while Alta California became part of the U.S.A.

BALBOA   Orange

Commemorates Vasco Nunez de Balboa (Spanish explorer). It was named by E. J. Louis, Peruvian Consul in Los Angeles, 1905. Balboa Island, named after the older settlement across the channel in 1912.

BALLAST POINT   San Diego Bay

That was Cabrillo's first landing place September 28, 1542. The stones at this place were suitable for ballast and the Spanish called them "Los Guijarros" (cobblestones) "o Lastre" (ballast). The Spaniards used to refer to Punta de los Guijarros; it was referred to Guijarros. In 1851 Ballast Point became the official name.

BALLAST POINT   Catalina Island

It was named first in 1852 after Ballast Point of San Diego Bay.

BALLENA   San Diego

Spanish meaning whale. It derives from mountain nearby, the sky line outline of which resembles in shape a hump-backed whale. The Spaniards used to call Lower California "Puerto Balenas, Punta de la California, Playa Balenas (the present Punta de San Lucas or Cabo San Lucas).

BALLENA VALLEY   San Diego

Named after the Indian "rancheria de la Ballena". It was the near-by hill shaped like a whale which suggested the settlers to choose this name.

BALLONA CREEK AND BALLONA LAGOON   Los Angeles

The Talamantes family grantees of the rancho Ballona or Paso de las Carretas grant dated November 27, 1839, named the place after the city of Bayona in northern Spain, the town of their ancestors.

BANDINI   Los Angeles

Is located a short distance from Los Angeles on the Santa Fe Railroad. The founder of this family was Jose Bandini, a sailor of Spanish birth who came to California and settled at San Diego. His son Juan Bandini, held several public offices. He was an eloquent speaker and became a prominent citizen.

LOS BANOS   Merced

Founded by Henry Miller of Miller and Lux ranch 1889. Name from nearby Los Baños Creek. First named Arroyo de les Baños del Padre Arroyo meaning "Creek of Baths of Father Arroyo" because the pools in the creek were used for bathing purposes by Father Felipe Arroyo de la Cuesta who came to California in 1808 as Franciscan missionary.

BARRANCA COLORADA   Tehama
Named after a Mexican land grant of December 24, 1844. The name means "red bank or red ravine".

BARTOLO VIEJO, PASO DE   Los Angeles
In 1838 the San Antonio grant bears Paso de Bartolo. We notice that the Camino Viejo crosses the Rio de San Gabriel. It must have meant "Bartolo's Crossing on the old road". In 1816 we find Bartolo Tapia as the owner of a rancho in Los Angeles district.

BATEQUITOS LAGOON   San Diego
Corrupt diminutive of bateas which means "flat-bottomed boats". Word should be spelled with penultimate "a". On January 10, 1776, Font writes about "Los Batequitos", a watering place. Different spellings are notice: Batiquitos, Batiguitos. Batequi means "water hole" in the Cahita language of Sinaloa. Batequito is the diminutive of batequi.

BAULENES   Marin
A Mexican land grant dated October 19, 1841 and November 29, 1845. Also spelled Bolinas. The Spaniards used to call this place "La Cáñada que llaman los Baulenes (the valley called the Baulenes) we are not certain of the meaning of Baulenes. On the map which includes now Bolinas Point, Duxbury Point, Bolinas, had the word "Baulenes".

BAUTISMO (CANADA DEL)   San Diego
Spanish meaning "glen of the baptism". Miguel Costanso tells in his diary that two Indian children were dying and were baptized by the padres, and thus the naming of this site.

BAUTISTA CANYON   Riverside
Juan Bautista de Anza went across the canyon on journeys between Sonora and California in 1774 and 1775-76. The Canyon was probably named for him, however, on certain early maps the defile is designated as Baptiste Canyon.

BEAN HOLLOW LAKE   San Mateo
Was named after the "Arroyo de les Frijoles" (Kidney Bean Creek). Several Bean Creeks and Bean Canyons are in the state.

BELL CANYON   Orange
Known in Mexican times as: Canada de la Campana (Canyon of the Bell) so named because of the sound made by a granite rock, when founded, that filled the canyon.

BELLA VISTA   Shasta
Origin unrevealed. Spanish for beautiful view.

BELLOTA   San Joaquin
Origin unrevealed. Spanish for acorn. At one time known as Fishers Bridge for at this point William V. Fisher settled 1861 and erected a bridge and stage station.

BENICIA   Solano
Named for Dona Francisca Benicia Carrillo Vallejo. City located on the north shore of Carquinez Strait founded in 1847 from land deeded to Robert Semple and Thomas Larkin by General Mariano G. Vallejo. Population 8,783 in 1970. The city was first called Francisca. At that time San Francisco was called Yerba Buena, then named San Francisco. Dr. Semple was so outraged at their changing the name to one so nearly to his town that he, in turn, changed his town's name to the other name of MRS. Vallejo and "Benicia" it has been to this day.

BERENDA   Madera
Corruption of Berrenda - Berrendo for native antelope of Northern Mexico. One of the diarist of Portola expedition of 1769 named Miguel Costanso writes "Hay en la tierra Venados, verrendos (or berrendos) muchos liebres, conejos, gatos monteses y ratas" (there are in the land deer, antelopes, many hares, rabbits, wild-cats and rats.) On August 4 the expedition reached a site forty leagues from San Diego which they called "Berrendo" because they caught a live deer. Antelope Creek (Tehama County) was originally named "El Rio de los Berrendos" (the river of the antelops) because of the profusion of

antelopes which came to drink at this place.

BERROS　　　　　　　　　　　　　　　　　　San Luis Obispo
　　Spanish meaning watercress. Was section of Nipomo Rancho. Granted to William G. Dana in 1847. Los Berros Creek was called Arroyo de los Berros. The town was founded and named in 1891.

BERREYESA　　　　　　　　　　　　　　　　Santa Clara
　　Commemorates Nicolas Berreyesa grantee of San Vincente Rancho in 1842 who became insane and died in 1863 as a result of a chain of tragic circumstances. He was the descendant of Nicolas Antonio Berry-essa (1761-1804) who took part of Anza expedition (1776).

BERRYESSA VALLEY　　　　　　　　　　　　Napa
　　Jose Jesus and Sisto Berryessa were grantees of Rancho Las Putas in 1843.

BIXBY SLOUGH　　　　　　　　　　　　　　Los Angeles
　　Was known as Cañada de Palos Verdes "Green Stick Valley"; then as Lagunita. In 1900 it was named Bixby Slough for Jotham Bixby a landowner.

BLANCO　　　　　　　　　　　　　　　　　Monterey
　　Named for Thomas White sailor who deserted from the St. Louis in 1840 and became lumberman and Mexican citizen. He changed his name to Tomas Blanco and was granted a rancho on Salinas River. People used to call his place "Blanco Crossing" and in 1872 the name was given to the Southern Pacific Station.

BLOODY ISLAND　　　　　　　　　　　　　Tehama
　　The "Isla de la Sangre" of the Spaniards, of Rancho Buenaventura because of the attacks by Indians here, was named in 1844 by Samuel I. Hensley of Sutter's Fort.

BLUE
　　Some names may be translations as Spanish adjectives of colors (blue, white, etc. were used). Sierra azul, for instance. (See Azul)

BOCA　　　　　　　　　　　　　　　　　　Nevada
　　Spanish for mouth. Probably applied to this locality because it is situated at the mouth of Little Truc-kee River.

BOCA
　　Spanish for mouth; concerns geographical features: entrance or outlet of a river, estuary, port or valley. We find "Boca" in three land grants of different counties: 1) Boca de Santa Monica (Los Angeles) of June 19, 1839. 2) Boca de la Cañada del Pinole (Contra Costa) June 21, 1842. 3) Boca de la Playa (Orange) April 18, 1845 and May 7, 1846.

BODEGA　　　　　　　　　　　　　　　　　Sonoma
　　Takes name from Bodega Rancho. Spanish for wine cellar, however, probably named after Spanish explorer Bodega y Cuadra who discovered Bodega Bay October 3, 1775. Maps of the times show Puerto y Rio del Capitan Vodega (Bodega); then the maps mention Puerto de la Bodega. In 1850 it was named Bodega Bay. In 1797 the French explorer La Pérouse called Pointe Bodega; Duflot de Mofras in 1844 calls Pointe de la Bodega or Cap Romanoff. Then it became Bodega Point (1850) and Bodega Head (1851).

BOGA　　　　　　　　　　　　　　　　　　Butte and Sutter
　　Spanish for the prickly envelop of the chestnut, buoy, act of rowing. The exact origin of the naming is not exactly known. It is assumed that an Indian word was corrupted by the Spaniards. The land grants of the region show on their map an Indian village by the name of Boga; the rancho was called "Rio de las Plumas" (it was located on the Feather River).

BOLANOS BAY　　　　　　　　　　　　　　Marin
　　Named for Francisco de Bolanos chief pilot of Vizcaino expedition of 1602 and commander of the San Diego.

BOLINAS   Marin

In 1834 Ignacio Martinez mentions it "La Cañada que llaman los Baulenes" (the Valley that they call the Baulenes); it is found on a map of the time "Baulenes" where now we have Bolinas Point, Duxbury Point and the town of Bolinas. We are not certain of the meaning of Baulenes, we can only assume it was an Indian word, apparently corrupted by the Spaniards. (See Baulenes)

BOLIVAR LOOKOUT   Siskiyou

This name has been changed to Craggy Peak, however, the ranger station preserves the name of the South American revolutionary hero, Simon Bolivar.

BOLSA   Orange

Spanish for purse or pocket. Name appears on first map of San Joaquin Rancho where entire Newport Bay area is designated as Bolsa de San Joaquin. The name appears also in the following counties: San Luis Obispo, San Benito and San Mateo.

BONANZA

Spanish for prosperity. It appears in four counties: Kern, Lake, Merced, San Bernardino.

BONITA   San Diego

Community established in Sweetwater Valley on portion of Nairional Rancho and means pretty in Spanish.

BONITA CHANNEL   Marin

(See Bonita Point).

BONITA COVE   Marin

(See Bonita Point).

BONITA POINT   Marin

In 1775 Ayala explored the region. He named the point Punta de Santiago. It is also recorded as Punta Bonete because of its particular shape of the bonnet of a clergyman. It is also found around 1809 as Punta de Bonetas. We find also the following spelling: Punta Boneta; then Point Bonita and also Bonito. This last spelling is certainly in reference to the large bonito that lives in this particular water.

BOREGO, BORREGO, BORREGA

From the Spanish "borrego", lamb or sheep, a popular word in place names during Spanish times. It appears in many land grants in California counties: Contra Costa, Santa Barbara, Santa Clara, Santa Cruz, San Diego. For instance Sanjon de Borregas (ditch of lambs) in Santa Cruz county.

BORREGO VALLEY   San Diego

Spanish for a lamb less than one year old in reference to long existence in vicinity of desert of bighorn sheep. For years a corrupt spelling of Borrego was in vogue. A monument to Pegleg Smith (1801-66) the mountain man with a wooden leg, memorializes his mythic mine.

BORONDA CREEK   Monterey

Named after the Boronda family, early settlers of 1839 for the land grant of Rancho Los Laureles some nine miles north-west of the creek.

BOSQUEJO   Tehama and Butte

Land grant recorded 1844 as "Bosquejo del terreno solicitado por Pedro Lawson". This means a sketch of land solicited by Peter Lassen. In Spanish Bosquejo is a sketch or small tract of wooded land.

BOUQUET CANYON   Los Angeles

From the corrupted Spanish "buque" ship. In the early 1800's a French sailor by the name of Chari settled in the Canyon in the neighborhood of Mexican who nicknamed him "El Buque" (the vessel, the ship). The 1850's surveyors recorded it the French way "Bouquet". The name has kept its French flavor and spelling to the present.

BRANCIFORTE CREEK   Santa Cruz

Named after the Pueblo de Branciforte, located where the present town of Santa Cruz stands. It was named for the viceroy of New Spain, the Marques de Branciforte. The town was established in 1797. In 1802 its population was 101. The present county of Santa Cruz temporarily took the name of Branciforte (Feb. 18 - April 5, 1850).

BRAVO RIO   Kern

Origin unrevealed but in good Spanish means "valiant, wild or brave river."

BREA   Orange

Takes name from the Spanish word for tar or asphalt which is found there. Town was incorporated in February 23, 1917 but tar or oil deposits were known to Spanish California residents long before. Brea Canyon, Orange county was named after the "Gran Rincon de la Brea, Los Angeles Co., February 23, 1841. Brea appears as a geographical term in several land grants in Los Angeles, Monterey, Orange and Santa Clara counties, and Santa Barbara (Labrea Creek).

BRIONES HILLS   Contra Costa

Named for the family of Felipe Briones who settles in 1831 on Martinez' rancho. In 1840 Briones was ambushed and killed by Indians.

BUNCHON POINT   San Luis Obispo

Soldiers of Portola expedition seeking Monterey named locality when they camped here September 4, 1769 and met a chief with a large goitre hanging from his neck. Buchon comes from "Buche" meaning big craw or stomach.

BUENA PARK   Orange

Spanish for good. Originally Buena, when the town grew, it reached an important size and met with the existing railroad station Northam. The Santa Fe R.R. renamed it Buena Park in 1929. It is very well known for its tourist attractions including: California Alligator Farm, Enchanted Village of Wild Animals, Movieworld Cars of the Stars, Japanese Village and Deer Park, Knott's Berry Farm, and Movieland Wax Museum.

BUENA   San Diego

Spanish for good. Name applied to a rancheria called Buena Vista for a land grant dated June 17, 1845. With the extension of the San Diego Central a station was created and named Buena Vista, then in 1908 another station was created and two stations bore the names BUENA and VISTA.

BUENAVENTURA   Shasta and Tehama

Spanish for good adventure, good fortune. Named after an imaginary river that supposed to flow from the Rocky Mountains through the Great Salt Lake and through the Sierra Nevada into the Ocean. Bonaventura was used for the sacraments in the 1830's. The valley, at times was called the Buena Ventura Valley. As late as 1857 the Salinas was called San Buenaventura. Coincidentally the Mapa de los Estados Unidos Mexicanos (Paris 1837) has a Rio San Buenaventura emptying into the Ocean mouth of San Luis Obispo. The Mexican land grant of December 4, 1844 of the Sacramento River bears the name of Buenaventura. Buenaventura River was visited by Escalante (1776), Jedediah Smith (1827), John Work (1832) and Frémont.

BUENA VISTA

Spanish meaning beautiful view. It is the most common place name of Spanish origin in the U.S.A. Thus the peaks in Amador, Madera, Mariposa and Tulare counties were named because they were offering a beautiful view. In Spanish times the name was so popular that it was profusely used for geographic features as well as land grants. Buena Vista figures as an Indian village as far as 1772. Buena Vista Lake is recorded on a map of 1819 as Laguna de Buenavista. Buena Vista County was created April 30, 1855 but it did not materialize.

BUENA VISTA   Monterey

As far as April 1776 an agglomeration called Buenavista exists. Buenavista was applied to two land grants in 1794 and 1821. Also we find several Buena Vista Creeks and Buena Vista Hills.

BUENA VISTA CREEK   San Diego

On July 17, 1769 the Portola expedition camped on the banks of the creek. The site was named "Santa Sinforosa". The creek took the name of the place. St. Sinforosa is a saint of the Franciscan Calendar.

BUENOS AIRES (ARROYO)   San Joaquin

Spanish for creek of the good airs. Because of the richness of the surrounding area thanks to its regular flow.

CABAZON   Riverside

From Cabezon "collar, opening of a garment for the head to pass; by extension, big head". The station was named for the Indian rancheria Cabezone (1859). In 1884 the town was laid out and named after the station. The Cabazon Peak was named in 1901.

CABEZA DE SANTA ROSA   Sonoma

Spanish for head. Used as geographical term. Name of a land grant of September 30, 1841.

CABRILLO   Mendocino

Named in 1870 for Juan Rodriguez Cabrillo. Cabrillo National Monument, San Diego was certainly the first landing place of the Spanish explorer in California (Sept. 28, 1542). Cabrillo Point, Monterey. In November 16, 1542 Cabrillo anchored near it. This point was named in 1935.

CACHAGUA CREEK   Monterey

From a tributary of the upper Carmel River, unnamed but in the map, nearby appears the words Canada and Ojo de Agua, it would not be surprising that popular ears had put the words into Ca-cha-gua.

CACHE CREEK   Yolo

Before 1832 this stream was called Riviere la Cache by the trappers of Canadian origin of the Hudson Bay Company, because they had "a cache" (hiding places) for their traps on its banks. The Mexican documents of the 1840's bear the name of the creek called Rio de Jesus Maria (at times it appears under Arroyo de Jesus Maria), the name of the Sacramento river north of its junction with the Feather.

CADIZ   San Bernardino

This town commemorates in California the province of Cadiz. In 1749 Fathers Junipero Serra, Francisco Palou and other missionaries who founded the missions in California, sailed for the New World. The Cadiz station was named in 1883 by the Atlantic and Pacific Railroad, after a town of the eastern United States. Cadiz Dry Lake, named after the locality.

CAHUENGA PASS   Los Angeles

Portola traversed the pass in exploring the San Fernando Valley. This pass was famous for several battles: in 1831 Governor Manuel Victoria was defeated; in 1845 Alvarado and Castro overthrew Governor Micheltorena. In the surroundings Fremont and Andres Pico signed the Cahuenga Capitulation Treaty (Jan. 13, 1847) which ended the war between American and Mexican forces in California. The origin of the name is certainly a Shoshonean word.

CAJON

Spanish for box used as a geographical term to describe boxlike canyons. Cajon Camp, San Bernardino County (see Cajon Pass). Cajon de Muscupiabe, El (see Cajon Pass). Cajon, El town, San Diego County derives its name from El Cajon Rancho which was named for the valley where the ranch was located. The valley being a canyon hemmed in by mountains.

CAJON PASS   San Bernardino

The first white man who went through this pass was Don Pedro Fages, in 1772. It was nicknamed later El Cajon de los Mexicanos and ElCajon de Muscupiabe (Muscupiabe was the name of a Serrano Indian rancheria located at present Camp Cajon) or El Cajon de Muscupiavit. Mormon emigrants who founded the city of San Bernardino in 1851, entered the valley through it. Jedediah Smith traversed it in 1827.

CAJON RANCHO, EL San Diego

An area of 11 leagues were granted in 1845 to Maria Antonio Estudillo de Pedrorena. Presently on this land stand modern El Cajon, Bostonia, Santee and Lakeside.

CALABASAS Los Angeles

An hispanicization of the Chumash Indian village name "Calahoosa" meaning "place of wild gourds". Calabazas in Spanish mean pumpkin, squash or wild gourd. The history of the town goes back prior to August 18, 1795 when it is recorded that Padre Santa Maria slept here.

CALABASAS RANCHO, LAGUNA DE LAS CALABASAS Santa Cruz

An area of two leagues granted December 17, 1833 to Felipe Hernandez. The name means "the lagoon of the pumpkins or gourds". In Los Angeles county there is a name of Peak and Canyon using the word "Calabasas".

CALABAZAS CREEK Santa Clara

CALABAZAS CREEK Sonoma

CALABOOSE CREEK Monterey

From the Spanish "Calabozo" jail, comes the colloquial western American term for "jail". There is a Jail Canyon in Inyo County. Calaboose Creek was put on the map in 1917.

CALAVERAS COUNTY

Spanish word for "skull". Created February 18, 1850, chap. 15. 1028 sq. mi. Takes its name from the Calaveras River which flows west to empty into the San Joaquin River near Stockton.

CALAVERAS RIVER

Was discovered by Alférez Gabriel Moraga and Father Pedro Muñoz in 1806, it was named Rio de la Pasion. Later on Moraga renamed the stream Rio de las Calaveras, (Sp. River of the skulls). On Wilkes' maps of 1841 and 1849 the river appears under the name of Rio San Juan. On maps of Fremont (1845) one finds Rio de las Calaveras. A Parage de las Calaveras is mentioned in 1809 and Monument Peak was known at one time as "Cerro de las Calaveras". Calaveras is found in association with: Creek, County Dam, reservoir, river, State Park, and Valley. In 1837 John Marsh discovered a great number of skeletons on the banks of the river to which he gave that name.

CALAVERITAS (GHOST TOWN) Calaveras

Is an historic landmark. Takes its name from Calaveritas Creek, a tributary to the South Fork of Calaveras River. Calaveritas is a Spanish diminutive meaning "Little Calaveras".

CALERA

Spanish meaning "lime-kiln" a word often used in Spanish times for place names. It is found in Santa Clara County: Arroyo Calero, Calero Reservoir. The mispelled word "Calero" means lime-burner, lime-maker. Calera Creek in Santa Clara County is a tributary to Coyote River. Calera Valley, San Mateo County is shown as Cañada de la Calera. La Calera y las Positas Santa Barbara County. Land grant of May 8, 1843 and July 1, 1846. Meaning in Spanish "limekiln and water holes".

CALEXICO Imperial

Is the international border with Mexicali as its Mexican counterpart across the line. Once it was the site of a Salvation Camp founded by Cave J. Couts. The town was founded in 1908.

CALIENTE (TOWN, CANYON, AND CREEK) Kern

Stems from Caliente Creek Community. It was named by laborers building the Tehachapi section of the Southern Pacific railroad stationed there in about 1875. Name is from Spanish meaning "hot" which is appropriate in summer months. The name was certainly given because of the hot springs in the Canyon.

CALIENTE MOUNTAIN San Luis Obispo

Caliente Range: between the Cuyama River and the Carrizo Plain. The name meaning "hot" in Spanish owes its origin to the Ojo Caliente and refers to the hot springs in the Cuyama Valley.

CALIFA   Madera

Origin unrevealed. Spanish for caliph, a title applied to successors of Mohamet.

CALIFORNIA

Origins of the name: 1) Captain Frederick William Beechey, an English explorer who visited San Francisco and Monterey in 1826-27 was the first to record the belief that the name came from Latin words "calida" and "fornax" meaning heat and furnace. 2) M. G. Vallejo and Juan B. Alvarado said word stemmed from lower California Indian term "kali forno meaning "high hill" and "native land". 3) Other possible origins from Greek and Latin roots: calidus fornus, caliente fornalia, caliente horno, kala phor nea, kala chora nea, etc. In April 1862 Edward Everett Hale solved the origin of the name to everyone's satisfaction. He reported that the name was contained in the romantic novel, *Las Sergas de Esplandian* which comprised the fifth book of omnibus novel, Amadis de Gaula, a 16th century tale. The author, Garcia Ordonez de Montalvo published his book in 1510 in Seville, Spain. "The name California described the land of black women living like the Amazons. . ." Who was responsible and who decided upon the name of California for what is now called Lower California is not known. In 1601 the historian Antonio de Herrera stated that it was Cortes himself who placed this name upon it. Other historians ascertain that Fortún Jiménez, the pilot of the Becerra expedition, in the winter of 1533, discovered the peninsula and named it. On several maps of 1562 and 1569 the name California appears; by 1705 the French cartographer Guillaume Delisle considered the present state of California in the name. In 1769 the Spaniards differentiated Baja California and Alta California.

CALIFORNIA HOT SPRINGS   Tulare

Located in Deer Creek Canyon. Formerly known as Deer Creek Hot Springs. It is a popular resort built in 1908 on the site of seven sulphuretted hot springs.

CALIFORNIA REDWOOD PARK   Santa Cruz

Was established in 1902 to protect a forest of coast redwoods. At present it contains 9,997 acres and is known as the Big Basin Redwoods. It is a part of the California State Park system.

CALIPATRIA   Imperial

Certainly a coined name from "Cali" California and "patria" for the Spanish "homeland". The townsite was first laid out in 1914 and was known as Date City. The town was incorporated in 1919.

CALLEGUAS (CREEK, RANCHO)   Ventura

Several versions surround the origin of this name: 1) From a land grant in 1837 to Jose Pedro Ruiz, the name may stem from the Spanish "calleja" meaning a lane or a narrow passage. 2) In 1795 Padre Vicente de Santa Maria visited an Indian rancheria called "Cayegues". The name would derive from a Chumash word meaning my head.

CAMAJAL Y PALOMAR   San Diego

Known originally as Mesa de Camajal and Cañada de Palomar (Valley of the dovecot, pigeon house), appears on the land grant dated August 1, 1846.

CAMARILLO   Ventura

From Camarillo family. The first was Juan Camarillo who arrived with the Hijar Padres colony in 1834. He became trader at Santa Barbara, was "sindico and juez" at different times. He purchased the Calleguas Rancho in which the present city of Camarillo is located.

CAMINO   El Dorado

The origin is unrevealed. Spanish meaning road. It is a very popular name applied in El Dorado and Los Angeles counties. From there derives "El Camino Real" (the royal highway" a term for public road used in California in the 18th century for the road from Baja to Alta California linking the presidios and missions. It began with the Sacred Expedition of Portola (1769).

CAMPBELLS (POINT AND COVE)   Sonoma

Known in Spanish times as Punta de Bodega (Bodega Head), the spot where Bodega anchored in 1775. Today known for Captain John Campbell, a pioneer.

CAMPHORA   Monterey

In 1873 Camp Four had been set up in this location. Mexican workers referred to it as Camphora. The railroad administrators named the station according to the Mexican spelling and pronunciation.

CAMPITO (MEADOW AND PEAK)   Mono

Spanish for little field or little camp. Origin unrevealed.

CAMPO

Spanish for field, camp.

CAMPO   San Diego

Originally an Indian settlement where the first Spanish visitors made camp. In 1870 settlers from Texas came. The town was then known as New Texas or Little Texas.

CAMPO DE LOS FRANCESES   San Joaquin

Spanish for Camp of the Frenchmen, because in the 1830's the French-Canadian trappers camped there.

CAMPO SECO   Calaveras

Spanish for dry camp. Named for an old mining town, because of the high and dry gold deposits in which they could work when the lower part of the gulch bars were flooded.

CAMUESA (CANYON AND PEAK)   Santa Barbara

Name derived from the Spanish Gamuza or camusa (chamois). The squaws tanned buckskin brought to them by the hunters. It was a very important Indian camp because the chamois were numerous.

CAÑADA

One of the most common generic term of the Spanish times. It means "valley".

CAÑADA DEL PINOLE RANCHO, BOCA DE LA   Monterey

Two leagues along the coast in northern Monterey county. The rancho is often referred to as La Sagrada Familia (the sacred family ranch). In 1822 the land grant went to José Joaquin de la Torre.

CAÑADA DEL RINCON EN EL RIO DE SAN LORENZO DE SANTA CRUZ

Santa Cruz

Spanish - San Lorenzo of Santa Cruz's glen of the corner of the river. A land grant of two leagues was awarded in 1846 to Pedro Sainsevain.

CAÑADA DE SAN MIGUELITA RANCHO   Ventura

Spanish for Little San Miguel's Valley. A land grant of two leagues awarded in 1846 to Ramon Rodriguez.

CAÑADA, LA   Los Angeles

Named after "La Cañada Rancho" the land grants of March 25, 1838. The post office was established circa 1890.

CAÑADA LARGA OVERDE RANCHO   Ventura

Spanish for Long or green Valley Rancho. Land grant dated January 30, 1841 to Joaquina Alvarado; it was an area of half a league in western Ventura County.

CAÑADA RANCHO, LA

A part of San Rafael Rancho, bequeathed to Dona Catalina Verdigo for an area of 5,800 acres. La Crescenta is located on the site of the rancho.

CAÑADA VERDE   San Mateo

Spanish for green valley. From a land grant dated March 25, 1838.

CAÑADA VERRUGA   San Diego
Named for an old Indian squatter who settled here in 1864. Spanish verruga means wart. He had a large wart on the side of his neck. His ranch was nicknamed Verruga Rancho and the canyon became Cañada Verruga.

CANOAS
Spanish for canoes or troughs (in Mexico) is found in two creeks in Fresno and Santa Clara counties and in Cinco Canoas Campo (Monterey County). Pueblo de las Canoas, Ventura (See Hueneme)

CANOGA PARK   Los Angeles
It seems to be a corruption of the Spanish "canoa" (canoe). It is because of the trough shaped like a canoe, that this site was so named. The idea was to create a popular reservoir under the good guidance of San Fernando Mission fathers. Thus for many years the cattle herders as well as the Los Angeles-Santa Barbara stage coach used it regularly. In 1913 the town changed its name to Owensmouth; but a few years later it returned to its present name. Another historian claims that it was probably named after Canoga, New York, from the Indian village GANOGEH, (place of floating oil).

CANTARA   Siskiyou
Origin unrevealed. Spanish for liquid measure of two gallons.

CANTIL   Kern
Spanish for steep rock. The origin is unrevealed but we believe that the naming is due to the fact that the mouth of the Red Rock Canyon is nearby. The station was named when the Nevada and California Railroad was extended from Owens lake to Mojave in 1909.

CANTU   Imperial
In honor of the Mexican Colonel Esteban Cantu, a governor of the northern district of Lower California from 1915 to 1920. The name was applied to the station of the Inter-California Railroad in 1909. To be noticed that the post office name is not Cantu but Andrade.

CANTUA CREEK   Fresno
Was named after a member of the Cantua family, prominent in Mexican times in the district of Monterey. In 1850's Cantua Creek was one of the retreats of the famous bandit Joaquin Murieta.

CANYON
From the Spanish cañon for "pipe, cannon, narrow watercourse between mountains, etc." The word has become a true generic term and it is used more often than the English term.

CANYON   Contra Costa
Is abbreviated from New Redwood Canyon post office established in 1911. Changed its name to Sequoya in 1923.

CAPAY   Yolo
Named after Canada de Capay Rancho, granted to Santiago Nemesio and Francisco Berreyesa in 1846. It was an area of nine leagues. The name "Capay" or "Kapai" in Wintun Indian, means stream. The town was first called Munchville then Langville. The modern communities of Rumsey, Guinda, Tancred, Brooks, Capay, Esparto and Madison are located on this site of the original grant.

CAPITAN   Santa Barbara
Spanish for captain. It is said that the point was named after Captain José Francisco Ortega who participated in the founding of the presidio of Santa Barbara. Also Canada del Capitan El Capitan Beach.

CAPITANCILLOS, CANADA DE LOS   Santa Clara
Capitancillo is a diminutive of Captain or chief. The name means "The Valley of the little chiefs or captains". Land granted to Justo Larios on June 16, 1842.

CAPITAN GRANDE INDIAN RESERVATION   San Diego
Was named by executive order of President U. S. Grant, December 27, 1875.

CARBONERA, LA Santa Cruz

Spanish meaning coal-house; a place where charcoal is made, coal pit. An area half a league, north of Santa Cruz granted Feb. 3, 1838 to William Buckle.

CAREAGA Santa Barbara

Named for Juan B. Careaga who cultivated a tract near Los Alamos in the early 1880's (Co. Hist., 1883, p. 295). Another version is that Careaga is a corruption of Cariaga, the family name of Saturnino Cariaga, grantee of the Real de las Aguilas Rancho, (Hanna, 1951, p. 55).

CARMEL Monterey

Carmel Bay; Carmel Mission; Mount Carmel, Carmel River, Carmel-by-the-Sea. The River rises in Santa Lucia Mountains to empty at Carmel Bay near San Carlos Borromeo del Carmelo Mission, south of the village of Carmel. It was discovered by Vizcaino, January 3, 1603 and called Rio del Carmelo because of the friars of the Carmelite order who accompanied him. Malaspina's map of Monterey Bay (1791) records "Rio del Carmelo; Punta del Carmelo, Ensenada de Carmelo." Modern Carmel-by-the sea was so named to distinguish it from another Carmel located about ten miles inland.

CARMENITA Los Angeles

Spanish for country home, garden, diminutive meaning little country home. This town was laid out in the land grant Los Coyotes in 1887; three miles east of Norwalk.

CARNADERO CREEK Santa Clara

Spanish for butchering place. It is recorded as early as January 23, 1784. We find the name later on maps and in documents and was used also for the Las Animas grant. In 1854 and 1873 we find on maps Carnadero River.

CARNE HUMANA RANCHO Napa

Spanish for human flesh. A land grant dated March 14, 1841 to Dr. Edward Turner Bale, the builder of grist mill of same name. It appears in the record with various names: Caligolman, Colijolmanoc, Huilic Noma. It was an area of four leagues on which the present cities of Calistoga and St. Helena are located.

CARNEROS RANCHO, LOS Monterey

Spanish for sheep. Land grants dated May 13, 1834, August 16, 1839 and October 5, 1842 were named Los Carneros. The area of one league was granted in 1834 to David Littlejohn. The name "carneros" appears in several places: Los Carneros (1836) Arroyo de los Carneros (1844), Carnero Creek and Carnero Mountain (1850), Carnero Ridge. Carneros Spring, Kern county. Carneros Canyon, 1909. Carneros Valley, Santa Barbara (1842) Arroyo de los Carneros (1846).

CARPENTERIA RANCHO, CAÑADA DE LA Monterey

Spanish for the valley of the carpenter shop. Land grant dated 1845 awarded to Joaquin Soto. An area of half a league.

CARPINTERIA Santa Barbara

On August 17, 1769 the Portola expedition camped here. It was then an Indian village very busy in the building of canoes. The soldiers named this town La Carpinteria (the carpenter shop), but Father Crespi, the missionary diarist, christened it with the name of San Roque, for St. Roch, a 14th century French monk, whose day falls on August 16. The name La Carpinteria is mentioned in several early manuscripts. The post office was named Carpinteria in 1868. A land grant Canada de la Carpinteria in Monterey Co., was dated October 12, 1831 and September 25, 1835. Carpinteria Beach State Park, Santa Barbara was created and named in 1932, it has an area of 16.88 acres.

CARQUINEZ: Strait, Point, Bridge, Contra Costa and Solano counties

The name is derived from the Karquin (or Carquin) Indians. The strait was discovered by Captain Pedro Fages on March 29, 1772 during an expedition on the east side of San Francisco Bay. In March 1776 Father Font, who accompanied Juan Bautista de Anza named the strait as "Boca del Puerto Dulce" (mouth of the fresh-water port). Father Abella who explored this region in 1807 referred to it in his diary as "Rancheria de los Karquines, and Estrecho de los Karquines. Ignacio Martinez who had a rancho at the narrows spelled the name as it appears presently. Until 1905, however it was spelled Karquines.

-18-

CARRISALITO, SPRING, CREEK   Merced
Carrisalito from the Spanish carrizo "Reed grass'. The original land grant dated February 10, 1844 was named "Panoche de San Juan y Los Carrisalitos."

CARRIZO   San Diego
Spanish for reed grass which exudes a sap containing a sweet substance. The Indians made a form of sugar from the sap which they traded with Mexico. Much of the grass once grew in this locality. It was first recorded by Father Font who accompanied the Anza expedition during their stay at the junction of Carrizo and San Felipe Creeks, Dec. 13, 1775. Different spellings are encountered such as: Carizal (1844), Cariso Creek (1848), Carrizo Creek, Carical (1844) and Carrisa. The name can be found in Riverside and San Luis Obispo counties. Carrizo Station, Imperial county.

CARTAGO   Inyo
Spanish name for the ancient city of Carthage in North Africa that was applied to the station by the Southern Pacific in 1909. The name was given to the post office in 1919. It was the southern terminus for the "Bessie Brady," a steamboat operating on Owens Lake at that time. A creek and a settlement nearby, bear the name Carthage.

CASA BLANCA   Riverside
Because of a white house which stood nearby the railroad station of the Santa Fe. (1887). Casa is found also in Riverside and Orange counties: Casa Loma (instead of Casa de la Loma) house of the rising slope.

CASA DIABLO HOT SPRINGS   Mono
Casa, Spanish word for house is one of the favorites applied to American times. Casa Diablo means Devil's House, because of sporadically erupting geyser for so many years. Casa Diablo Mountain, Mono county, named after the Casa Diablo Mine. Casa Diablo Lake, Mono county named for the Mine.

CASCO, EL   Riverside
The word casco has several meanings: the skull, the helmet, the wine cask, and the horse's hoof. The origin of the name is not known.

CASITAS PASS   Ventura
In 1812 an earthquake damaged San Buenaventura Mission and a chapel, San Gertrudis, was built at the mouth of the pass. It took several years before the mission was rebuilt. The Indians lived in huts or adobes, what the Spaniards of the times called "Casitas" (little house), hence the name. In 1864 we find recorded on a plat of the land of Ex-Mission San Buenaventura "The Arroyo de las Casitas" (Creek of the little houses).

CASLAMAYONI RANCHO   Sonoma
This is an Indian name and its meaning is not known, except for the ending - yomi meaning place. The ranch was known as Laguna de los Gentiles (Lake of the Heathen) (Gentiles meant unbaptized Indians). A land grant was awarded March 21, 1844 to Eugene Montenegro, for an area of eight leagues.

CASMALIA   Santa Barbara
It is probably an Indian word rendered Spanish. It appears on maps and on a land grant dated April 6, 1837 for Antonio Olivera. The grant awarded an area of two leagues. The name appears under different spelling: Casmali, Casmaria, Casmale, it applied to a town and hills.

CASTILLEJA LAKE   Sequoia National Park
It is the name of a flowering plant of the figwort family. The plant name has been used for the naming of a lake.

CASTRO
This Spanish family name is common in California. Several places bear this name.

CASTROVILLE   Monterey
Town founded and laid out by Juan B. Castro in honor of his father Jose Simeon Nepomuceno Castro on the Bolsa Nueva y Moro Cojo Rancho on which the present community is located. The original

parcel is dated February 14, 1825. The grant was made in parcels from 1825 to 1844.

CASTRO CREEK, POINT, ROCKS   San Francisco Bay
Perpetuate the name of Joaquin I. Castro, proprietor of Rancho San Pablo.

CASTRO VALLEY   Alameda
For Guillermo Castro grantee of the San Lorenzo and San Leandro lands Feb. 23, 1841.

CASTRO FLATS   Santa Clara
On Las Animas Rancho, of August 17, 1802, to Jose Mariano Castro, son of Joaquin Castro who served in the Anza expedition in 1776. The name is also found in Los Angeles county, for a peak, in Santa Barbara, for a canyon, and a village, Santa Clara county.

CATALINA ISLANDS
There are four islands discovered by Cabrillo (1542) but named by Vizcaino (1602): Santa Barbara, the smallest, San Nicolas, the farthest offshore, Santa Catalina, the largest (developed as a tourist resort) and San Clemente a U.S. Naval training ground.

CAVALLO POINT   Marin
Spanish for point of the horse. In a document from Padre Payeras in 1819 it is said that the name arose because horses were kept here for travel. On the Tamalpais grant of 1845 we read "Punta de los Caballos" (Point of the Horses); later on a "Plaza de los Caballos" appears on Duflot de Mofra's Plan 16 (Gudde, p. 61).

CAYUCOS   San Luis Obispo
The present community has been named after the Moro y Cayucos Rancho dated December 28, 1837 and April 27, 1842 an area of two leagues granted to Vicente Felix. The word "Cayucos" designated fishing boats in American Spanish taken from the Eskimo "Kayak". As far as March 1776 documents mention canoas o cayucos de las que usan en noka. (canoes or kayaks, the kind they use in NOOTKA.) We find it also the word employed to describe the bidarkas of the Aleuts who hunted the sea otter along the shores of the Pacific. The present settlement was started by Captain James Cass who built a wharf here; the town was laid out and named in 1875.

CAZADERO   Sonoma
Spanish for hunting place, hunting ground. The station of the North Pacific Coast Railroad was said to be plentiful with wild game.

CAZADORES   Sacramento
Spanish for hunters. The name of land grant dated July 26, 1844.

CEBADA CANYON   Santa Barbara
Spanish for barley. Named after the immense fields of barley that were the chief crops of this region.

CEDROS ISLAND
In 1539 Cortez sent out Ulloa with three ships to explore the Mexican coast northward. Ulloa rounded and sailed along the outer coast as far as Cedros Island, in latitude 28 . Ulloa never returned from his expedition, only one surviving vessel reached Mexico the following year.

CENTINELA   Los Angeles
The town never materialized under this name. The site was laid out on a portion of the Aguaje de la Centinela Rancho, in 1875 by the California Immigrant Union. The project contemplated the subdivision of 25,000 acres of land into farms, surrounding the colony which, it was promised, would contain a college and a farm school. The name stems from the original ranch. (Hanna, p. 60).

CENTINELA CREEK   Los Angeles
From the Spanish "Aguaje de la Centinela' (Spring of the Sentinel) from a land grant of September 14, 1844. Centinela POST OFFICE was established in 1892.

CENTRO (EL)   Imperial

County seat. It was named and laid out in 1905 by W. F. Holt. Its population in 1970 was 19,272. It is known as the "largest city below sea level in the Western Hemisphere".

CERRITO

Diminutive from Spanish Cerro (hill) hence "little hill" or "hillock". We find several Cerro or Cerrito Creeks, Cerrito Hill (a tautology little hil hill).

CERRITO (EL)   Contra Costa

Mentioned in documents as Cerrito de San Antonio (1820) after the Patron Saint of the Franciscans, Anthony of Padua, named by the padres of Mission Dolores.

CERRITOS RANCHO, LOS   Los Angeles

Land grant dated May 22, 1834 to Manuela Nieto. An area of five leagues. Previously known as Signal Hill. The present towns of Bellflower, Clearwater, Hynes and Signal Hill are located on the site of the grant.

CERRITOS RANCHO, POTRERO DE LOS   Alameda

Spanish for Pasture of the hills from a land grant of March 21, 1844 to Tomas Pacheco and Augustin Alviso.

CERRO

Spanish for mountain or high hill, a commonly geographic term as survived as a generic term in the names of several mountains and eminences in San Diego and San Luis and Inyo counties. Several Cerros were followed by adjectives such as alto (high), lodoso (muddy), ultimo (last, remote).

CERRO GORDO   Inyo

Spanish for fat hill. Probably refers to mineral riches of the mountains that bear it rather than its physiography. It was named in 1865 when Pablo Flores and two Mexicans discovered the rich ore here. It was originally known as the Lone Pine Mining District, that was renamed Cerro Gordo and reorganized in 1872.

CERRO ROMUALDO   San Luis Obispo

Named after an Indian, Romualdo, who was the owner of the Huerta de Romualdo or Chorro land grants of 1842 and 1846. (Huerta means orchard; chorro means spout of water.)

CHAMISAL, CHAMISE, CHAMISH, CHAMISSO, CHEMISE

From Chamiza meaning kind of wild cane or reed. The name was very popular in Spanish times and appears in such places as: Chamisal (Monterey), Bolsa del Chamisal (San Luis Obispo), Chamisal de Los Lobos (San Francisco). In American times it was used as a generic term. Chemisal and Chemissal Creeks (Colusa), Chemise (San Benito), Chemise Creek (Mendocino), Chemisal Ridge (Monterey), etc.

CHAMISAL RANCHO (BOLSA DE)   San Luis Obispo

A land grant dated 1837 to Francisco Quijada.

CHAMISAL RANCHO, EL   Monterey

Land grant dated 1835 to Felipe Vasquez for an area of one league.

CHAPARRAL   Butte

Meaning an area of dense underbrush or dwarf trees. Also plantation of evergreen oaks.

CHAVEZ RAVINE   Los Angeles

Named for Julian Chavez an early owner. The land was used as a potter's field before the 1800's. During the smallpox epidemics of 1850 and 1880 it served as the county infirmary farm. Elysian Park absorbed part of it in the 1880's.

CHICO   Butte

Name from Arroyo chico "small stream". Very popular term during Spanish times, where it appears in more than twenty places. William Dickey and Edward Farley gave the creek this designation in course of a journey into northern end of Sacramento Valley in 1843. The land was granted November 7, 1844. The present city was laid out in 1850. It contains a 2,400 acre park as an urban preserve.

CHICO RANCHO   Arroyo, Butte
Spanish meaning small stream; land granted to William Dickey November 7, 1844.

CHICO MARTINEZ CREEK   San Luis Obispo
Named for Chico Martinez a mustang breeder.

CHILENO
Spanish for a native of Chile. The term appears in several places Chileno Canyon (Los Angeles) Chileno Creek (Merced), Chileno Valley (Marin).

CHILE GULCH   Calaveras
or CHILI GULCH
One of the richest placer mining sections, took its name from a great number of Chilean miners who worked here in 1848-49.

CHINO   San Bernardino
Spanish for Chinese; in Mexico "curly hair"; in Spanish times derogatory "mixed blood" named after Santa Ana del Chino Rancho granted March 26, 1841 in two parcels of five and three leagues to Antonio Maria Lugo and Isaac Williams. The present town was laid out by Richard Gird on the site of the Rancho. The term Chino appears in several places: Chino Creek (Butte county), Chino Rodriguez (San Mateo), Rancheria del Chino (Santa Clara county).

CHIQUITA, CHIQUITO
Spanish for little, small and is found in several places. Its origin goes back to the Chiquito Joaquin (tributary of the Joaquin River).

CHIQUITA STATION   Sonoma

CHIQUITO CREEK   Shasta

CHIQUITO CREEK   Madera

CHIQUITO LAKE, PASS, RIDGE   Madera

CHOLLAS VALLEY   San Diego
Spanish meaning skull or head. Steep-walled valley west of La Mesa so named for presence here of numerous specimens of cholla cactus. We must note that Choya (a frequent spelling for (jackdaw or crow) sounds as chollas. Originally it was named for an Indian village in 1775. Appears under the name of Rancheria de las choyas (1782). There are also:

CHOLLAS STATION   San Diego

CHOLLAS RESERVOIR   San Diego

CHOYAS VALLEY, LAS   San Diego

CHORRO
Spanish meaning a gush of water or rapids. Chorro creek, San Luis Obispo county appears on land grant dated 1842 and 1846 under the name of Huerta de Romualdo o del chorro and Aguaje del Chorro.

CHORRO RANCHO, EL   San Luis Obispo
Land grant dated 1845 to James Scott and John Wilson for an area of one league.

CHUALAR
Spanish for site where the chual (white pigweed) grows.

CHUALAR RANCHO   Monterey
Granted in 1839 to Juan Malarin from the Santa Rosa de Chualar for an area of two leagues.

CHULA VISTA   San Diego
From the Mexican words meaning beautiful view or attractive, pretty view. It was granted from a part of the Nacional Rancho, to Juan Forster in 1858. It was laid out and named by the San Diego Land and Town Company in 1888. Before 1906 the post office was written Chulavista. It has become not only a large residential area but a center for aircraft parts production and other industry. Its population in 1970 was 67,901.

CHUPADERO   Monterey
From the Spanish sucking, sucker, absorbent. In Spanish American it is a "brackish pool where animals come to drink. It existed before 1795.

CHUPINES
From the Spanish Chopoa meaning black poplar tree, black cottonwood.

CHUPINES CREEK   Monterey
Recorded in 1854 as Arroyo de los Chupines.

CIENAGA
From the Spanish word Cienaga meaning moor, marsh. The term used as a generic is still seen in several places such as:

CIENAGA CREEK, CIENAGA VALLEY   San Benito

CIENAGA SECA   San Bernardino

COOPER CIENAGA   San Diego

CIENAGA CANYON   Los Angeles

CIENEGUITAS
Diminutive meaning little marshes from a land grant in Santa Barbara county of October 10, 1845, under the name of Paraje de la Cieneguita, or Suerte en las Cieneguitas (Place of Cieneguita or luck, chance or luck of the Cieneguitas.)

CINCO   Kern
Origin unrevealed. Spanish for five.

CIERVO
Spanish for elk used often in Spanish times and still remains in our times.

CIERVO HILLS   Fresno

CIERVO MOUNTAIN   Fresno

CIERVO, ARROYO   Fresno
It is also spelled cierbo as in Cañada del Cierbo (Contra Costa).

CIMA
Spanish for summit of a mountain, hill, top of a tree.

CIMA   San Bernardino
Name of the station of the San Pedro-Los Angeles-Salt Lake Railroad (1907).

CIMA MESA   Los Angeles
Located above Antelope Valley.

CIPRESES (PUNTA DE LOS)   Monterey

Spanish for point cypress. The Cypress Point extends along the cliffs and low bluffs from Pescadero Point to Cypress Point, a distance of two miles. As a result of their struggle with violent storms from the Pacific Ocean which break on the unprotected cliffs, they present a variety and singularity of form connected with their exposed habitat.

CISCO   Placer

Town situated at an altitude of 5934 ft. Its origin has been dispute: it has been said to be derived from the Algonquin word cisco meaning a sort of oily fish found in the Great Lakes. It is believed that the word derived from the Spanish cisco (broken pieces of coal.) There is another theory which is that the town was named for John Cisco, at one time connected with the U.S. government.

COAHUILA or COACHELLA   Riverdale

From the Spanish onomatopoeic rendering of an Indian word Ka-wia, name of Shoshonean tribe in Colorado desert. Variants of the name are: Caguilla, Cahuillas, Coahuillas, Cohuilla, and Coahuila.

COCHE RANCHO, OJO DE AGUA DE LA   Santa Clara

Spanish for coach; hence the spring of the coach. Land grant dated August 4, 1835 to Juan Hernandez, for an area of two leagues. Present Morgan Hill is located on the site of the grant.

COCHES

Spanish "coach"; Mexican "hogs". The term is used on several land grants:

COCHES CANYON, COCHES CREEK   San Diego

CANADA DE LOS COCHES (1843)   Los Coches, Monterey

LOS COCHES   Santa Clara

COCHENITOS

(diminutive for coches) "little pigs" became Las Pulgas

ARROYO DE LOS COCHES or
ARROYO DEL MONTE DE LOS COCHES: COCHE CANYON
                    Ventura

LOS COCHES MOUNTAIN, CAÑADA DE LOS COCHES Santa Barbara

COCHE POINT

COCHES PRIETOS

CODORNICES VILLAGE   Alameda

Named by Jose Domingo Peralta in 1818 when he and his brother found a nest of quails eggs (codorniz).

COJA CREEK
"Lame woman Creek"   Santa Cruz

COJO

Spanish for lame man.

CANADA DEL COJO   Santa Barbara

Discovered by Portolas expedition August 26, 1769. The Indian chief was lame in one leg and the soldiers of Portola called the place "Rancheria del Cojo", however, the Spanish leader christened it Santa Teresa.

COLORADO RIVER

The Little Colorado was named so because of the red coloration of its water said Onate in 1604 when he met the stream; the larger river was named Rio Grande de Buena Esperanza by Onate in January 1605. It has had many names: Rio de Buena Guia (good guide river); Rio del Tizon (firebrand river); Rio de los Martires (Martyrs River), Colorado River (about 1806). We find the Spanish adjectives in several counties: Alpine, Contra Costa, Imperial, Mariposa, Riverside, San Benito, Tehalma.

CONCEPTION POINT   Santa Barbara
Juan Rodriguez Cabrillo discovered it in October 18, 1542 and named it: Cabo de Galera because of its resemblance to a galley. On December 7, 1602 Martin Palacios Vizcaino's cartographer gave the name Punta de la Limpia Concepcion or Punta de la Purisima Concepcion (Immaculate Conception) because it was the day of the Immaculate Conception. Later on upon reaching an Indian village where a native stole a sword of a soldier, Crespi called the place "Rancheria de la Espada y Concepcion de Maria Santisima". The present town of Concepcion stands on the land grant "Punta de la concepcion". It is after 1793 that the Anglicized name Point Conception appears.

CONCORD   Contra Costa
In 1834 Salvio Pacheco was granted Rancho del Diablo of 18,000 acres. In 1862 he selected there the site of town and named the new settlement Todos Santos. But the name was changed to the present by 1873.

CONEJO GRADE   Ventura
Spanish for rabbit because of the great number found by Spanish explorers. It stems from El Conejo Rancho upon which grade is situated.

CONEJO RANCHO, EL   Ventura
Spanish for rabbit was often used in Spanish times and has been well preserved in the following counties: Fresno, Monterey, San Diego, Stanislaus, Ventura. As far as 1776 the name appears in a singular or plural form. El Conejo Rancho was granted in 1803 to Jose Polanco and Ignacio Rodriguez. In October 10, 1822 the grant was known as El Conejo or Nuesta Senora de Altagracia (Our Lady of High Grace) and a portion of it was given to Captain Jose de la Guerra y Noriega. The present Newbury Park is located on the site of the grant.

CONTRA COSTA COUNTY
Spanish for "opposite coast" to San Francisco, explored by Fages (1772), Anza (1776) and Duran (1817). Created February 18, 1850, chap. 15. Area 434 sq. mi.

CORONADO BEACH   San Diego
This long spit of land forming the outer shore of the harbor of San Diego, derives its name from the Coronado Islands nearby. These islands were originally named in honor of Coronado. The four islands, also it is said were named "Los cuatro Martires Coronados" (the four crowned martyrs) Severus, Severianus, Carpophorus and Victorius, scourged to death in Rome during Diocletian in 303 A.D. Father Antonio de la Ascension named them November 8, 1602 because they were four islands which were sighted on the saints' day of the four martyrs. The town was named in October 1887 by the Coronado Beach Company. The 1870 population of the town was 20,910.

CORDILLERAS
Spanish for mountain ranges (South America). In 1846 the word cordilleras appears "Cordilleras of California or Sierra Nevada".

CORDILLERAS CREEK   San Mateo

CORONA
Spanish for crown. A popular name in the U.S. Six communities bear the name in California.

CORONA   Riverside
The town was founded by the South Riverside Land and Water Co., in a form of a circle one mile in diameter (1886). At that time it was named South Riverside. The city was incorporated in 1896 and named Corona in 1916.

CORONA DEL MAR Orange

Origin unrevealed, meaning crown of the sea. Named in 1904 by George E. Hart. In 1905 the name waschanged to Balboa Palisades. But people did not like the name and the old one was brought back.

CORRAL

Spanish for poultry yard, enclosed space; a term widely used in the western U.S. which has survived as a place name. The word appears as far as 1769 at the time of Portola expedition; a village near Castaic, in Los Angeles county is named "Rancheria del Corral".

CORRAL DE PIEDRA CREEK San Luis Obispo

Land grant of February 11, 1841.

CORRAL CANYON Alameda

First named Portezuela de Buenos Ayres (1834), then Arroyo de Buenos Ayres (1852).

CORRAL RANCHO, CANADA DEL Santa Barbara

By land grant of November 5, 1841 to Jose Dolores Ortega for an area of two leagues.

CORRALITOS Santa Cruz

Little corrals.

CORRALITOS RANCHO, LOS Santa Cruz

Land granted to Jose Amesti in 1844 for an area of four leagues.

CORRALITOS LAGOON Santa Cruz

Named by Portola expedition "Laguna del Corral" October 1769. The present name appears in 1807. There is a creek and a town of the same name.

CORALILLOS CANYON Santa Barbara

Previously known as Corral de Guadalupe on the map of Rancho Guadalupe (1837).

CORTE MADERA

From Spanish "Corte de Madera" (a site where lumber is cut). A very popular name in California where the name appears in several counties.

CORTE MADERA Marin

Was named "El Corte de Madera del Presidio". A saw mill operated by the grantee John Reed (around 1834) was the most important lumber supplier for the Bay district.

CORTE DE MADERA CREEK San Mateo

Crosses through two grants: Canada del Corte de Madera (May 18, 1833) and El Corte de Madera (May 1, 1844) for Domingo Perralta and Maximo Martinez.

CORTE MADERA MOUNTAIN San Diego

CORTE MADERA VALLEY San Diego

CORTE DE MADERA CREEK Santa Cruz

COSTA MESA Orange

Costa meaning coast, mesa meaning table. Post office established in 1921. Was previously known as Harper.

COTATE RANCHO Sonoma

Today Cotati. Land grant of July 6, 1844 to Juan Castañeda, for an area of four leagues. It is designated on early maps as Lomas de Cotate, this word is an hispanicization of Kotati (Cotati), the name of a coast Miwok Indian village.

COTATI VALLEY Sonoma (See Cotate Rancho)

COVELO   Mendocino
It could be a misspelled name for Covolo, an old Tirolian fortress. There is a Covelo in Spain. The origin is unrevealed. The California town was recorded on the land office map of 1879.

COVINA   Los Angeles
Applied to subdivision of La Puente Rancho in late 1880's. Spanish for locally - place of vines. It was named in 1882 by J. S. Phillops of Los Angeles. It is assumed that the name was coined because the region was "cove-like" and because there were some vines planted by the Badillo brothers of Costa Rica who had purchased a part of La Puente Rancho in 1870.

COYOTE
A kind of wolf or fox generic hispanicized from the Aztec name Coyotl. Very popular, this generic term has become the place name of many American features mostly in the southwestern regions.

COYOTE RIVER   Santa Clara
Known in early Spanish times as Arroyo del Coyote or Arollo del Coyote (1776, 1781). Anza visited it in 1776.

LOS COYOTES   San Diego

COYOTE WELLS   Imperial
Because of the wells discovered there where a coyote was scratching the ground for water.

COYOTES RANCHO, LOS   Orange and Los Angeles
Land grant dated in 1834 to Juan Jose Nieto. The present cities of Buena Park Cypress and Los Alamitos are located on the site of the grant.

LA CRESCENTA   Los Angeles
(See La Cañada Rancho).

CRUCERO   San Bernardino
Spanish meaning crossing. It is appropriate where north and south bound Tonopah and Tidewater and east-west Union Pacific railroad once crossed. The previous name Epsom was changed to the present in 1900.

CRUCES, LAS   Santa Barbara
From former Canada de las Cruces Rancho. Spanish for the crosses.

CUATE
From the Mexican word taken from the Aztec "coatl" (twin) appears in several land grants.

CUATI RANCHO, HUERTA DE   Los Angeles
Huerta is Spanish for orchard, garden. Granted in 1830 Victoria Reid.

CUCA RANCHO, or EL POTRERO   San Diego
Spanish meaning a kind of fruit or root used as a substitute for coffee. From a land grant named "Los Gentiles de Cucam". (The heathen Indians of Cucam) dated May 7, 1845 granted to Maria Juana de los Angeles for an area of half a league.

CUCAMONGA   San Bernardino
Named from the Cucamonga Rancho, which in turn was named for the Cucamonga Rancheria. The name Cucamonga Rancheria appears first in 1821; in 1819 it had been named "Nuestra Señor del Pilar de Cucamunga". The land grant is dated from January 25, 1839. The present town was laid out around the oldest winery in the state in 1854. The post ffice was established in 1867.

CUCAMONGA PEAK   San Bernardino
Takes its name from the Cucamonga Rancho, it has an elevation of 8,911 ft. and is located in the San Bernardino National Forest.

CUCAMONGA RANCHO   San Bernardino
    In the beginning it was under the jurisdiction of San Gabriel Mission. The mission was secularized in 1834; three leagues of land were granted to Tiburcio Tapia in 1839. The present communities of Alta Loma, Cucamonga and Upland are located on the site of the grant.

CUESTA PASS   San Luis Obispo
    Portola, Anza and Fremont traveled through it. It is located in the northern part of Los Padres National Forest. Spanish meaning grade or slope and is appropriate for the steep hill nearby. Cuesta appears very frequently in Spanish times. In 1842 it was called "Cañada de la Cuesta".

CUESTA, CAMP AND STATION
    (1887). The Cuesta Pass was previously called San Luis Pass.

CUMBRE PEAK, LA   Santa Barbara
    Cumbre is Spanish for summit, top.

CUPERTINO   Santa Clara
    Anza expedition camped at the creek, March 25, 1776 named Arroyo de San José Cupertino (present Stevens Creek) in honor of an Italian Saint (1602-1672) of Brindisi. A post office was established in 1882 until it was discontinued in 1895. In the 1960's it acquired an electronics and aerospace industry. In 1970 its population was 18,216.

DANA POINT, town   Orange
    The bay was called Bahia (or Ensenada) de San juan Capistrano at the time of the mission circa 1830. Named in memory of Richard Dana, (1815-82). The post office Dana Point was established in 1929. It is now a residential and resort area with an important yacht harbor.

DEER
    A second place after "bear", deer is found in more than 150 place names: creeks, canyons, flats, parks, etc. Some of the names are translations from the Spanish: Arroyo de los Venados, Rio de los Venados (Thehama county).

DEHESA   San Diego
    Spanish for pasture - ground. Name applied to a post office 1890.

DELGADA POINT   Humboldt
    Spanish meaning narrow point. Applied 1775 by Bodega. In 1792 Vancouver changed this name to Barro de Arena.

DELGADA CANYON
    Name approved 1938.

DEL LOMA   Trinity
    Spanish for the hill. Post office named in 1927.

DEL MAR   San Diego
    Spanish for of the sea, from the sea. Resort and residential community north of San Diego on the ocean side. There are a Turf Club for horse racing and an annual County Fair. It is located near Torrey Pines State Park.

DEL NORTE COUNTY
    Spanish for of the north. The name was chosen in preference to Alta, Altissima, Rincon and Del Merritt, the other suggested names. It was created March 12, 1857, chap. 52. Area 1,003 sq. mi.

DEL PASO   Sacramento
    From a Mexican Grant, Rancho del Paso, of Dec. 18, 1844, which was named after El Paso de Los Americanos. The post office was opened in 1904 and was named after the Mexican Grant. The present post office name is : Del Paso Heights.

DELPIEDRA Fresno

For the terminal of the Santa Fe. Spanish "piedra" means stone. The post office was named Del Piedra in 1923.

DEL REY Fresno

When the railroad reached this station in 1898 the present name was adopted from the nearby Rio del Rey (King's River) ranch.

DEL ROSA San Bernardino

Incorrect combination of a feminine noun with a masculine article. Should have been De La Rosa, unless it was a family name Delrosa. Post office and town.

DE LUZ San Diego

Named after an English pioneer Luce who built an enclosure for his horses. The Mexican neighbors called it "Corral de Luz". The present name was adopted by the post office and town circa 1880.

DESCANSO San Diego

Possible origin of name Descanso "place of rest". Local historians say because a party of surveyors running the lines of old ranch grants stopped here each day for their lunch. Name applied to the post office in the 1880's. It contains 6,000 roses, 100,000 camellias and diverse other flowers and trees.

DESCANSO BAY Catalina Island

DIABLO MOUNT Contra Costa

In the early days (1790) the mount was called San Juan Bautista. The name changed (1811) to Cerro Alto de los Bolbones; then to Sierra de los Bolbones. In 1824 the name Monte del Diablo (mount or wood of the Devil) appears on the map of the Mission San Jose. A legend attributed to General Mariano Guadalupe Vallejo tells us that "a military expedition from San Francisco in 1806 marched against a tribe known as the Bolbones, who were encamped at the foot of the mountains. The Indians were victorious and at the conclusion of the skirmish, a plume-bedecked figure appeared, which the Indians designated as Puy, their superhuman leader. The Spaniards translated "puy" as diablo or devil and so named the mountain. (Hanna p. 86). It was also named Monte Diavolo or Diabolo (1837); Monte del Diablo and Sierras de los Bolbones (1844); Mount Diabolo (1848); Diablo Range (Geographic Board, May 15, 1908). Diablo Post office was established in 1917. The popularity of the Spanish word diablo appears in land grants: Rincon del Diablo, San Diego county, May 18, 1843. Canada del Diablo, also called San Miguel, in Ventura county May 30, 1845. Point Diablo in Marin county and Diablo Point in Santa Cruz island.

DIAZ CREEK, STATION Inyo

Named after the brothers Rafael and Eleuterio Diaz who operated a cattle ranch on the creek in the 1860's.

DOLORES MISSION San Francisco

Named after a small spring "Los Dolores or Nuestra Senora de los Dolores" (Our Lady of Sorrows) by Anza on March 29, 1776.

DOMINGUEZ Los Angeles

Dominguez was a family name. Juan José Dominguez (1736-1809) was first of line in California and was grantee of San Pedro Rancho November 20, 1784 upon which the locality is situated. Several names were given to the station: Davidson City, Elftman. Several cities are now located on the original land grant which extended from Wilmington to Los Angeles, Compton, Dominguez, Gardena and Redondo Beach.

DOMINGUEZ, LAGUNA Los Angeles

Has replaced the muddy lake formerly known as Nigger Slough (March 30, 1938).

DORADO, EL County

Spanish for the gilded one. Takes its name from the mining camp. Created February 18, 1850. Chap. 15. Area 1,725 sw. mi.

DORADO, EL   El Dorado
Mining camp of 1849. Spanish contraction of el hombre dorado meaning gilded man. Refers to pre-historic custom of a sacrifice made in behalf of the community by Indians of Guativita, New Granada, South America. After ceremonies the chief was smeared with gum and powdered pure gold dust on himself. Later he would wash it off by jumping into a lake from a raft. This act completed the sacrifice. (Hanna, 89) Area was first named Mad Springs.

DORADO CREEK, EL   Placer
A gold mining community near Michigan Bluff. Previously known as El Dorado Canyon.

DORADO NATIONAL FOREST, EL
Named and created by presidential proclamation in 1910. There are several communities: El Dorado (Calaveras county), El Dorado Creeks in Mariposa, Placer and Santa Barbara counties.

DOS CABEZAS SPRINGS   San Diego
Origin unrevealed. Spanish for two heads.

DOS PALOS   Merced
Spanish for sticks, lumber, trees hence two sticks was applied to the station of the Southern Pacific in 1889. In 1892 a Dos Palos Colony was established. The previous spelling was Dospalos. The present name was adopted in 1905. The town was founded in 1907.

DOS PUEBLOS   Santa Barbara
Name derived from two Indian villages located at the entrance of the canyon. As far as 1542 these two villages were noted by Cabrillo, and noticed also by Anza on April 28, 1774. The Creek and Canyon of the same name were named on April 18, 1842.

DOS RIOS   Mendocino
Spanish for two rivers because of the location of the town on the fork of the Eel River.

DRAKES BAY   Marin
Drakes Bay was discovered by Sebastián Rodriguez Cermeño on Nov. 6, 1595; and was named San Francisco (Puerto y Bahia de San Francisco) the following day. On January 8, 1603, Vizcaino renamed the bay Bahia de Don Gaspar. It was not until 1625 that the name of Drake appears on the maps (Puerto St. Francisco Draco). Then comes San Francisco Bay in 1790.

DUARTE   Los Angeles
Named for Andrés Duarte grantee of Azusa Rancho on May 10, 1841. The present town is located on the site of the grant. Once noted for citrus groves, it has become a residential area. The City of Hope National Medical Center is located on the site of the original grant.

DULAH   Ventura
Seems to be a corruption of the Spanish dula meaning a pasture. The origin and meaning of the name are unknown.

DULZURA   San Diego
Spanish for sweetness. Obtained its name because it was a center for milk and honey production in 1869. One can find a Honey Spring Ranch and a Bee Canyon nearby. The post office was established in 1887 and was named by Mrs. Hagenbeck.

DUME   Los Angeles
Named by Vancouver to honor his distinguished host Padre Francisco Dumetz of Mission San Buenaventura. The name was corrupted into Dume. Later on it became Duma and in 1869 it took its present spelling.

ELMIRA   Solano
Was known as Vaca Station until 1852. When Stephen Hoyt came from New York State, to California in 1853 he laid out the townsite around the former locality. He named it "Elmira" from the name of his hometown of New York State.

EMBARCADERO Santa Clara
Named by a land grant of June 18, 1845 Embarcadero de Santa Clara. Spanish meaning landing place or wharf.

ENCANTO San Diego
Miss Ella Klauber named it in 1889 because of salubrious climate with enchanting views of San Diego. Spanish for charm or fascination.

ENCINITAS San Diego
Spanish for little evergreen oaks. We find this word in titles of several land grants. The present city of Oakland was once called "Encinal de Temescal" (Oak grove of Temescal) Encinitas Creek, San Diego bore the name of Cañada de los Encinos at the time of Portola's expedition. The land grant related to this area was applied July 13, 1842 under the name of Los Encinitos. Encinitas (Town) dates from 1881. The Santa Fe railroad station was named Encenitos in 1881. Encino, Los Angeles county - Portola called the San Fernando Valley Santa Catalina de Bononia de los Encinos, August 5, 1769. The station was established in 1892; the post office in 1939. It was an area of one league granted to Ramon Francisco and Roque on July 18, 1845. Note that the correct spelling would be La Encina.

ENTRE NAPA RANCHO Napa
Land grant dated 1836 to Nicolas Higuera. Spanish for "between or within" Napa.

ESCALON San Joaquin
Named by James W. Jones who laid out the town on his land in 1895-96. Spanish for step of a stair.

ESCARPINES Monterey
The name is first seen in 1837. Bolsa de los Escarpines grant. Several meanings are given to the word: escarpin: sock or light shoe, by extension escarpe: bluff, steep slope; or escorpina, a small salt water fish.

ESCONDIDO San Diego
Spanish for hidden. Located on Rincon del Diablo Rancho. The Spanish word used in a geographical sense with watering places. On February 22, 1776 tthe Anza expedition set camp there; they called the place "Agua Escondida". There are Escondido Creeks in San Diego, Santa Barbara and Los Angeles counties.

ESCORPION Los Angeles
Spanish for scorpion. Mentioned by Fages as a place name as early as September 1783. An area of one and a half leagues granted to three Indians Manuel, Odon and Urbano August 7, 1845. Scorpion Hills also known as the Sierra Santa Susanna.

ESMERELDA Calaveras
From the Spanish word "Esmeralda" (emerald) named after Esmeralda Mine from a land grant of 1891. In 1892 it was mispelled and never corrected.

ESPADA CREEK Santa Barbara
Spanish espada meaning sword. Named because an Indian stole the sword of a Spaniard. Named after "Rancheria de la Espada". Two and a half leagues northwest of Point Conception.

ESPARTO Yolo
Botanical term for form of grass known as "matweed" or "feather grass". When the railroad reached the place in 1875 it called it Esperanza. In 1881 the post office was named Esparto.

ESPERANZA, RAILROAD STATIONS Orange and Siskiyou

ESPERANZA CREEK Calaveras
Named after the mine of same name.

ENCINAL Y BUENA ESPERANZA Monterey
Spanish meaning oak grove and good hope. From a land grant dated November 29, 1834.

-31-

ESPINOSA LAKE   Monterey

To honor José and Salvador Espinosa, cattle breeders. El Rancho de los Espinosas Llamado San Miguel, whose forebear was Jose Joaquin Espinosa, a soldier on the Sacred Expedition.

ESPIRITU SANTO   San Benito

Spanish for Holy Ghost. The name appears in two land grants: Lomerias del Espiritu Santo (San Benito county) granted August 26, 1842. Loma del Espiritu Santo grant dated April 15, 1839 for Maria del Espiritu Santo Carrillo.

ESTANILAO, RANCHERIA DEL RIO   Stanislau

Named for the Stanislau River. Land grant dated December 29, 1843 to Francisco Rico and José Antonio Castro for an area of eleven leagues.

ESTANISLAO, RANCHO DEL   San Joaquin and Stanislau

Granted in 1846 to Alpheus Basilio Thompson for an area of eight leagues. Named after the Stanislau River. The river was discovered and named Rio De Nuestra Señora de Guadalupe by Gabriel Moraga (October 1806). An Indian leader Estanislao fought bravely against Mariano Vallejo and the river was know by his name. In 1839 we find "Rio Estanislao"; then the American version Stanislau appeared in 1844.

STANISLAUS, Town   (Alta California)

STANISLAUS STATION (1879)

STANISLAUS POST OFFICE   Tuolumne county 1912

STANISLAUS COUNTY

Created April 1, 1854 from part of Tuolumne county.

NATIONAL FOREST

Created and named in 1897.

ESTERO

Spanish for estuary, deep cover, creek, salt marsh. It was frequently applied as a geographical term in Spanish times. As far as 1769 we find "Punta del Estero"; then as "Los Esteros", "Esteros Point", "Ponto del Esteros", "Esteros Point", "Point Esteros", "Esteros Bay", and "Estero Bay".

ESTERO AMERICANO RANCHO   Sonoma

Granted in September 4, 1839 to Edward McIntosh for an area of two leagues.

ESTERO BAY   San Luis Obispo

Large lagoon whose interior portion is Morro Bay. Estero "estuary" was used as early as 1769 during Costanso's expedition.

ESTEROS RANCHOS, RINCON DE LOS

For three land grants with this name grouped around the estuary of Alviso Creek and San Francisco Bay. The name means "the inside corner of the estuary". The grants were made in 1838 to Ignacio Alviso.

ESTRELLA   San Luis Obispo

Spanish for star. Named for Estrella Rancho located on Estrella River.

ESTRELLA CREEK   San Luis Obispo

A tributary to the Salinas Creek.

ESTRELLA (Town)

Mispelled Estrelta (1850).

FALDA   San Diego

From the Spanish word skirt.   It designates the lower part of the steep slope of Loma Alta. The name was applied to the station of the San Diego Central.

FAMOSO   Kern

Spanish for famous, great. It was previously known as Poso named after Poso Creek. In 1890 with the creation of the post office it became Spottiswood. But the residents did not like the name and they had it changed to Famoso.

FANDANGO   Modoc

A lively Spanish dance. The name was given by an immigrant party of 1849 who had to dance all night in order to keep warm, hence the name of Fandango Valley. Also:

FANDANGO CREEK

FANDANGO MOUNTAIN

FANDANGO PASS

(6,250 feet elevation) allowing travel between Nevada and Oregon. For its naming, see Fandango.

FARALLONES, THE   San Francisco

Sebastian Vizcaino, Spanish explorer, named these islands Los Frayles or the friars when he visited them in 1602. Juan Francisco de Bodega y Cuadra 1775 renamed "cliffs of the friars" which is the complete translation of "Farallones de los frayles". One has to note that "farallon means small rocky island. Drake called them Islands of Saint James. The name appears also as "Farallones (1579) de San Francisco", North Farallon, South Farallon, Middle Farallon. In 1909 the islands were made a bird sanctuary. Since 1856 they have been part of the city and county of San Francisco.

FALSE CAPE   Humboldt

The Punta Gorda of Hezeta (1775). One finds in 1851 "False Cape Mendocino" in 1854 it appears under "False Cape", or "Cape Fortunas".

FEATHER RIVER   Butte and Plumas

The river was known by the present name as well as by its Spanish name "Rio de las plumas", because the Indians went profusely decorated with feathers, and feathers were seen everywhere. It was Captain Luis Arguello who in 1821 named the place "Rio de las plumas". Frémont camped on its banks before the beginning of the Bear Flag Revolt. Rich Bar on its banks was very famous during the gold rush as the site of mining camps. Power developments on the river created Lake Almanor and Oroville Dam.

FEATHERTON   Plumas

A mining locality. (See Feather River).

FELIPE LUGO RANCHO, POTRERO DE   Los Angeles

From a grant dated 1845 to Teodoro Romero. The name means "The pasture of Felipe Lugo".

FELIS RANCHO, LOS   Los Angeles

From a land grant dated 1843 to Maria Ygnacia Verdugo, for an area of one and a half leagues. Named after Jose Vicente Felix (Felis, or Feliz) who was with Anza expedition (1774). He was the founder of Los Angeles pueblo and owned a rancho in this area.

FELIZ RANCHO   San Mateo

For a lang grant dated April 30, 1844 to Domingo Felix or Feliz, an area of one league. It was also called Cañada de las Auras.

FELIZ CREEK   Mendocino

Named for Fernando Feliz, land grant of Nov. 9, 1844.

FERMIN (or FIRMIN) POINT   Los Angeles

Named in 1793 after Father Fermin Francisco Lasuén by Captain Vancouver who established eight

California missions. Vancouver admired so much Father Fermin that he named a second point for him. Point Lasuén.

FERNANDEZ   Butte
Named after the brothers Dionisio and Maximo Fernandez who received a grant on June 12, 1846.

LAS FLORES   San Diego
Don Gaspar de Portola and Father Juan Crespi named this region Santa Praxedis de los Rosales for July 21 was Saint's day of the second century holy one and Crespi related "the spot was full of grape vines and innumerable Castilian rosebushes and other flowers."

FLORES
Spanish "flowers" used widely in Spanish times appears in numerous place names, titles of claims and land grants.

LAS FLORES   Tehama
The town was laid out in 1916 and named after the Las Flores land grant (1844). The name is also found in Los Angeles and Santa Barbara counties.

FLORES PEAK   Orange
In honor of the famous Juan Flores the Mexican outlaw (1836-57) who was publicly hanged in Los Angeles. The peak is located in Santiago Canyon.

FONTANA   San Bernardino
Some evidence called "fountain" because of abundance of water that issued from nearby Lytle Creek. It is also possible that Mike Fontana gave his name to the land he subdivided to start a new settlement in 1913. The previous name was Rosena.

FORTUNA   Humboldt
Spanish for fortune. The two previous names of this locality "Springville and Slide" did not survive. The owner of this land, thought about the name Fortune for it was a good place in which to live, or after the goddess "Fortuna" of good fortune.

FRANCESES RANCHO, CAMPO DE LOS   San Joaquin
In memory of a French trappers' camp for the land grant of 1844 to William Gulnac for an area of eleven leagues. The present city of Stockton is located on the site of this grant.

FRESNO COUNTY
Spanish "ash" because of this tree which flourished along the San Joaquin and Kings rivers. It is important in food processing and as an oil producer. Created April 19, 1856, chap. 127, 5,985 sq. mi.

FRESNO   Fresno
Named because of the great number of ashes. As far as 1851 the Rio Fresno appears on maps. (Also in the American version Fresno River; in 1856 it appears with a different spelling Frezno.) Since 1872 the present name has been adopted for the city and county.

FRUTO   Glenn
Spanish for fruit. It is descriptive of horticultural products of this region in locality, post office listed in 1890.

GABILAN PEAK   Monterey
Spanish meaning sparrow-hawk (gavilan). A popular name in Spanish times for mountains, peaks. Captain Fremont erected a fort on Gavilan (Gabilan) Peak, March 6, 1846. Already in 1828 it figures on Registro, p. 14. "Un gran cerro llamado del "Gavilan". (A high hill called of the hawk).

GABILAN PEAK   Riverside
"Sparrow-hawk Peak". Located in Western Riverside county (2,439 ft. elev.)

GABILAN RANCHO, CIENEGA DEL   Monterey
Granted in 1843 to Joseph Yves Limantour. Spanish for "the swamp of the sparrow-hawk" for an area of eleven leagues.

GALLINAS   Marin
Spanish for "hens". As far as 1819 the name appears as "Sitio de las Gallinas" (Place of the hens).

GARAPATA CREEK   Monterey
Corruption of "garrapata" meaning sheep or cattle tick. Because of the great number of ticks found in the region. Known in 1835 as "Arroyo de las Garrapatas".

GARAPITO CREEK   Los Angeles
Spanish for waterbugs, ticks; named because of the great number of ticks swarming the place.

GARCIA RIVER   Mendocino
For Rafael Garcia who was granted nine leagues on the coast north of Presidio Ruso (Fort Ross) November 15, 1844. (Gudde, p. 124)

GARROTE   Tuolumne
Spanish for the scaffold where the capital punishment called garrote is inflicted (by strangulation). Named because some angry miners hanged a thief here in 1850. The post office disappeared in 1875. The name was replaced by Groveland around 1879.

GARZAS CREEK   Stanislaus and Merced
Spanish for herons. Already in 1840 it appears in documents as "Parage llamado las Garzas" (a site called the herons), and in 1843 it is shown as "Arroyo de las Garzas".

LOS GATOS   Santa Clara
Spanish for cats. Taken from name "Rinconada de los Gatos Rancho". Corner of the Cats. First known as Forbes Mill. From a land grant of May 21, 1840 to Sebastian Peralta and José Hernandez for an area of one and a half leagues.

LOS GATOS   Monterey
Land grant of 1820 and 1837 to Jose Trinidad Espinosa for an area of one league. Los Gatos means "the cats, bob-cats or mountain lions". It was also known as Santa Rita Rancho. Gatos was often found in geographical names: Los Gatos, Gatos Creek, Cuesta de los Gatos.

GAVILAN, see Gabilan

GAVIOTA   Santa Barbara
Spanish for sea-gull. The soldiers of Portola expedition 1769 called it "Gaviota" when they saw a seagull on the spot. The name was popular in Spanish times: "Elcajon de la Gaviota", El Cañon de la Gabiota".

GAVIOTA PASS   Santa Barbara
Elevation on 918 ft. Mexican forces were expected to ambush Fremont there (Dec. 25, 1846) during his advance on Santa Barbara, but he avoided them by using San Marcos Pass.

GAZOS CREEK   San Mateo
A corruption of the Spanish "garzas" meaning herons. The Portola expedition found herons on the creek and named it "Arroyo de las Garzas".

GLENDALE   Los Angeles
Previously known as Verdugo before 1883; in 1886 the town was subdivided and incorporated in 1906; it absorbed the small town of Tropico in 1918.

GOBERNADORA CANYON   Orange
Named after a Mexican plant (zygophyllum tridentatum) commonly named gobernadora. "Cañada de la Gobernadora"; or Cañada Gubernadora; also in Santa Barbara County under "Gobernador Creek", or

even Governador.

GOLETA   Santa Barbara
Spanish for schooner. Suburb of Santa Barbara. Named for first vessel of any size built in California. In 1829 construction for a vessel of 33 tons was designed for otter catching. Another source says that an American schooner went aground in the estuary and lay there for years. A Japanese submarine shelled an oil field near there (Feb. 23, 1942).

GOLETA RANCHO   Santa Barbara
Land grant of June 10, 1846 to Daniel Hill for an area of one league. The town was laid out on the site of the grant La Goleta.

GONZALES   Monterey
Named for Teodoro de Gonzales, twice Alcade of Monterey and active in Spanish-California political affairs. In 1836 he was granted Puente del Monte Rancho an area of seven leagues.

GORDO
Spanish for fat or big used in geographical terms for mountains, hills, promontaries.

GORDA, PUNTA   Humboldt
Name originally applied to the point farther north now known as Table Bluff by exploring expedition of Bruno Heceta in 1775. Some unknown map maker later moved it to this landmark. Spanish maritime usage meaning massive cape.

GORDA   Monterey
There are a school, a mine and a settlement that preserved the name Gorda. In 1862 the Coast Survey changed it to Cape San Martin.

GORDO BASIN
Spanish for big, fat. Underwater ocean plain extending from a deep sea area off Cape Mendocino north nearly to the Canadian border. It is subject to frequent earthquakes.

GORDO, CERRO
Appears in Cerro Gordo Peak (peak big peak), Cerro Gordo Mountain, Cerro Gordo Mine and Cerro Gordo Spring in Inyo county.

GRACIOSA   Santa Barbara
Spanish for graceful; named after Indian women who performed dances at times of Portola expedition. The soldiers found them "graciosas" (graceful). In 1776 Font says "La Laguna Graciosa" (The Graceful Lagoon). The ridge of La Graciosa appears first on March 19, 1824 "La Cuesta de la Graciosa".

GRACIOSA CANYON
Appears in 1841 "la Cañada de la Graciosa". In 1882 La Graciosa Station was named when the Pacific Coast Railroad reached this area.

GRANADA, EL   San Mateo
Post office named 1910. It was named for the last Moorish stronghold in Spain. If it is named for the Spanish word meaning "pomegranate" the article "la" should have been used.

GRANDE
Spanish for Great or large. It is found in several geographical names as a descriptive adjective.

GRANDE, ARROYO   San Luis Obispo

GRANDE, MESA   San Diego

GRAPE, Grapevine   Kern
The names of Grape and Grapevine Canyon and Creek in Kern county can be traced back to Spanish times under the word "uvas" example "Cajon de las Uvas" (canyon of the grapes) (See Uvas).

GREEN
The name is occasionally a translation from the Spanish. Example: "Cañada Verde" Green Valley, Contra Costa. Cañada Verde, Green Valley, Santa Cruz.

GROVELAND   Tuolumne
During the gold rush it was known as "Garotte" from the French "garrot' (Instrument of torture) or from the "garrotte" (French, death by strangulation) or from the Spanish "garrote" (Capital punishment used in Spanish territories consisting in strangling a criminal); the Spanish origin of the word is more obvious than the French. The name was given to this locality as "Garotte" because it witnessed several hangings among the miners. The community was referred to as "First Garotte" because of the establishment a few miles away of another camp named "Second Garotte". Later on the settlers adopted the name of Groveland.

LAS GRULLAS   Monterey
Spanish for the cranes. As early as 1769 Portola expedition diarist writes "On October 7 we pitched our camp between some low hills near a pond, where we saw a great number of cranes, the first we had seen on this journey. This took place about four leagues from the Pajaro River.

GUADALASCA   Ventura
The name looks Spanish but the meaning is unknown; the root guad-from the Arabic "wad" (oued) for river or stream is found in many Spanish names i.e. Guadalquivir. Also spelled Guadalaesa. Land grant of May 6, 1836 to Isabel Yorba.

GUADALUPE   Santa Barbara
Name is from Guadalupe Rancho on which area is located. The rancho is named after Nuestra Senora de Guadalupe patron saint of Mexico.

GUADALUPE, RIVER, CREEK, SLOUGH   Santa Clara
The river owes its name to the Anza expedition of March 30, 1776, in honor of the Mexican saint. "Rio de Nuestra Senora de Guadalupe"

GUADALUPE, LAKE, POST OFFICE   Santa Barbara
"Laguna Grande de San Daniel" and "Laguna Larga" were the names born by the lake.

GUADALUPE VALLEY   San Mateo
As far as 1835 we find in documents "Cañada de Guadalupe y Visitacion".

GUADALUPE VALLEY   Mariposa

GUADALUPE MOUNTAINS   Mariposa

GUADALUPE Y LLAMITOS DE LOST CORREOS   Monterey

GUALALA RIVER, POST OFFICE, POINT   Sonoma and Mendocino
The name seems to be an Hispanicization of "wa-la-li" an Indian word meaning the "meeting place of the waters of any inflowing stream with those of the stream into which it flows or with the Ocean, in short, a river mouth." (Hanna 129) Some anthropologists insist that it is the Spanish version of "Walhalla". It appears as early as 1846 under "Arroyo Valale". In 1867 the Spanish name Gualala was used for the post office.

GUEJITO Y CAÑADA DE PALOMEA   San Diego
A Spanish diminutive of "guijo meaning pebble, gravel) appears in a land grant of September 20, 1845 to Jose Maria Orozco, for an area of three leagues from a land named "Sierra de Guejito".

GUENOC   Lake
A Spanish rendering of a Lake Miwok place name Wenok. An area of six leagues granted in 1845 to George Rock.

GUIJARRAL   Fresno
Spanish for place where cobblestones are found.

GUILICOS   Sonoma
Spanish word derived from the name "Willikos" the Miwok Indians, from a land grant of November 13, 1837 to John Wilson for an area of four leagues. The present community of Kenwood is located on the site of the original grant.

GUINDA   Yolo
Spanish for cherry. The name of the Southern Pacific Station in 1891 for an old cherry tree standing at the side of the station.

HABRA, LA   Orange
Named for Habra Rancho. Originally name applied to the whole valley. The modern Spanish spells it without the initial H. It refers to the Pass or Gorge traversed by Portola expedition July 30, 1769.

HABRA RANCHO, LA   Los Angeles and Orange
From a land grant dated 1839 to Mariano Roldan for one and a half leagues, named for the pass "abra" used many times by the Portola expedition (1769). The present locality has been laid out on the grant.

HACIENDA
From the Spanish farm or estate . Is found in many place names in Alameda, Kings, Los Angeles and Sonoma counties.

HACKAMORE   Modoc
Corruption from the Spanish "jaquima" (headstall of a bridle) was applied to the station of the Nevada-California-Oregon Railroad in 1910. Also Hackamore Reservoir.

HALF MOON BAY   San Mateo
This community was established in 1863 under the name of Spanishtown because of the great number of Spanish speaking people. Circa 1905 the post office was listed as Half Moon Bay, but for many years the residents of the locality disregarded the new name.

HAMBRE (See Alhambra)

HARPERS WELL   Imperial
Originally it was named San Sebastian when Juan Bautista de Anza, Spanish explorer stopped here March 10, 1772. It is said that he named the site after his guide Sebastian Tarabel. Around 1891 a well was drilled by the Harper Brothers, thus the present name.

HEDIONDA CREEK   Santa Clara
Spanish adjective for fetid. It applied to creeks or ponds with unpleasant odors.

HERMOSA BEACH   Los Angeles
Spanish for beautiful. Seashore community originally promoted by Hermosa Land and Water Company. Incorporated 1907. The name is popular in southern California.

HERNANDEZ   San Benito
Apparently named after two brothers, Rafael and Jesus Hernandez (1879).

HERRERA ,CAÑADA DE   Marin
For a land grant dated August 10, 1839 to Domingo Sais for one half league. Herrera is the name of a Spanish soldier who sponsored the baptismal of four Indians in 1817. No one is certain that the valley was named after him.

HIGH SIERRA WILDERNESS AREA
Established in 1931 it is the largest primitive preserve in California (615 sq. mi.). It is located within the Kings Canyon and Sequoia National Parks. In the Sierra Nevada it extends from Tioga Pass to Walker Pass.

HONDA   Santa Barbara
    Clipped from nearby La Cañada Honda. The word used as an adjective means "deep". It is very popular
    with the combination of Creek, or Arroyo. It appears in more than ten Californian place names.

(LA)HONDA CREEK   San Mateo
    Previously known as "Arroyo Ondo" or "Hondo".

(LA)HONDA
    The post office has existed since 1880. Its name changed to Lahonda until 1905 when the former
    name was restored.

HONDO   Los Angeles
    Post office since 1919, name for the Rio Hondo. The creek appears as "Rio de San Gabriel, Rio Hondo
    de Azuza" and "Zanja Onda" (deep ditch).

HOPE RANCH
    On a land grant "La Calera y las Positas" or "Cañada de Calera", on June 10, 1870 to Thomas W. Hope
    for more than 3,000 acres. He changed the original name to his.

HORNITOS   Merced
    Spanish for little ovens. Most credible legend has it that Mexican miners evicted from Quartsburg
    settled here in '50's; the ground was so rocky that dead inhabitants were buried above ground with
    mounds of stone covering them. This resembled Mexican ovens, hence the name. It is also possible
    that the name was brought by Mexicans who named the site in reference to Los Hornitos of Durango
    because it had once several reduction furnaces.

HORSE (See Cavallo)
    The name horse appears on several documents of Spanish times. When the Europeans and Mexicans
    arrived in the Mexican province they gave the name to Canyons, Creeks, Flats, Lakes, etc. We find in
    today's toponymy of California five hundred Horse names, including numerous places named for dead
    and blind horses, Sometimes the name was transferred to post offices and communities: Horse Creek
    (Siskiyou county), Horse Lake (Lassen county); White Horse (Modoc county). About twenty Horse-
    thief Creeks, Canyons, Points, etc. commemorate the hideouts of horsethieves or places where they
    were caught and punished. (From Gudde's California Place Names, p. 154).

HOSPITAL CREEK   San Joaquin, Stanislaus
    From the Indian sweathouses (temescales) near the spring in the canyon. Hospital Creek is represented
    on maps as early as 1843 under the name of El Pescadero Ospital; in 1860 a new name appears as Arroyo
    del Osnito.

HOYA (See JOLLA)
    In Spanish means a hollow worn in a river bed, hole, cavity or pit. The correct spelling should be
    Hoya; Jolla seems to be a corruption of the Spanish word; it is found in several counties, with its differ-
    ent spellings Hoya and Jolla.

(LA)HOYA CREEK   Santa Barbara

HUASNA RIVER   San Luis Obispo
    The Chumash name of an Indian village, from the Huasna land grant of Dec. 8, 1843, to Isaac Sparks
    for an area of five leagues. As early as 1842 we find on documents: "Lomeria colindante con Guasna"
    (Hills adjacent to Guasna (or Huasna)" also "Arroyo del Huasna" or even as "Rio Wasna".

HUECOS   Santa Clara
    Spanish for gap, hollow, hole. Name of a land grant dated May 6, 1846 to Luis Arenas and John Roland
    for an area of nine leagues.

HUENEME Ventura

The name is derived from the Chumash village Wene me. Juan Cabrillo was the first white man to sight it. He called the Indian village "Pueblo de las canoas" because of the numerous canoes used by the Indians for fishing. In 1870 W. E. Barnard, G. S. Gilbert and H. P. Flint founded the present city.

HUENEME POINT AND CANYON

The name was applied to the Point and Canyon in 1856.

HUERHUERO CREEK San Luis Obispo

From a land grant May 9, 1842 and March 28, 1846, derived from "Huergüero" place recorded May 26, 1843 to Mariano Bonilla for an area of one league. The origin of the name is not known. It is assumed that it was for the Mexican Spanish "Huero" (putrid) perhaps in reference to the Soda Springs.

IGNACIO Marin

Honors Don Ignacio Pacheco grantee of San Jose Rancho.

IMPERIAL BEACH San Diego

It was named after the "Imperial Valley". The land promoter E. W. Peterson tried to encourage the nearby residents to build summer homes here (1906). The site was first known as South San Diego.

INDIO Riverside

Spanish for Indian. Named for the station of the Southern Pacific (1876). It is now a resort, travel and trade center whose important industry is the capital for the production of dates. In 1970 its population was 14,459.

ISABEL MOUNT Santa Clara

Formerly Sierra de Santa Isabel.

ISABEL CREEK Santa Clara

ISABEL VALLEY Santa Clara

ISABELLA Kern

Named for the Spanish Queen, by Stephen Barton, in memory of "the good Queen who financed the expedition of Columbus.

ISLA PLANA Solano

Was the named given by Ayala in 1775 to what is today Mare Island; the island was once called "Isla de la Yegua" (isle of the mare).

JACALITOS CREEK Fresno

"Jacalito" a diminutive for the Mexican Spanish "Jacal" (little Indian hut, Wigwam).

JACALITOS HILLS Fresno

"The wigwam hills".

JACINTO Glenn

Named for Rancho which in turn was named for Jacinto Rodriguez to whom it was granted on September 2, 1844.

JACINTO RANCHO Glenn

Named after Jacinto Rodriguez who served in the Mexican army under Alvarado. He was granted an area of eight leagues.

JALAMA CREEK Santa Barbara

Jalama Mission, La Purisima exists as early as 1791 in official documents; also under "Cañada Jalama". Although it is hispanicized, the meaning is unknown.

JARRO POINT Santa Cruz

Spanish for jug or pitcher. From an early land grant El Jarro (or Tarro) of October 12, 1839, which became the Agua Puerca y las Trancas. Early documents show in Santa Barbara county, Arroyo del Jarro (the Jug Creek). Jarro Point was officially named in 1911.

JAVON CANYON   Ventura

Javon or Jabon Spanish for soap. Named after the "natural soap" (infusorial earth) discovered by H. L. Bickford.

JESUS MARIA   Calaveras

Mining camp probably of the early '50's located near the north fork of the Calaveras River. It is named for Mexican Jésus María who raised melons at this point.

JIMENO RANCHO   Yolo

Named after the grant of the same name dated Nov. 2, 2844 to Manuel Jimeno Casarin for 11 leagues.

JOAQUIN MURIETTA CAVES   Alameda

Named after the famous Mexican bandit Joaquin Murietta who, according to tradition, used to hide there.

JOAQUIN ROCKS   Fresno

JOAQUIN RIDGE

Named after the famous Mexican bandit Joaquin Murietta of the early 1850's.

JOTA   Napa

In Spanish "Jota" (the letter "J" and "a dance"). From a land grant to George C. Yount, Oct. 21, 1843 for an area of one league.

JULIAN   San Diego

Named after a miner during the gold rush of the 1870's in the mountains north of Cuyamaca Rancho State Park.

JUNIPERO SERRA PEAK   Monterey

Honors Father Junipero Serra, President of Franciscan missionaries in California from the beginning of its colonization in 1769 until his death, August 28, 1784.

JUNTAS   Contra Costa

Land grant dated October 20, 1832 and February 12, 1844 granted to William Welsh for an area of three leagues. The name was probably derived from Junta de los quatro Evangelistas (Junction of the four Evangelists).

JURISTAC RANCHO   Santa Clara

For the name of a land grant of October 22, 1835 which includes a Costanoan place name. The grant was also known as La Brea and as Los Germanos. The land had an area of one league and was granted to Antonio and Faustino German.

KINGS RIVER   Fresno and Kings

On January 5, 1805 Gabriel Moraga discovered and named the river "Rio de los Santos Reyes" (The River of the Holy Kings), the day of the discovery being the eve of Epiphany. The river rises in the Sierra Nevada and empties into the Tulare Lake Basin.

LAGUNA

A favorite amongst the Spanish geographical terms which designates a small lake or a marsh. The word "laguna" appears in the names of more than thirty land grants and claims. It occurs as a tautology in the case of "Laguna Lake".

LAGUNA DAM   Imperial

Built between 1980 and 1911 on the Colorado River. Named after Lake Laguna on the lower Gila River.

LAGUNA BEACH   Orange

Named because it lies at the mouth of the Laguna Canyon which in turn is named for small lagoons located at its head. An 1841 map names it as Cañada de las Lagunas. Its population in 1970 was 14,550.

LAGUNA, ARROYO DE LA   Alameda

Appears as far as 1834 under "Laguna Permanente que es nacimiento de este Arroyo".

LAGUNA CREEK Santa Cruz
In 1836 it is shown on maps as "Arroyo de la Laguna".

LAGUNA HONDA San Francisco
"Deep lake", named because of a deep reservoir that existed (1839).

LAGUNA MOUNTAINS San Diego
Named for the two lakes located on top of the mountains (1871).

LAGUNA PEAK Ventura
Named after the Mugu Laguna (previously called "Laguna" of the Guadalasca Grant of 1836.

LAGUNA SALADA San Mateo
"Salt Lake" of the San Pedro grant of 1838.

LAGUNA SECA Monterey
From the Laguna Seca grant of May 18, 1833.

LAGUNA SECA Santa Clara
As far as 1797 the Laguna Zeca is already mentioned on documents.

LAGUNA RANCHO Riverside
A land grant to Julian Manrique in 1844 for an area of three leagues. Elsinore Lake and the present town of Elsinore are located on the site of the grant.

LAGUNITAS Marin
Spanish for little lagoons or little lakes.

LAGUNITAS CREEK Marin
From the Laguna de la Canada de Herrera Grant.

LAGUNITAS, PUERTO ZUELO
From the Spanish "portezuela" little mountain pass, where little Carson Creek flows through its canyon.

LAGUNITAS (Town and post office) Marin
The post office was listed in 1900.

LAGUNITA LAKE Monterey
A tautology, literally "Little Lake Lake" appears in 1834 on the Vergeles Grant.

LA HABRA VALLEY Orange
From the Spanish "Abra" (pass, gorge) in reference to Portola expedition going through the Puente Hills on July 30, 1769. Named for a land grant, La Cañada del Habra October 22, 1839. The post office was listed in 1912.

LA JOLLA San Diego
Spanish for the hollow. Oceanside community known for its five residences, the Salk Institute, the Scripps Institution of Oceanography, its beaches and famous caves. In 1970 the population was 28,790.

LA JOLLA BAY San Diego

LA JOLLA CANYON San Diego

LA JOLLA CAVES San Diego

LA JOLLA CREEK Fresno

LA JOLLA INDIAN RESERVATION San Diego

LA JOLLA MESA San Diego

LA JOLLA POINT San Diego

LA JOLLA VALLEY San Diego

LA JOYA PEAK Ventura
Crespi mentions in his diary "La Hoya de la Sierra de Santa Lucia" (Sept. 17, 1769).

LANCHA PLANA Amador
Spanish for level slabs or barge. First settled by Mexican miners in 1848 and flourished until the middle '60's. It is said that a barge used to ferry miners across the river, the origin coming from the point where the flat-boat tied up.

LA MIRANDA Los Angeles
Spanish for the glance or the gaze. Named for the station of the Santa Fe in 1888.

LA PALETA VALLEY San Diego
Spanish for fire-shovel, iron ladle or artist's palette. It is named for the shape and coloring of the valley.

LA PALETA CREEK San Diego
(See La Paleta Valley).

LA PANZA San Luis Obispo
Also spelled on maps La Pansa. From the Spanish belly or paunch. In 1878 gold was discovered. A settlement was laid out after the establishment of a post office. Named after the Panza Range because of its shape like a paunch.

LA PATERA Santa Barbara
Name applied in 1880's with the station of the Southern Pacific. Spanish for place where ducks congregate. It was good duck hunting area until the airport was built.

LA QUINTA Riverside
Spanish for country house, country seat, villa, or the sequence of five cards in the game of piquet. Named after the Quinta Hotel. It is a winter resort and residential community in desert country surrounded by the Santa Rosa Mounts.

LARGO Mendocino
Spanish for long. Largo honors L. F. Long who settled 300 acres at this locality. Long served as county supervisor for two terms and in the State Legislature in 1878.

LAS AGUILAS CANYON San Benito

LAS AGUILAS CREEK San Benito

LA AGUILAS MOUNTAINS San Benito

LAS AGUILAS VALLEY San Benito
Named after the land grant of January 16, 1844 called Real de las Aguilas "Camp of the Eagles".

LAS TRAMPAS RIDGE Contra Costa
Spanish trampas meaning snare or trap. From the early name Sierras pequenas del arroyo San Ramon alias las Trampas. Later on the long name was abbreviated in Las Trampas.

LAS TRAMPAS PEAK Contra Costa

LAS TRAMPAS CREEK Contra Costa

TRAMPA CANYON Monterey
Same origin.

LAS VIRGENES CREEK Ventura and Los Angeles
"Virgen" plural form is "Virgenes" from the early name El paraje de las virgenes (the residence, or place of the Virgins). From two grants in 1802 and 1867.

LAURELES   Monterey

Spanish for laurels or bay tree. From two grants along the Carmel River: one for Jose Agricia for 2,000 varas, in March 4, 1844; the second to Jose Manuel Boronda for one and a half leagues on September 19, 1839. (Laurels appears mispelled in some documents as "laurelles").

LAURELES CANYON   Santa Barbara

From Laureles Arroyo.

LAVIGIA HILL   Santa Barbara

Spanish for look out "vigia". From an early document on which it appears as El Cerro de la Vigia.

LECHUSA CANYON   Los Angeles

Spanish for barn owl. Named because of the great number of owls. The Spanish word is "lechuza".

LERDO   Kern

Spanish for heavy or dull, lumpish. First applied to locality by Henry Martens who established a colony of Mennonites here on April 20, 1909. Difficulties developed after the land titles and the colony dispersed.

LIEBRE MOUNTAIN   Los Angeles

LIEBRE GULCH   Los Angeles

Spanish "liebre" meaning hare. Named after early documents mentioning: "El paraje que llaman la Cueba de la Liebre" (the place called the burrow of the hare). Land grant of April 21, 1846. Named because of the great number of hares.

LIEBRE RANCHO, LA   Kern and Los Angeles

Granted April 21, 1846 to Jose Maria Flores for an area of eleven leagues.

LINDA   Yuba

Named after the "Linda" a small river steamer designed for operation from San Francisco to Marysville. The community was founded in January 1850 and laid out by John Rose.

LINDA, RIO   Sacramento

Linda, lindo is Spanish for beautiful, pretty, handsome.

LINDA CREEK   Placer

LINDA VISTA   San Diego

LINDA VISTA   Santa Clara

LINDO LAKE   San Diego

LINDERO CANYON   Los Angeles

Spanish for contiguous, bordering. From an early grant on which it figures as "Cañada del Lindero" (boundary Valley).

LION ROCK   San Luis Obispo

This rock was named El Lobo (wolf) in Spanish times.

(LAS) LLAGAS   Santa Clara

Spanish for the wounds. In reference to the legend that St. Francis was supposed to have received, after a fast of fifty days, the miraculous imprint of the Savior in his hands, feet and side. It was the name of a site near Gilroy. It was also given by the Padres to "Alameda Creek".

LLANADA   San Benito

Spanish descriptive for plain, level-ground. Post office established in 1901.

LLANO   Los Angeles

Spanish for plain, level ground. Commonly used as a generic geographical term. Named after Llano del Rio.

LLANO DEL RIO
Communal society established in 1914 by Job Harriman, a leader of the Socialist Labor Party.; located in Antelope Valley between the Mojave Desert and the San Gabriel Mounts. It dwindled away in 1918.

LOBITOS CREEK   San Mateo
Spanish for little wolves in reference to coyote. The stream appears as Arroyo de los lovitos (1838) as well as Arroyo de los lobitos (1839).

LOBO   San Francisco
Spanish for wolf; geographical term which occurs mainly in reference to the "sea wolf" (lobo marino) corresponding to the seal or sea lion).

POINT LOBOS   San Francisco

LOBOS CREEK   San Francisco
In reference to the westernmost point of San Francisco. "Punta de los Lobos" appears circa 1816.

POINT LOBOS   Monterey

LOBOS ROCKS   Monterey
As far as 1770 Crespi writes of a great number of sea wolves observed along the coast.

POINT LOBOS RESERVE   Monterey
Established in 1933 by the California Park Commission.

LOLA MOUNT   Nevada
Named after the great courtesan Lola Montez who in the 1850's made a name as a voluptuous and fiery courtesan in the mining camps of California.

LOMA DEL   Trinity
Correct Spanish is de la loma meaning of or by the hill.

LOMA ALTA   Marin
Spanish for high hil.

LOMA ALTA   Monterey
Spanish for high hill.

LOMA ALTA   Santa Barbara
Spanish for high hill.

LOMA ALTA   San Diego
Spanish for high hill.

LOMA ATRAVESADA   Fresno
Spanish for oblique hills.

LOMA CHIQUITA   Santa Clara
Spanish for little hills.

LOMA LINDA San Bernardino

Was previously named Mound Station. Present name was given in 1900.

LOMA PELONA San Luis Obispo and Santa Barbara

Spanish for bald.

POINT LOMA San Diego

Appears first in 1782 "Punta de la Loma" it became subsequently Loma Point then Point Loma. The post office is listed in 1895.

LOMA PRIETA Santa Clara

Named for the high chaparral-covered point which looks black in the distance. In 1861 it was first named Bache Mountain.

LOMA VERDE Los Angeles

Spanish for green hills.

(LAS)LOMAS Kings

(LAS)LOMAS MUERTAS San Diego

For "bare hills.".

LOMERIAS MUERTAS San Benito

Spanish for dead hills because they are without trees. Land grant of August 16, 1842 to Jose Antonio Castro for an area of one and a half leagues.

LOMITA Los Angeles

Spanish Mexican for long little hill. Named thus when founded by W. I. Hollingsworth Company of Los Angeles in 1907.

LOMITA PARK San Mateos

Modern locality.

LOMO Sutter

Spanish for back in man and spine in animals. Origin not known.

LOS ANGELES COUNTY

Spanish for the angels. Very famous for orange growing, motion picture producing. Created February 18, 1850, chap. 15. Area 4,071 sq. mi.

LOS ANGELES Los Angeles

The expedition of Gaspar de Portola named the river Nuestra Señora la Reina de los Angeles de Porciúnculas. The previous day, August 1, had been jubilee day of the Lady. In Porciuncula, Italy, in a church dedicated to the Lady that St. Francis is said to have gained his jubilee, or a year of remission from penal consequences of sin. Founded September 4, 1781. (From Hanna p. 176).

LOS ANGELES AQUEDUCT Los Angeles

Starting at Aberdeen in Inyo county, the aqueduct is 233 miles long. It was started in 1908 and completed in 1913.

LOS BANOS CREEK   Merced

Spanish for the baths. Named for the pools near its source called "Los Baños del Padre Arroyo" (1841). A post office was established in 1874 and named Los Baños. The present town was laid out in 1889.

LOS BUELLIS HILLS   Santa Clara

Mispelled Spanish word for buelles (or buyes) "oxen". It is assumed a herd of "wild oxen" were seen there, thus the name.

LOS GATOS   Santa Clara

Spanish for the cats. Community established in 1850 in the Santa Cruz Mountains. The profusion of wild cats (gatos) in this area was responsible for its naming. A utopian colony "Holy City" was established by William E. Riker (1918). It lasted until 1950. The community was once very active in lumbering. Famous people spent some time here: Josiah Royce, Charles Erskine, Scott Wood, Yehudi Menuhin, etc.

LOS NIETOS   Los Angeles

For the Nieto family, pioneers. The first was Manuel Nieto who was granted Los Nietos Rancho (1784). The huge rancho (33 leagues) was regranted to his five heirs on May 22, 1834. The Santa Fe Station was named Los Nietos in 1887. The post office was established in 1892.

LOS OLIVOS   Santa Barbara

Spanish for olive trees. It was named because Alston Hayne Jr., owned an orchard of 6,000 olive trees. The olive was introduced into California by the Franciscan padres. In 1887 the Pacific Coast Railroad area flourished and opened a station there.

LOS PADRES NATIONAL FOREST   Santa Barbara

Named by order of President F. D. Roosevelt, to honor the Franciscan Padres who founded the California Missions.

LOS PENASQUITOS CANYON   San Diego

Spanish for small rocks. Appears as far as June 15, 1823 on a land grant of Santa Maria de los Penasquitos.

PENASQUITOS CREEK   San Diego

LAS TRANCAS   Napa

Tranca is Spanish for bar. From the land grant "Trancas y Jalopa" of September 21, 1838.

TRANCAS CREEK   Los Angeles

TRANCAS CANYON   Los Angeles

LOS TRANCOS CREEK   Santa Clara

Also recorded as Strancos Creek.

LOS VIEJOS   Kings

Spanish for the old ones. Because of the hills which are older physiographically than those directly north. (Geographic Board, no. 20).

LUCIA   Monterey

Name stems from Santa Lucia Range near this locality. Spanish for Lucy.

LUGO   San Bernardino

Renowned California family name. The first of the family, Francisco Salvador de Lugo came to Sinaloa shortly after 1769. He participated to Rivera y Moncada's expedition of 1774. Several of his sons were soldiers; one of them Antonio Maria (1778-1860) was an "alcade" of Los Angeles.

LUNADA BAY   Los Angeles

Spanish for shaped like a half-moon. Applicable to the crescent-shaped bay.

LUZ, DE   San Diego

Spanish for of light or from light. Perhaps because warm sulphur springs exist there. Point was popular spa circa 1890.

MADERA COUNTY

Spanish for timber or wood. In the 1850's it was the scene of gold mining; later it became the site for lumbering. Created March 11, 1843, chap. 143. area 2,148 sq. mil.

MADERA   Madera

Spanish for wood. Established by W. H. Thurman, manager of California Lumber Company.

MADERA CREEK   Santa Clara

Recorded in 1830 as Arroyo del Matadero. The name was changed after 1870.

MADRONE   Santa Clara

A mispelled word for "madroño", a beautiful native tree "Arbutus menziesii". The word is found in numerous place names: valleys, foothills, mountains, etc.

MALAGA   Fresno

Named for the malaga grape which is grown in the region. The malaga grape was brought to California from Malaga, Spain in 1852.

MALPASO CREEK   Monterey

From a diseño of the Sur Chiquito grant of April 2, 1885, where it appears as "Arroyo de mal paso" (Creek of difficult crossing).

MAL PASO, MALLO PASO CREEK   Mendocino

MAL PASS   Humbold

MANTECA   San Joaquin

Spanish for layer of fat nearest hide of cattle. Settlement was center of productive cattle region. The railroad station took its name for the Spanish word because of a local creamery which had taken its name from the Spanish word "manteca" (lard or butter).

MANZANA CREEK   Santa Barbara

Spanish for apple for an important apple orchard along the creek.

MANZANAR   Inyo

Spanish for apple orchard. Originally it was a horticultural community. The finest apples in California were grown here. Post office listed in 1912.

MAR, DEL   San Diego

Spanish for "of or by the sea". In 1885 the community was established. The name was given by Mrs. I. M. Loop for Bayard Taylor's poem, "The Fight at the Paso del Mar" (1849).

MARE ISLAND   Solano

Part of the peninsula was called "Isla Plana" (Flat Island) by Ayala in 1775. It is said that the island was called "Isla de la Yegua" (isle of the mare) because one of Vallejo's mares swam to the island when the boat on which it was being carried capsized. Mare Island Navy Yard was established and named by act of Congress, August 31, 1852.

MARIN COUNTY

Named for the chief of the Licatiut Indians, Marin, who was baptized "El Marinero" (the sailor, or the Mariner, in Spanish). Created Feb. 18, 1893, chap. 15, 521 sq. mi.

MARIN ISLANDS   Marin

The bay in which the two islands lie was called "Bahia de Nuestra Señora del Rosario la Marinera" by Ayala in 1775. It is possible that "La Marinera" was applied to the islands. On a map of the Grant

Corte Madera del Presidio of 1834 and 1850 the islands appear as "Marin Islands".

MARIN PENINSULA   (See Above)

MARIPOSA   Mariposa
Stem from Arroyo de las Mariposas, Spanish for "brook of the butterflies". Discovered and named by Alferez Gabriel Moraga, September 27, 1806 because of so many butterflies.

MARIPOSA COUNTY
Spanish for butterfly. Created February 18, 1850, chap. 15. Area 1,455 sq. mi.

MARIPOSAS RANCHO, LAS   Mariposa
From a land grant dated 1844 to Juan Bautista Alvarado for an area of ten leagues. In 1849 John Charles Fremont acquired a large portion of the rancho which yielded him a fortune when gold was discovered here. (Hanna, p. 186).

MARTINEZ   Contra Costa
Named for Ignacio Martinez, a native of Mexico City in 1774. He came to California in 1799 as "comandante del Presidio de San Francisco". He settled in "La Cañada del Hambre" (Canyon of Hunger). The town was laid out in 1849.

MAR VISTA   Los Angeles
Changed from Ocean Park Heights in 1904 to avoid confusion with Ocean Park. Spanish for view of the sea. Post office established in 1925.

MATANZAS CREEK   Sonoma
As far as 1859 the stream appears as Matanza Creek. The name was given because of the slaughter of cattle every killing season took place on this particular site.

MATURANGO PEAK   Inyo
The word seems to be a mispelling of "maturrango" (colloquial Spanish for poor horseman, brutal person). The peak is situated in the Argus Range; 8,850 feet.

LOS MEDANOS   Contra Costa
Spanish for sand banks or dunes. Name was applied 1878 because it is situated on the land grant "Los Medanos" dated November 26, 1839 to Jose A. Mesa for an area of two leagues. The present cities of Pittsburg and Antioch are located on the site of the original grant.

MEDANOS POINT   San Diego
Name given to the Cape by the Coast Survey. A mispelling such as "meganos" is shown near Punta Falza (False Point). Medanos means in Spanish "dunes, sand-bars, sand banks".

MELONES   Calaveras
Spanish for melons. Named because Mexican miners found gold in flakes like melon seeds. The original name of the town was Robinson's Ferry. The post office changed its name from Robinsons to Melones in 1900.

MENDOCINO COUNTY
Named for the Spanish viceroy of Mexico (New Spain) Antonio de Mendoza (1485-1552), for whom was named Cape Mendocino. He summoned Coronado to explore Colorado and New Mexico. Created April 19, 1855, chap. 107. Area 1,983 sq. mi.

MENDOCINO (Town, Canyon, National Forest)
For origin see Mendocino county. The town was settled in 1852; the post office was established in 1853. The National Forest was created in 1907, present name 1908. Mendocino Cape, Humboldt county.

MERCED COUNTY
Spanish for "Mercy" is derived from "El Rio De Nuestra Señora de la Merced" (River of Our Lady

of Mercy). Created April 19, 1855, chap. 104. Area 1,983 sq. mil.

MERCED RIVER   Merced
    See origin of Merced county.

MERCED FALLS, CITY, and POST OFFICE   Merced
    Founded in 1853, post office established in 1858. The present city was laid out in 1872.

MERCED GROVE, LAKE, PASS, PEAK   Yosemite National Park

MERCED LAKE   San Francisco
    The Anza expedition named it in 1775 "La Laguna de Nuestra Señora de la Merced" (The Lake of
Our Lady of Mercy). In the 19th century it became part of the reservoirs of the Spring Valley Water
Company.

MESA
    Spanish for table used in American Southwest as a generic term.

(LA)MESA   San Diego

(THE)MESA   San Diego

(LA)MESA BATTLEFIELD   Los Angeles

MESA COYOTE   Monterey

MESA DE BURRO   Riverside

MESA DE COLORADO   Riverside

MESA DE LA PUNTA   Riverside

MESA GRANDE   Monterey

MESA GRANDE   San Diego

MESA PEAK   Los Angeles

(LAS)MESAS POTRERO   Monterey

MESAVILLE   Riverside

(BURTON)MESA   Santa Barbara

(MOUNT)MESA   Los Angeles

MESQUITE   Imperial
    From the Mexican "Mezquite" which in turn, stems from the Aztec "Mizquitl" a deciduous shrub of
the Southwest deserts. There is a considerable amount of Mesquite in this area.

MEXICALI
    Mexican border city across the street from Calexico in Imperial County. It is the northern terminus
of a major Mexican railroad and a free port. It is the capital of Baja California with a population of
392,324 in 1970.

MILAGRO VALLEY   San Mateo
    Spanish for miracle. Sometimes spelling is corrupted in "milagra" apparently the naming is recent.

-50-

MILPITAS   Santa Clara

A diminutive of "milpas" (cornfields). Named after Milpitas Rancho that comprehended two grants one to Jose M. Alviso (1835) for one league and the other to Ignacio Pastor (1838). The modern town of Milpitas is located on the site of the original grant.

MINDEGO HILL   San Mateo

Named for Juan Mendico in 1877. The mispelling has remained until now.

MIRA

Spanish command for "look! or behold!" A popular word with coined name such as: Miramonte, Miramar, Miraloma, Miraflores . . .

MIRADOR   Tulare

Spanish for gallery or balcony. That was the name of the Santa Fe station in 1923.

MIRALESTE   Los Angeles

For Spanish "look at the eastern wind!"

MIRA LOMA   Riverside

Changed name several times from its original Stalder, then to Wineville, to finally the present name in 1930.

MIRAMAR   San Diego

Name given to the Linda Vista Ranch belonging to E. W. Scripps. Post office established in 1892.

MIRAMONTE   Fresno

Spanish for mountain view.

MIRA MONTE   Ventura

Spanish monte meaning mountain or woods.

MIRAMONTES POINT   San Mateo

Named after the Miramontes family of San Francisco.

MISSIONS

Some fifty place names in the western part of the U.S.A. are still the witness of the importance mission played in the life of early New Spain. The Spanish Kings found the mission system a very convenient means to extend and reinforce their authority in the American colonies mostly in California. The 21 California missions were founded by Franciscan missionaries, or members of the Third Order of Friars Minor, between 1769 and 1823. But when on August 17, 1833 the Mexican Congress decreed that the missions of Upper and Lower California should be secularized, this marked the end of the mission system. As we are progressing in our reading we will find the names of the missions in their proper alphabetical order.

MISSION BAY   San Diego

Formerly called "Puerto Anegado" (overflowed port); Puerto Falso (False port) 1782; then Missions Bay (June 2, 1915) adopted by the Geographic Board.

MISSION BAY STATE PARK   San Diego

Named in 1929.

MISSION CREEK   San Francisco

Was known as "Estero de la Mission" (1842). Later on the Geographic Board gave its present name. IN 1775, Ayala had it called "Ensenada de los Llorones" (Creek of the Weepers).

MISSION SAN JOSE   Alameda

(See San Jose). Post office established in 1851 and named after the mission.

MISSION VIEJA DE LA PURISIMA RANCHO, LA   Santa Barbara
Spanish for the old mission of the Purest Virgin Mary. Land grant to Joaquin and Jose Antonio Carrillo, in 1845 for an area of one league.

MISSION VIEJO O LA PAZ RANCHO   Orange
Spanish for Old Mission or the peace Rancho. Land grant to Augustin Olvera (or Olivera) in 1845.

MOCHO ARROYO   Alameda
Spanish for shorn, cut-off creek. For a creek seeming to sink into the ground during the dry season.

MOCHO MOUNTAIN, PEAK   Santa Clara
Named after the arroyo.

MODESTO   Stanislaus
Spanish for modest. Station of the Central Pacific that received the name because of its president W. C. Ralston who modestly declined the honor of having the place named after him. The name was changed to the Spanish "Modesto".

MOJAVE RIVER (or MOHAVE)   San Bernardino
"The name is an Hispanicized phonetic rendering of the name of an Indian tribe of Yuman lineage which the Franciscan missionary-explorer, Father Francisco Garces, in 1775 first called JAMAJAB, but which is more accurately rendered in English as "Hamakhava", the Indians' name for themselves. The name was first applied to the river under the erroneous impression that it drained into the Colorado in Mohave territory. The Mojaves of today do not know the meaning of their tribal name." (Hanna, p. 197). Father Garces called the river "Arroyo de los Martires" (March 9, 1776), and "Rio de los Animas", however, Fremont calls it "Mohahve River" (1853). Previously the same stream had been called "Inconstant River" by the traveler Jedediah Smith (1826); as for the Mohave Valley it appears on several maps as "Sink of Mohave" or "Soda Sink" (1860); as for the famous "Mohave Desert" it was surely known under the name long before the 1870's.

MOLATE POINT   Contra Costa
From the Mexican "Moleta" a conical stone used to grind colors. It was by mistake that "moleta" became "molate". Molate Point was named by the Coast Survey in 1854 and Molate Reef in 1864.

MOLINO   San Bernardino
Name of the Santa Fe Station because a mill had been built here in 1896.

MOLINO   Sonoma
Spanish for mill; often used as a geographical term. Place located on the Molino grant of February 24, 1836.

MOLINO CREEK   Santa Cruz
It appears in early documents as Arroyo del Molino (1846).

MOLINOS, LOS   Tehama
Spanish for mills, or mill-stones. From important flour mill that existed here in '50's and '60's from a land grant dated December 20, 1844. Original name "El Rio de los Molinos" (The river of the mill-stones; present name Mill Creek.

MONO COUNTY
Spanish for monkey. The Spanish called an Indian tribe of the Shoshonean Indians by this name. The county was called for the Indians. Created April 24, 1861, chap. 233. Area 3,045 sq. mi.

MONO LAKE
Saline lake east of Yosemite and south of Bodie is so alkaline that only one kind of shrimp and one kind of fly can live in it.

MONSERRATE MOUNTAIN   San Diego

Named after Montserrat (Spain). The name was derived from the Monserrate land grant of May 4, 1846.

MONSERATE RANCHO San Diego
From a land grant of 1846 to Isidro M. Alvarado for an area of three leagues.

MONTALVO Ventura
Named for Garcia Ordoñez de Montalvo, the father of the famous novel *Las Sergas de Esplandian* (1510) in which the name California appears for the first time. Established as a town in 1887.

MONTARA POINT San Mateo

MONTARA MOUNTAIN
Spanish "Montaraz" (mountain, mountainous, wild). It is possible that the word "montara" is mis-pelled. It could stand for "Montana, montaraz or montuoso and montosa". As far as 1838 the word appears on documents: "Una Cañada Montosa" (A valley full of thickets).

MONTE
Spanish word for grove, woods, thickets, mountain; a very popular generic geographic term in Spanish times. The term is used in combination with adjectives for specific meanings related to woods or mountains, also for communities: Monte Arido (Santa Barbara), Monte Bello (Santa Clara, Monte Cristo (Los Angeles, Mono and Sierra counties), Monte Nido (Los Angeles), Monte Rio (Sonoma), Monte Vista (Placer, San Bernardino, Santa Clara counties).

MONTE, DEL Monterey
Spanish for "of the mountain". Community of private homes developed by Del Monte Properties Company. Name derived from De la Puente del Monte Rancho granted to Teodoro de Gonzalez in 1836.

MONTE, EL Los Angeles
Settled 1851 by mixed American emigrants. Area was known as "Monte" meaning wooded place referring to dense willow thickets that once grew there. Post office established 1857. It was considered the terminus of the Santa Fe trail. It is now a residential suburb with a population in 1970 of 69,892.

MONTEBELLO Los Angeles
"Beautiful woods" applied by Harris Newmark and Kaspare Cohn in 1899 who purchased the Repetto Ranch. The entire settlement was named Montebello (should have been written in two words Monte Bello).

MONTECITO Santa Barbara
Spanish diminutive meaning little mountain. A favorite amongst the diminutive of Spanish times it appears on several land grants. Mission Santa Barbara was founded there in 1844. The modern town of Montecito is on Santa Barbara pueblo lands. The name at time was spelled Monticito.

MONTE OAK PARK, EL San Diego
Located at the foot of El Capitan Mountain in the San Diego Valley. The mountain was named for "El Capitan Grande" (Spanish for the great captain).

MONTEREY BAY Monterey
On November 16, 1542 Cabrillo discovered the bay which he named "Bahia de los Pinos"; on December 10, 1595 Cerineno explored it and named it San Pedro. Vizcaino who visited the harbor on December 16, 1602 named the harbor Puerto de Monterey.

MONTEREY COUNTY
When Sebastian Vizcaino landed in California in 1603 he named this region "Monterey" for the Spanish viceroy of Mexico: Gaspar de Zuniga y Azevedo Count of Monterey (1540-1606). Created Feb. 18, 1850, chap. 15.

MONTEREY HARBOR Monterey

Sebastian Vizcaino explored upper California and mapped carefully the harbors of Monterey and San Diego on December 16, 1602--03. But it was not before 1770 that Monterey was occupied and became the capital of Upper California. Thus the process of the missionary and military occupation was begun.

MONTEREY PRESIDIO AND MISSION Monterey

On June 3, 1770 a presidio and a mission were established and named San Carlos Borromeo. The presidio was known as Monterey.

MONTEREY RIVER

On March 4, 1776, Font called the Salinas River "Rio de Monterey", which in turn became Monterey River.

MONTEREY PARK Los Angeles

Named for the nearby Monterey Hills. It was incorporated May 29, 1916.

MONTE RIO Sonoma

Corruption of monte del rio which in Spanish is mountain by the river.

MORAGA Contra Costa

Named for Joaquin Moraga who was granted land on which the area is located. His son Gabriel (1765-1823) also a member of the Anza expedition became the leading explorer of the central Valley (1805-17). The post office was established in 1916.

MORAGA VALLEY Contra Costa

Named after Joaquin Moraga, a soldier in the San Francisco Company 1819; grantee of the "Laguna de los Palos Colorado".

MORENA LAKE San Diego

Artificial reservoir of 21,900,000,000 gallons capacity and vital part of San Diego's water system. "Morena" is feminine of "Moreno" for brown, dark, tawny. It is assumed that the name is a family name rather than the Spanish descriptive adjective.

MORENO Riverside

Spanish for brown. Named for F. E. Brown who owned 1,500 acres here in 1881. He is the first who suggested the possibility of a dam in Big Bear Valley in San Bernardino Mountains.

MORO ROCK Sequoia National Park

From the Mexican Moro (bluish color). Named after Mr. Swanson's horse which was a blue roan mustang.

MORO COJO SLOUGH Santa Cruz

MORO Y CAYUCOS RANCHO San Luis Obispo

Land grant of 1840 to Vincente Felix. Moro means "a horse of bluish color", but it could stand for nearby Morro Bay. Cayugos are small fishing boats.

MORRO

The Spanish geographical term for "anything that is round", very popular in Spanish times. It is still found in San Diego, San Luis Obispo, and Ventura counties.

MORRO BAY San Luis Obispo

Named from rounded rock that lies offshore which at high tide is separated from the coast by little less than a gunshot - description by Crespi of Portola expedition. It appears written with one "r" in some documents of 1837: Moro y Cojo, or Moro y Cayucos.

MUERTAS, LAS LOMAS San Diego

Noun "muerto" refers to place where corpse was found or to burial ground. Used frequently in Spanish times. It has survived and can be found with a generic orographic term to designate a "barren place".

MUERTAS, LAS LOMAS	San Diego
MUERTAS, LAS LOMERIAS	San Benito
(PUNTA DE LOS)MUERTOS	San Diego Harbor

MURIETA
> See Joaquin Murieta.

MURRIETA   Riverside
> Named after John Murrieta who owned part of the Temecula Rancho. Post office established in 1885.

NACIMIENTO RIVER   San Luis Obispo and Monterey
> Spanish for birth or nativity. Portola expedition camped on the river on September 21, 1769. Crespi wrote about its source "Nacimiento". Anza visited the same place and called it "Nacimiento" for "Nativity". (1774). In 1850 the Rio Nacimiento was named Nacimiento River. Crespi had called the river, where the expedition camped on September 21, 1769 "Las Truchas de San Elceareo". It is also referred as "Rio de Las Truchas". (River of the Trouts).

NACION RANCHO, LA   San Diego
> Granted to John Forster in 1845 for an area of six leagues. Several towns are presently located on its site, they are: Bonita, Chula Vista, Lincoln and National City. Spanish for "National Ranch"; in Spanish times it was known as "Rancho del Rey" (The King's Ranch).

NACIONAL RANCHO   Monterey
> Granted to Vicente Cantua in 1839 fro an area of two leagues.

NARANJO   Tulare
> Spanish for orange tree. The area is an important orange-growing center since 1900. The town and the Visalia Railroad took their name from the orange-grove of "Naranjos". Post Office established in 1904.

NATIVIDAD RANCHO, LA   Monterey
> Spanish for nativity. Land granted to Manuel Butrón and Nicolas Alviso, November 16, 1837 for an area of two leagues. Font named it on March 23, 1776 two days before the "Anmunciation". Anza calls the same place "La Assumpcion".

NAVARRO   Mendocino
> Local legend says that it was named for Pedro Navarro (1460-1528) Spanish soldier famed for his development of use of mines in warfare. The name had several spellings: Nevarra, Novorro, Novarra, Navarra. Another source mentions that the naming was for the Spanish province of Navarra.

NAVARRO RIVER
> Named for the above.

NAVARRO (Town and Post Office)
> The town became a center for lumbering operations in the late 1879's. Its name then was Wendling. Around 1914 the name of the town and the post office became Navarro.

NEGRO
> The name is found in Spanish times: "Arroyo de los Negros" was the old name for Lytle Creek; "El Puerto de los Negros" was the pass northwest of San Bernardino. We find also: "El Cajon de los Negros" (1846).

NEVADA CITY   Nevada
> Had several names: Deer Creek Dry Diggings (1849), Caldwell's Upper Store (1849); in May 1850 it became Nevada. In 1858 the name is shown on maps as present one. Named for the Sierra Nevada.

NEVADA COUNTY

Spanish for snow-covered. Gold was discovered along the Yuba River. The towns which sprang up included the colorful names of "Rough and Ready", "Whiskey Bar", "Jackass Flat", etc. Created April 25, 1851, chap. 15. Area 979 sq. mi.

NEW ALMADEN   Santa Clara

Named after the quicksilver mines of Almaden, Spain. The American mines were known to the Indians who used the cinnabar ore they contained for ceremonial paints. New Almaden Rancho was granted to Andres Castillero in 1846. He had claimed the mines in 1845. Almaden comes from the Arabic word "Almadin" (the mine).

NICASIO   Marin

Named after Nicasio Rancho an area of 20 leagues granted to Teodosio Quilaguegui, in 1835. The name Nicasio is Spanish for Nicasius, one martyr from the Roman times. It was also a second land grant given to Pablo de la Guerra and Juan Cooper for an area of 16 leagues, in 1844.

NIDO, EL   Merced

Spanish for nest. The name is said to have resulted from the discovery of an eagle's nest on the river bank.

RIONIDO or RIO NIDO   Sonoma

Pseudo Spanish for "El Rio Del Nido" (The river of the nest). See above Nido for origin.

NOCHE BUENA RANCHO   Monterey

Spanish for "Christmas Eve". Granted to José Antonio Muñoz, November 15, 1835 for an area of one league. Present Seaside and Del Monte are located on the site of the original grant.

NOGALES   Los Angeles

Spanish for "walnuts". Two land grants, one to José de la Cruz Linares in March 1840 for an area of one league, in eastern Los Angeles county. The other to Jose M. Aguila of August 30, 1844 in Los Angeles county, near Alhambra. This last one was named "Canadas de los Nogales Rancho."

NOVATO   Marin

Spanish for commencing, new. Name from Novato Rancho granted 1839 to Fernando Felix for an area of two leagues.

(CORTE MADERA DE) NOVATO RANCHO   Marin

A land grant of 1839 to John Martin for an area of two leagues. The Spanish name means "wood pile of Novato".

NUECES Y BOLBONES   Contra Costa

From "Arroyo de las Nueces y Bolbones" (Creek of the nuts and the Bolbones (Indians)). Land grant to Juan Sanchez Pacheco of July 11, 1834 for an area of two leagues.

NUESTRA SEÑORA

Spanish for Our Lady. It was commonly done by the Franciscan Fathers to use this title in naming their missions. It became popular to combine the title with "Nuestra Señora" for instance: Nuestra Señora de Altagracia, Nuestra Señora de los Angeles, Nuestra Señora de los Dolores, Nuestra Señora de la Merced, Nuestra Señora del Rosario. However with the coming of modern times we notice that "Nuestra Señora" part of most of these names was dropped, and only the title has been kept.

NUESTRA SENORA DE LA ASUNCION   Ventura

See Ventura.

NUESTRA SEÑORA DEL REFUGIO RANCHO   Santa Barbara

Spanish for Our Lady of Refuge. Land grant to Captain Jose Francisco Ortega in 1797 for an area of six leagues. Present Gaviota and Port Orford are located on the site of the original grant.

NUESTRA SEÑORA DE LA SOLEDAD MISSION   Monterey

This mission was established by Fathers Buenaventura Sitjar, Fermin Francisco Lasuen and Diego Garcia, on October 9, 1791. This mission meaning in Spanish "Our Lady of Solitude" was the thirteenth mission founded by the Franciscan Order in California.

NUESTRO PADRE SAN FRANCISCO, CAÑADA DE   Calaveras

(See San Andreas Lake).

NUESTRO PADRE SAN FRANCISCO, LAS LLAGAS DE San Martin

(See San Martin).

NUEVO, NUEVA

Spanish for "new". An adjective very much used in Spanish times which has survived modern place-naming. For instance: Nuevo Canyon (Ventura), Nuevo Creek (Santa Barbara).

NUEVO   Riverside

Named after the "San Jacinto Nuevo Y Potrero Rancho" on which it is located. The post office was officially named in 1916.

OCEANO   San Luis Obispo

Spanish for ocean. Named after the Pacific Ocean by the first settlers.

OJITOS   Monterey

Spanish for "little eyes" or "little springs". From the land grant "Ojo de agua de los Ojitos" of April 5, 1842 to Mariano Soberanes for an area of two leagues. The geographical term widely used in Spanish times, has barely survived in modern times except in 'Ojo".

OJO

Spanish "eye" or "Spring" used mostly in "ojo de agua" was a very popular geographical term during the Spanish times. It appears widely in land grants: Ojo de l'Agua de la Coche (sow spring) in Santa Clara county; Ojo de Agua de Figueroas in Sonoma county, Tres ojos de agua in Santa Cruz county, etc. Some terms did not survive the 1880's such as "El ojo de la Coche Peak" or "El Toro" or the spring "El Ojo Grande".

OLD BALDY

Common name given to the Mt. San Antonio, the highest point of the San Gabriel Range, so called because its wind wept peak was without vegetation.

OLD SPANISH TRAIL

Name given to a caravan route to Los Angeles from Santa Fe and Taos. An attempt to reach the California missions by that route was made by Silvestre Escalante and Francisco Dominguez, two friars in 1776.

ORO

Spanish for gold. The most luring Spanish geographical term used in the southwestern part of the U.S.A., particularly near mining settlements. In the beginning the term was given only to a gold mine in a diversity of combinations without respect to idiomatic usage, thus: "Oro Chino" (mariposa county), Oro Fino (Siskiyou county), Oroleeve, Monte de Oro (Butte county), Orocopia Mountains (Riverside), etc.

ORO GRANDE   San Bernardino

Named for the Oro Grande Mill and Mining Company which developed gold mines in the vicinity in 1880. The Spanish name means "big gold," or "coarse gold". It was previously known as "Halleck".

OROFINO   Siskiyou

Should be oro fino meaning fine gold. A mining camp of the early fifties near Fort Jones.

ORTEGA HILL   Santa Barbara and Ventura

Named after the Ortega family well known in the history of the county. The Mexican born founder was José Francisco Ortega (1734-98).

ORTEGA CREEK
Formerly known as "Arroyo de las Ortegas".

ORTEGA STATION   San Joaquin county

ORTIGALITA PEAK   Merced

ORTIGALITA CREEK
Spanish diminutive for "ortiga" meaning little nettle.

ORTIGALITO
Post Office established in 1880.

OSO
Spanish for "bear". Was frequently used for place names in Spanish times. We can still find it in the place-names of a dozen of geographic features in California.

OSO FLACO LAKE   San Luis Obispo
Commemorating an encounter of soldiers with California bears. Popular name given by Crespi expedition "lean bear" and also "Las Vivoras" (the Vipers). But "Oso Flaco" survived the holy name given by Crespi and the other names given by soldiers and travelers. There are an "Oso Flaco Valley", an "Oso Flaco Creek" and a Lake of the same name. Father Crespi mentions in his diary that he gave the holy name of "San Juan de Perucia" and "San Pedro de Sacro Terrato".

(CAÑADA DE LOS) OSES Y PECHO Y ISLAI   San Luis Obispo
Spanish for "Valley of the bears and beast and islay". Land grant to Victor Linares in 1842-43 and September 24, 1845. In the diary of Portola 1769 we read stories of fierce fights with bears, which then haunted this place in such numbers that the explorers gave it the name of "La Cañada de los Osos" (the glen of the bears). Later on Captain Fages and Miguel Costanso make the same remarks in their reports.

PACHECO HILL   Marin
Named for Ignacio Pacheco (1808-1864) a grantee of the San Jose land grant, on which the hill is located.

PACHECO PASS   Merced
Named for Francisco Perez Pacheco who received the land grants of San Luis Gonzaga and Ausaymas y San Felipe of 1833, 1836 and 1843. He became one of the largest langholders in Monterey district.

PACHECO PEAK   Merced
(See Pacheco Pass).

PACHECO CANYON   Merced

PACHECO CREEK   Merced
See Pacheco Pass.

PACHECO VALLEY   Contra Costa
Honors Salvio Pacheco who was given in 1833-34 Monte del Diablo Rancho. He was a California and a soldier in Monterey county as early as 1810. The town was laid out in 1857 and took the name of Pacheco the following year.

PACHECO CREEK   Contra Costa
See Pacheco Valley.

PADRE BARONA VALLEY   San Diego
In honor of José Barona, a friar at San Diego (1798-1811) and at San Capistrano (1811-1831). The
name was applied to the mesas in the region; as well as to the Creek. A land grant was established
under the title "Cañada de San Vicente y Mesa del Padre Barona", January 25, 1846.

PADRES NATIONAL FOREST, LOS
Is located partly in Kern, Los Angeles, Monterey, Santa Barbara, San Luis Obispo and Ventura counties. Created by President William McKinley (1898-99) and by President Theodore Roosevelt (1906-
07). The present name honors the sacrifices of the Franciscan missionaries in California. The area
contained in 1946, 1,775,894 acres of government land.

PAJARO RANCHO, BOLSA DEL   Santa Cruz
Spanish for the pocket of the Pajaro River. Named after the Pajaro River which was named by the
soldiers of the Portola expedition on October 8, 1769. Land grant to Sebastian Rodriguez in 1837
for an area of two leagues. The present town of Watsonville is located on the site of the original land
grant.

PAJARO RANCHO, VEGA DEL RIO DEL   Monterey
Meaning "the plain of the Pajaro River". Land grant to Antonio M. Castro given in 1820 for an area
of 8,000 acres.

PAJARO RIVER   San Benito, Santa Clara, Monterey, Santa Cruz
                                                   counties
Was named "Rio del Pajaro" to which Father Crespi, diarist of Portola expedition added "La Señora
Santa Ana". The name appears also as "Llano del Pajaro" (Plain of the bird), and as "Rio de los Paxa-
ros". The original name comes from a big bird (an eagle certainly) that the Indians had killed and
stuffed with straw. "Pajaro" was given to the river, the town and islands.

PAJARO VALLEY
Located between Monterey Bay and the Santa Cruz mountains. Is watered by the Pajaro River, named
by Portola's soldiers (1769). The valley is noted for its orchards and vegetables. The river forms the
boundary between Santa Cruz and Monterey counties and between Santa Clara and San Benito counties.

PALA   San Diego
Often misspelled "palo" (Stick) is located fifteen miles to the northeast of San Luis Rey, and is the
site of the submission of San Antonio de Pala founded in 1816 by Father Peyri. A coincidence about
the name is that "pala" in Spanish means a "spade" and in Indian "water".

PALA RANCHO   Santa Clara
A land grant to Jose Higuera of November 5, 1835 for an area of one league. There is a slight contro-
versy as for the name. The first source states that "Pala" stands for Spanish "shovel". Second source
says it was named for an Indian word meaning water. Third source states, the name stands for an
Indian chief named Pala.

PALA RANCHO, CANADA DE   Santa Clara
Land grant given to José Jésus Bernal in August 1839 for an area of 8,000 varas. The translation of the
name is "Valley of the Shovel". As for its naming, nobody knows for sure.

PALMAS SPRING, DOS   Riverside
Spanish for two palms. Was a station on stage line, San Bernardino-LaPaz (established 1863) and des-
cribes nearby native Washingtonian palms. Also Valle de las Palmas, Santa Barba county and Las Palmas,
Fresno county.

PALO
Spanish for stick, log, mast, timber, or tree. Was very popular in use with descriptive adjectives in
Spanish times. It has survived to our present age: Palo Colorado (redwood), Palo Prieto (dark tree),
palo seco (Drywood, or dry tree), Palo verde (green tree).

PALO ALTO   Santa Clara
Spanish for big tree or big stick. Refers to the tall coast redwood discovered by Juan Bautista de Anza March 26, 1776. The present community was established in 1891.

PALO CEDRO   Shasta
Spanish for cedar tree, named after a cedar tree standing on this site. The town was laid out in 1891; the post office was listed 1893 and until recently was spelled "Palocedro".

PALO COLORADO CANYON   Monterey
Early known as "Arroyo del Palo Colorado".

PALO ESCRITO PEAK   Monterey
Because of a tree engraved with symbols and names. As far as 1833 we found "un terreno llamado palo escrito"; "Cañada de Palo Escrito" (1840).

PALOMA
Spanish for dove, pigeon; the locative ending "r" stands for "place of the doves" or "pigeons". It was very popular for place names in Spanish times. The name Paloma is found in: Calaveras, Los Angeles, Monterey, Riverside, San Diego and San Luis Obispo counties.

PALOMARES CREEK   Alameda
Named after Francisco Palomares, a very famous Indian fighter circa 1833.

PALOMAR MOUNTAIN   San Diego
In Spanish times was known as "Cañada de Palomar" Spanish meaning "Valley of Pigeon-roost". During Spanish days the peak was known to be the home of band-tailed pigeons hence the name.

PALOMAR MOUNTAIN STATE PARK   San Diego
The park was created in 1933. It has a wooded area of 1,684 acres.

PALOMAS CANYON   Los Angeles
Named after the great number of pigeons found in the area.

PALO VERDE   Imperial
Named after a small green tree (Cercidium Torreyanum) native to the region.

PALOVERDE
Post office established 1904. Became Palo Verde in 1905.

PALO VERDE LAGOON

PALO VERDE MOUNTAIN
See above.

PALOS COLORADOS, LAGUNA DE LOS   Alameda and Contra Costa
From the original "Bosques de Palo Colorado" for a lake and several redwoods standing nearby. Land grant of October 10, 1835 to Joaquin Moraga.

PALOS, DOS   Merced
The origin is obscure. The meaning from Spanish "two trees or two sticks". Local legend says the name developed when surveyors officially marked the boundary of Sanjon de Santa Rita Rancho with two sticks.

PALOS VERDES   Los Angeles
Spanish for green trees. Name is from Palos Verdes Rancho. The area borders the ocean in Los Angeles county and was granted in 1824 to heirs of Jose Dolores Sepulveda. The present Walteria, Lomita, San Pedro, Wilmington and Palos Verdes Estates are located on the site of the original grant.

PAMO, VALLE DE or SANTA MARIA RANCHO   San Diego
Land grant to Jose Joaquin Ortega and Edward Stokes.

PANAMA   Kern
It was known in 1865 as Mexican Settlement at the time of its foundation by Dolores Montano. Before 1874 the name Panama was given to the land because ot its resemblance with an isthmus created by two river channels.

PANOCHA GRANDE RANCHO   San Joaquin
Land grant to Vicente P. Gomez of 1844 for an area of four leagues. Spanish Panocha (for ear of grain) it is also a confection of coarse sugar. Several titles mention the word "panocha". "El Punto de la Panocha", "Paraje llamado la Panocha", "Panocha de San Juan y Carrisalitos" (Merced county), "Panoche Grande (San Benito county). The name appears with several corruptions: Paneche Pass; Penoche Valley. The name "Panochita" also appears on several diseños.

PANZA, LA   San Luis Obispo
Origin legendary meaning the paunch. Began with Spanish Californians who placed paunches of beef here as bait for bears.

PARAISO SPRINGS   Monterey
Spanish for paradise. It was a popular place name during Spanish times but it has barely survived in modern times. One can find in documents of 1775 a "Cañada del Paraiso" which is presumably the present upper San Jacinto Valley in Riverside county.

PASO
Spanish for pass, passage, or ford, crossing, channel, narrows. One of the most geographical terms used in Spanish times as a generic in several land grants and place names.

PASO MOUNTAINS, EL   Kern

PASO PEAKS, EL   Kern

PASO CREEK, EL   Kern
Named because there were passes nearby.

PASO, EL   Sacramento
Name is from the Del Paso Rancho. Meaning of the Spanish word is "of or from the pass", upon which it is located.

PASO RANCHO, DEL   Sacramento
Land grant of May 12, 1844 to Eliab Grimes for an area of ten leagues. The present city of Sacramento is located on the Southwest corner of the original grant.

PASO ROBLES   San Luis Obispo
Named for Paso de Robles Rancho covered with fine specimens of Valley Oak or Roble (Quercus lobata). Already on March 4, 1776, Font mentioned "Paso de Robles" (passage through the oaks). The city was founded in 1886 and incorporated in 1889.

PASTORIA DE LAS BORREGAS   Santa Clara
Spanish for "sheep pasture". For a land grant of January 15, 1842.

PASTORIA CREEK   Kern
This creek crosses a plateau used as pasture lands for the sheep of the nearby Indian Reservation.

PECHO ROCK   San Luis Obispo
Spanish "pecho" means breast. Geographical term for hills and rocks shaped like a woman's breast; commonly used with "Arroyo del Pecho", "Cañada del Pecho", "Arroyo del Pecho".

PECHO CREEK   San Luis Obispo
   See above.

PEDERNALES, PUNTA   Santa Barbara
   The Portola expedition camped near Point Arguello on August 28, 1769, where flints (pedernales)
   for their weapons were found. That seems to be the origin of the name. Punta Pedernales coincides
   with Punta (or point) Arguello. Thus Punta Pedernales means Point of Flints.

PEDRO POINT   San Mateo
   The name appears as far as 1791 under "San Pedro" and it is a rancho of Mission Dolores. A grant
   was issued January 26, 1839 and the point which is seen is named Punta del Angel Custodio (Point of
   the guardian angel) as well as Punta de las Almejas (Point of the Mussels).

PELONA
   Spanish for bald used as a descriptive name for orographic features where trees are non-existent. We
   find it in "Sierra Pelona", "Sierra Pelona Valley" (Los Angeles), in Loma Pelona (Monterey and Santa
   Barbara counties).

PENASQUITOS   San Diego
   Spanish diminutive for "peña", rock. It was applied to a land grant named "Santa Margarita de los
   Penasquitos" under the jurisdiction of Santiago Arguello, in 1831.

PENON BLANCO   Mariposa
   Spanish for white gold. It was a gold mining site of the '50's in the Merced River area. As late as 1863
   locality yielded gold valued at $16,000 to two men in two months.

PENITENCIA CREEK AND CANYON   Santa Clara
   Named after the adobe house "La Penitencia" which had been used as a house of confession and peni-
   tence in mission times. We find also on maps "Arroyo de la Penitencia" circa 1840.

PENON BLANCO   Mariposa
   A gold mine of 1850's in the Merced River area. Spanish for large white rock.

PENON BLANCO POINT   Mariposa

PENON BLANCO RIDGE   Mariposa
   Named after the Penon Blanco gold mine.

PERAL   Tulare
   Spanish for pear tree or pear orchard. Name applied to the Santa Fe Station when the line was built
   circa 1895. Takes its name from the pear orchards of the region.

PERALTA   Orange
   Named after the Peralta family. The ancester Luis Peralta came to California from Sonora in 1776
   with the expedition of Juan Bautista de Anza. One of the Peraltas, Juan Pablo in 1810 was co-grantee
   of the Santiago de Santa Ana grant. The settlement founded circa 1892 is located on the original
   land grant.

PERMANENTE CREEK   Santa Clara
   As far as 1839 it appears as "Arroyo Permanente". "Permanente" a Spanish adjective used as a geographical term to designate a surface of water which keeps its flow during the dry season.

PESCADERO POINT   Monterey

PESCADERO ROCKS   Monterey
   Appears in 1835 as "La Punta del Pescadero". For origin see below.

PESCADERO CREEK   San Benito
   Appears on early documents as "Sanjon del Pescadero".

PESCADERO CREEK   Santa Clara
    Named for the salmons the settlers caught there. Spanish "Pescadero" means fishing place. As far
    as 1830 we find on documents "Arroyo del Pescadero" and in 1854 "Pescadero River".

PESCADERO (Town)   San Mateo
    Name comes from Pescadero Rancho. Spanish meaning fishing place or fisherman.

PESCADERO CREEK

PESCADERO POINT   San Mateo
    For origin see Pescadero (Town).

PESCADERO RANCHO, EL   San Joaquin
    Land grant to Antonio Pico in 1843 for eight leagues; an eight leagues area was granted to Valentin
    Higuera and Rafael Felix in 1843, three-quarters of a league to Fabian Baretto in 1836. The name
    was given to this area by Fernando de Rivera in December 1776.

PICACHO PEAK   Imperial
    Spanish for sharp pointed peak, top, summit. Gold was first discovered there in 1860; the Picacho
    mining center took its name from the Peak (Elevation 1,945 ft.). The peak is shaped like an obelisk.
    Early documents name it "La Campana" (the bell), or "El Peñon de la Campana" (the rock of the
    bell). The local American settlers called it "Chimney Rock". "Picachos" was the name given to the
    Sutter Buttes. There is also a "Picacho Hill" nearby Arroyo Grande in San Luis Obispo county.

PICO   Los Angeles
    Named for Pio Pico penultimate Governor of California 1845-46 during Mexican regime.

PICO CANYON   Los Angeles

PICO OIL FIELD   Los Angeles
    Named for Andres Pico, brother of Pio Pico.

PICO HEIGHTS   Los Angeles
    Named for Pico family.

PICO BLANCO   Monterey
    Spanish for white peak. Pico for peak is a very popular orographic term preserved to our days.

PICO CANYON   Los Angeles
    Named for Andres Pico who produced coal oil in the region. "Old Pico" a pioneer well (now a National
    Historic landmark) was drilled in 1876.

PICO CREEK   San Luis Obispo
    Named for Jesus Pico, owner of the Piedra Blanca Grant (1840).

PICO RIVERA   Los Angeles
    Residential tract area that sprang after World War II. Named after the Pico family. In 1970 the popula-
    tion was 54,170.

PIEDRA PINTADA, LA   Santa Barbara
    Spanish for the painted rock. It is about eighty miles from Santa Barbara. Here there was a stone wig-
    wam, forty or fifty yards in diameter, whose walls were covered with paintings in the form of halos
    and circles, with radiations from the center. (*History of Santa Barbara County*).

PIEDRA
    Spanish for stone or rock. A very popular name from Spanish times has been preserved to our days:
    Piedras Altas (Monterey), Piedra Azul Canyon (Merced), Piedras Blancas Point (San Luis Obispo),
    Piedra Gorda (Los Angeles), Piedra de Lumbre Canyon (San Diego), etc.

PIEDRA, DEL   Fresno

Extensive rock crushing operations in this vicinity may have inspired the name. The proper rendering would be "De La Piedra". Spanish meaning is "of the rock, from the rock".

PIEDRAS ALTAS   Monterey

From the Spanish "high stones".

PIEDRAS BLANCAS POINT   San Luis Obispo

Spanish for white rocks. Named for the rancho on which the area is located. Land grant applied January 18, 1840 to Jesus Pico. Present town of San Simeon is located on the original site.

PIEDRA RANCHO, CORRAL DE   San Luis Obispo

Spanish "enclosure of rock". Land granted to José María Villavicencio in 1841 and 1846 for an area of two leagues.

PIGEON POINT   San Mateo

The original name before the 1850's was "Punta de las Ballenas (point of whales). After the clipper "Carrier Pigeon" was wrecked here on May 6, 1853, the Coast Survey gave the present name.

PILARCITOS CREEK   San Mateo

Spanish for little pillars or posts. The Portola-Crespi expedition passed here October 28, 1769; they saw many geese and called it plain of Los Ansares (Spanish for geese). It is not exactly known why the name "pilarcitos" was given except that a land grant of January 2, 1841 is recorded under "Arroyo de los pilarcitos". The same land was also known as "San Benito" and as "Rancho de Miramontes".

PILARCITOS LAKE

See above.

PILARCITOS CANYON   Monterey

As far as 1901 we find on documents a "Sitio de los Pilarcitos" or "Pilarcitos".

PILARCITOS RIDGE

See above.

PILLAR POINT   San Mateo

Spanish is "pilar." So named because of an elevated rock resembling a pillar. As far as 1796 some documents mention "Un parage llamado el Pilar" and we wonder if it was not named after "Nuestra Senora del Pilar"?

PINO GRANDE   El Dorado

Spanish for big pine. Named for the majestuous pines of the region.

PINOLE POINT   Contra Costa

In Spanish it is an aromatic powder used in making chocolate. Named by Jose de Canizares in 1775 who received a kind of mixture tasting like chocolate that the Indians gave him. He named the place "Campo del Pinole". In Mexican times it became known as "El Pinole"; several grants were issued under the names of "Pinole y Canada de la Hambre", "Boca de la Canada del Pinole". The name was mispelled later on as "Penoli", "Penole"; circa 1900 the present name was applied. Post office established circa 1870.

PINOLE CREEK

PINOLE RIDGE

See above.

PINOS, POINT   Monterey

Named Punta de Pinos or Point of Pines by Sebastian Vizcaino in December 1602 because of the forest of pines. Pinos (pines) is the most popular tree in place naming: Monterey Bay was "La Bahia de los Pinos"; Point Reyes was "El Cabo de los Pinos".

PINOS, POTRERO LOS   San Diego
From the land grant "The Potrero Los Pinos" which was part of the Potreros de San Juan Capistrano land grant (April 5, 1845).

PINTO MOUNTAINS   San Bernardino
Derives from corrupt Spanish pinto or mottled, occasioned by drab vari-hued colors of the range. Color applied to a piebald horse. As far as 1776 it appears on documents: "la sierra llamada Pinta . . . "

PINTO PEAK   Death Valley National Monument
The name was applied to the range north of Towne's Pass in 1871.

PINTO LAKE   Santa Cruz
Named after an early settler.

PINYON
For the Spanish piñon, the edible pine-nut seed.

PINYON PEAKS   Monterey
Named after the Pinus parryana and the Pinus monophylla, pine-trees bearing edible nuts, which grow in the area.

PINYON WELL   Riverside
Named because it is close to Pinyon Canyon where many piñones grow. See above.

PIOJO RANCHO, EL   Monterey
Spanish for the louse. Land grant to Joaquin Soto in 1842 for an area of three leagues. Named after El Piojo Creek.

PITAS POINT   Ventura
Spanish for whistle (pito). From an Indian village named "Los Pitos" by Portola expedition. Because of the Indians blowing some kind of pipes or whistles, all night. Crespi called the village "Santa Conefundis". It is not before 1822 that the name "de los Pitos" reappeared. In 1868 it is mentioned as "Las Petes". In 1889 it became "Las Pitas" (The Point Las Pitas).

PLACER COUNTY
French and Spanish word for "surface mining for gold". Because of the great number of placers in this county. The theory often advanced that the word "placer" is a contraction of "plaza de Oro" (Place of gold) is a fantasy. Created April 25, 1851, chap. 14. Area, 1,431 sq. mi.

PLACERITA CANYON   Los Angeles
In 1842 Francisco Lopez made its gold discovery. Several miners were attracted but it was not a gold rush. The Canyon was the scene of robberies by Tiburcio Vasquez. Presently it is a State Park.

PLACERITA CREEK   Los Angeles
For the discovery of gold in a placer belonging to Francisco Lopez, circa 1840.

PLACERVILLE   El Dorado
Was discovered by a party of three miners who had come to California. The settlement was first called "Dry Diggings". In 1850 rich placers were discovered and the town was called "Placerville". Among its early residents were Philip Armour, a butcher, and John Studebaker, a builder of wheel barrows, and Mark Hopkins, a grocery store owner. Armour became an important meat-packer, Studebaker an automobile manufacturer and Hopkins, a railroad magnate. In 1970 the population was 5,416.

PLANADA   Merced
In 1911 a contest to name the town decided on "Planada". Spanish name for plain or level ground. The locality was first known as Geneva and the railroad station was Whitton.

PLANO   Tulare
Spanish for flat, plain, or level ground. Post office established in 1871.

PLATINA   Shasta

Spanish for platinum ore. Named after the important platinum ore discovered in this area. Post office established in 1921.

PLAYA

Spanish for beach, strand. (Also a mud plain left by an evaporated pond.)

PLAYA, LA   San Diego

Was known in the 1820's as "Hide Park" when the area was used for drying hides.

PLAYA, BOCA DE LA   Orange

Spanish for mouth or entrance. From a land grant of May 7, 1846.

PLAYA DEL REY   Los Angeles

Spanish for King's Beach. New name for the unsuccessful Port Ballona.

PLEYTO   Monterey

Named for Pleyto Rancho and is usually spelled pleito meaning dispute, contest, or lawsuit.

PLEITO HILLS   Kern

PLEITO CREEK   Kern

See Pleyto, Monterey county.

PLUMAS COUNTY

Spanish for feathers from the first name of the river: El Rio de las Plumas (Feather River), from which the county takes its name. It became an important point of entry to California after the discovery of the pass Beckwourth in 1851. Created March 18, 1854, chap. 1. Area 2,570 sq. mi.

PLUMAS NATIONAL FOREST

Occupies portions of Butte, Lasse, Plumas, Sierra and Yuba counties. It was created by President Theodore Roosevelt in 1908. The forest contains 1,221,536 acres.

POINT ARENA (Town)   Mendocino

Named after the nearby cape. The post office was named Punta Arenas in 1867.

POINT ARGUELLO   Santa Barbara

Was named by Vancouver (1792) for Jose Dario Arguello. Vandenberg Air Force Base is located there.

POINT BONITA   Kern

Previous name of "Punta de Santiago".

POINT CONCEPTION   Santa Barbara

The point was discovered and named by Cabrillo (1542) "Cabo de la Galera" (Point of the seagoing galley). On December 8, 1602 Vizcaino sighted it, the feast of "La Purisima Concepcion" (Immaculate Conception) and therefore gave it the present name. The point itself has been anglicized to Point Conception.

POINT DUME

Located north of Malibu. The mispelled name honors Father Francisco Dumetz who entertained Vancouver during his visit at Mission San Buenaventura. It was Vancouver who named the Point.

POINT LOBOS   Monterey

Spanish for "Cape of the Wolves". It is a State Reserve since 1933 with an area of 1,250 acres. The offshore rocks are inhabited by sea lions and pelicans; sea otters and whales live in the surrounding waters. From 1861 to 1884 there was a whaling station very active on this site.

POINT LOMA   San Diego

See Loma.

POINT PINOS   Monterey
    See Pinos Point.

POINT REYES   Marin
    See Reyes Point.

POLITA CANYON   Inyo
    Named after the Poleta Mine. A Mexican named Poleta discovered the mine circa 1880.

POLITA STATION
    Was named after the Canyon.

POLVADERO GAP   Fresno
    From the Spanish "Polvadera" (Cloud of dust). Named for the numerous dust storms that Mexicans witnessed near Kettleman Hills.

PONCHO RICO CREEK   Monterey
    Named after Francisco Rico land owner of the San Lorenzo grant of November 16, 1842. Pancho, mispelled Poncho is a diminutive for Francisco.

PONTO   San Diego
    Poetical Spanish for the sea. The point was first known as La Costa as early as 1893 and was given the present name in June 1918.

PORCIUNCULA   Los Angeles
    In 1770 Costanso abbreviated the name of the river "Nuestra Señora la Reina de los Angeles del Rio de Porciuncula" when he camped on its banks August 2, which is the Feast Day of Our Lady of the Angels of the Portiuncula Chapel of the Franciscan Order near Assisi, Italy. The pueblo soon became called "Los Angeles" though named for the Virgin (La Reina) and for the river, not for the angels. (From Hart, p. 338).

PORTAL, EL   Mariposa
    Named by officials of Yosemite Valley Railroad when it reached the terminus here in 1907. The Spanish word means portal or gateway and El Portal is the natural water-level entrance to Yosemite Valley.

PORTOLA   San Mateo and Plumas counties
    Two localities with this name in California commemorate the first governor of Spanish-California 1768-70.

POSA   Santa Clara
    Also known as "Posa de San Juan Bautista" and "Posa de Chaboya" from a land grant dated March 10, 1839.

POSA DE LOS OSITOS   Monterey
    "Water hole of the little bears". From a land grant of April 16, 1839.

POSITA
    From the Mexican word for pond, water hole, a diminutive of "Pozo" (well).

POSITAS CREEK, LAS   Alameda
    As far as 1810 documents mention "una posa de buena agua" (a pool of good water) . . . and later ". . . un paraje nombrado de las positas del valle". (a site called a place of the little ponds of the valley.)

POSITAS RANCHO, LAS   Alameda
    From a land grant to Robert Livermore on April 8, 1839 for an area of two leagues. Livermore was associate to Noriega from whom he later bought his share.

POSITAS   Santa Barbara

From a land grant of May 8, 1843 under the title "La Calera y las Positas" granted to Narciso Fabregat and Thomas Robbins. In Spanish "La Calera" means lime kiln.

POSO CREEK   Kern

Called previously "Pose Creek"; after 1854 it appears as "Posa Creek"; in 1863 a French spelling is given "pose Flat" and "Little Pose"; Posey Creek circa 1880. The post office was established in 1915. Poso should be spelled Pozo in good Spanish. Garces named it "Rio de Santiago" in 1776.

POSOLMI Y POSITA DE LAS ANIMAS   Santa Clara

Spanish for Pool of the little pool of the "souls". Named after a land grant of February 15, 1844 given to Lopez Ynigo, an Indian.

POTRERO   San Diego

Spanish for pasture. One of the most common generic terms in California.

BIG POTRERO, ROUND POTRERO   San Diego

"Bih Pasture", "Round Pasture".

POTRERO CHICO, POTRERO GRANDE, POTRERO DE FELIPE LUGO
                                                 Los Angeles

"Small", "large", Felipe Lugo's pasture".

POTRERO SECO   Ventura

"Dry Pasture".

MILL POTRERO   Kern

"Mill Pasture".

LA CARPA POTRERO, MONTGOMERY POTRERO, SALISBURY POTRERO, PINE CORRAL POTRERO
                                                 Santa Barbara

Association of American words with the generic potrero. "La Carpa Potrero" (the carp's pasture) "Pine Corral potrero" (the pasture pine's enclosure).

POZA, POZO

Spanish poza meaning puddle, pozo meaning well. In California the spelling Posa, Poso is tolerated and used generally for "water-hole". The word is a very well used geographical term.

ARROYO LAS POZAS   Ventura

From a place called in 1819, "Las Pozas O Simi". In 1837 we find the following "Arroyo de las Pozas" and "Cuchilla de las pozas".

POZO   San Luis Obispo

Spanish for well. Named after a water hole in the valley.

PRADO   Riverside

Spanish for field or meadow.

PRADO STATION   Riverside

The station was given the name in 1907.

PRADO DAM

(See above).

PRADO, EL   Fresno

Name given to the station of the San Joaquin and Eastern Railroad.

PRENDA   Riverside

Spanish for security or pledge. For the development of the Santa Fe crossing the citrus district in 1907.

LA PRESA   San Diego

Spanish for dam, or dike. Located on the Sweetwater River, originally called "Agua Dulce" by the Spaniards, is found a few miles east of San Diego.

PRESIDIO

Spanish "fortified barracks", "garrison". There were four presidios: Monterey Presidio, 1770; San Diego Mission Guard, 1774; San Francisco, 1776; Santa Barbara, 1782. (Corte de Madera del Presidio Rancho, Marin county is an area of one league. The name means "wood pile of cut wood for the presidio).

PRIMER CANON RANCHO   Tehama

Land grant to Job F. Dyean May 22, 1844 for an area of six leagues. The grant is also known as "El Rio de los Berrenderos" "berrenderos" means antelopes.

PRIMERO   Tulare

Named in 1914 by Santa Fe Railroad because station was the first one north of Orosi on the Porterville branch of the road. Primero in Spanish means first.

PROVIDENCIA   Los Angeles

Spanish for providence, foresight. Land grant of March 1, 1843 to Vicente de la Ossa for an area of one league.

PUEBLO

In Spanish California "Pueblo" was a generic name equivalent to the American "town". The term "ciudad" (city) was occasionally used for Los Angeles, and "villa" (town) was used only once: "Villa de Branciforte" ancient name for the present Santa Cruz. "Pueblo de San José de Guadalupe" founded in 1777 is the oldest civic community. It is now the city of San José.

PUENTE   Los Angeles

From La Puente Rancho which means bridge. Named because an adjacent range of hills bridges the Santa Ana and San Gabriel Valleys. The rancho was established here originally in 1816 by Father Jose Maria Zalvidea under the jurisdiction of San Gabriel Mission. Land grant on July 22, 1845 to John Rowland and William Workman for an area of 48,000 acres. The name bridge "Puente" goes back to Portola expedition which camped at San Jose Creek on July 30, 1769, and it is mentioned as "Llano de la Puente" (The Plain of the bridge). The Railroad Station of the Los Angeles-Colton section of the Southern Pacific in 1875 bears the name "Puente". In 1887 the post office was established.

PUERTO, PUERTA

Spanish Puerto (port) was frequently used along the shore of California; it also means a mountain pass. Puerta feminine form of puerto indicates a door or gate. Hence we have Puerto, San Diego. Arroyo de la puerta (Rancho del) Puerto, Stanislaus county. Land grant of 1844 to Mariano Hernandez for an area of three leagues.

PULGA   Butte

Spanish for flea. At one time this was a populous mining settlement at the mouth of Flea Valley on the Feather River originally known as Big Bar. Changed to present name by Western Pacific Railroad Company.

PULGAS RANCHO   San Mateo

Spanish for the fleas ranch. Land grant given to Luis Arguello in November 1826 for an area of four leagues. Present Belmont, Menlo Park and Redwood City are located on the site of the original grant. The site takes its name because fleas and other vermin abounded in the habitations of the Indians living in squalid quarters. This mass of filth became soon too offensive even for savages and they adopted the very simple method of setting fire to the hut and erecting another one, in order to get rid of the fleas. In one instance the Spaniards took refuge in an Indian hut and a few minutes later came out screaming "Las Pulgas!" "Las pulgas!" (the fleas, the fleas) for this reason the soldiers called it "La Rancheria de las Pulgas."

PULGAS RIDGE   San Mateo

PULGAS CREEK   San Mateo
    For origin see above.

PULGAS CANYON, LAS   San Diego
    The former place of Mission San Luis Rey in 1828.

PUNTA
    Spanish point; the generic term also appears in the names of eight land grants. There is a Mesa de la
    Punta in Riverside county, a Punta Arena on Santa Cruz island, a station Punta in Ventura county
    and a Punta del Castillo in Santa Barbara county.

PUNTA GORDA   Humboldt
    See Gorda.

PUNTA DE LOS MUERTOS   San Diego Harbor
    Spanish for Point of the Dead, for the soldiers buried there because of an epidemic. Then on July 21,
    1905 an explosion on board of the U.S.S. Bennington caused the death of sixty-five sailors.

PUNTA DEL MONTE, RINCON DE LA   Monterey
    Is the name of a land grant of September 20, 1836.

PURIFICATION RANCHO, LOMAS DE LA   Santa Barbara
    Land grant of December 27, 1844 to Augustin Janssens for an area of three leagues. The word is in
    reference to the Purification of the Virgin Mary.

PURISIMA CONCEPTION DE MARIA SANTISIMA MISSION, LA
    A settlement with a tragic ending. Less than a year after its foundation on the site of present Yuma,
    the Indians attacked and killed 46 inhabitants. The other mission San Pedro y San Pablo de Bicuñer
    Mission founded by Fathers Juan Diaz and José Matias Moreno.

PURISIMA CONCEPTION MISSION, LA   Santa Barbara
    This eleventh mission was founded by Father Fermin Francisco Lasuen on December 8, 1787, the day
    of the Feast of the Immaculate Conception. The mission was secularized and sold on October 28,
    1845 to John Temple for $1,110.00. In 1935 it was made a State Park.

PURISIMA CONCEPTION RANCHO, LA   Santa Clara
    Land grant given to José Gorgonio dated June 30, 1840 for an area of one league. (For origin see
    above).

PURISMA CREEK

PURISIMA (Town)   San Mateo
    From the land grant "Cañada Verde y Arroyo de la Purisima" (green valley and Purisima Creek).

PUTAH CREEK, LAKE, NAPA, SOLANO counties
    The name may be Indian in origin, but the word likely is a corruption of the Spanish "puta" meaning
    "harlot, prostitute".

PUTAS RANCHO, LAS   Napa
    One land grant of eight leagues in 1843 to Jose de Jesus and Sexto Berreyesa. The name means "prosti-
    tutes" in Spanish.

PUTOS RANCHO, RIO DE LOS   Yolo
    Land grant of 1842 to Francisco Guerrero for an area of four leagues. "Puto" masculine for "putas"
    (prostitutes).

QUEMADO
Spanish for "burnt" used for several place names.

QUEMADO, ARROYO   Santa Barbara
Known as early as 1794.

QUIEN SABE CREEK   San Benito
Spanish for "who knows?"   Name of a land grant "Santa Ana y Quien Sabe" of April 8, 1839. Also mentioned "Canada de Quien Sabe", and "Sierra de Quien Sabe".

QUINADO CANYON   Monterey
A Spanish corruption of a Costanoan word meaning "evil-smelling" in reference to the sulphur springs.

QUINTA, LA   Riverside
Spanish for "country seat" or "villa". A deluxe resort in the Santa Rose Mountains near Indian Well.

QUINTIN, POINT   Marin
There are several versions as for the naming: 1) "Punta de Quintin" was thus named for an Indian thief and chief who redeemed himself. 2) For a Roman officer who became a Christian missionary. The name figures on a land grant of September 24, 1840. The name appears on "Punta Quintin", "Punta de Quintin". The Coast Survey of 1850 changed the name to its present form "San Quentin".

QUINTO CREEK   Stanislaus
Spanish "fifth"; may have referred to a share of land. Also spelled Kinto.

QUITO   Santa Clara
When the South Pacific was built from San José to Los Gatos in 1878 this location was named Quito because it was situated on the land grant of the same name dated March 12, 1841.

QUIT
An area of three leagues given to José Z. Fernandez.

RAIMUNDO, CANADA DE   San Mateo
Also spelled "Raymundo". The name appears on documents as far as 1797. Land grant of August 4, 1840.

RAMONA   San Diego
Named for heroine of Helen Hunt Jackson's long-selling novel of Indian oppression in California, *Ramona*, Boston, 1884). Post office established in 1892. Also:

RAMONA STATION   Sacramento

RAMONA PARK   Los Angeles

RAMONA HOT SPRINGS   Riverside

RANA
Spanish for frog. Several place names during Spanish times bore the term "rana". Cienega (Swamp or marsh) de las Ranas in Orange county.

RANA CREEK   Monterey

RANA STATION   San Bernardino

RANCHERIA, RANCHERIAS
Spanish for a group of ranchos also in modern times for village or hamlet. The word also applied to Indian villages. It is preserved as a specific term (not as a generic term) in twenty nine geographic features, such as creeks, on the side of which were groups of ranches. During Spanish California, the power of the crown grew with the power of the Church and the Franciscan fathers circulated among

the rancherias or villages of the natives to instruct the Indians in the ways of Christianity and civilization. Rancherias were numerous and they were under the jurisdiction of one or another of the missions and each had its individual name. La Purisima Concepcion Mission had 48 rancherias, Santa Ynez 57, Santa Barbara 212, San Fernando 184, San Juan Bautista 27, San Gabriel 19, San Luis Rey 110, San Diego 67, San Juan Capistrano 210, San Buenaventura 94, San Francisco Dolores 72, etc. (From Hanna, p. 249).

RANCHERIA CREEK   Yosemite National Park

RANCHERIA FALLS   Yosemite National Park

RANCHERIA MOUNTAIN   Yosemite National Park

RANCHERIA TRAIL   Yosemite National Park
For the four above see "Rancheria".

RANCHO, RANCHOS, RANCHITA
Spanish "rancho" means hut or group of huts in which farm employees used to live. In Mexican a rancho is a small farm or grazing place. Later on the meaning was extended to landed estate, called hacienda in Spain and other Spanish countries. It was used as a generic geographical term. "Ranchita" is a diminutive of rancho. These pasturages entitled the grantees to the use but not to the ownership of the land. Eventually these permits became actual transfers of ownership, and so California's more than 500 private land grants came into being. The first of these was the San Pedro Rancho granted in 1784 to Juan Jose Dominguez. The standard unit of measurement was the Mexican league, a matter of 2.63 miles and the league means a square league, though in the ancient documents the "square" is omitted. For small parcels the Mexican "Vara" of 32.99 inches was used, and here again the "square vara" is meant. The confirmed ranchos were described by the U.S. Land Commission in acres. (From Hanna, p. 249).

RANCHO SANTA FE   San Diego
Belonged to the Santa Fe purchased under the name of San Dieguito Ranch. The ranch was sold in 1927 to promoters who subdivided but kept the name.

REAL DE LAS AGUILAS RANCHO   San Benito
Spanish for the gathering, place of the eagles. Land grant of January 16, 1844 to Francisco Arias and Saturnino Cariaga for an area of seven leagues. The origin is not certain. One source says "the place named after two persons by the name of Aguila who made camp there . . ." Another source mentions the facts of having witnessed many eagles in the area.

REDONDO BEACH   Los Angeles
Spanish for round. Probably gained name from the Sausal Redondo Rancho (round willow grove). The city was founded in 1881 and incorporated in 1892. The town was developed as a seaside resort.

REFUGIO
Spanish for refuge. Refugio was often used as a place name. It is frequent in several counties (Santa Clara, Santa Barbara, Santa Cruz, Contra Costa, etc.)

REFUGIO PASS   Santa Barbara
From the land grant "Nuestra Señora del Refugio" of 1794 and 1834.

REFUGIO RANCHO   Santa Cruz
Spanish for refuge. A land grant to José Antonio Bolcof in 1841 for an area of three leagues.

RELIZ
A Spanish-Mexican term "landslide" used frequently in place-names. It was also spelled "Reliez".

RELIZ CREEK   Monterey
The name changed to "Release Creek".

RELIEZ VALLEY   Contra Costa
   The name is also spelled "Raliez" and "Reesley".

REPRESA   Sacramento
   Spanish for dam, dike or restriction. Post office designation for California State Prison, more familiarly known as Folsom Penitentiary. Outgoing prisons' mail always bears the cancellation "Represa".

RESEDA   Los Angeles
   Origin unrevealed. Both Latin and Spanish designation for Mignonette plant (reseda odorata).

REY, DEL   Fresno
   Spanish for "of or from the king" usually for a place belonging to the king.

REYES PEAK   Ventura
   One of the highest peaks (7,488 ft.) in San Rafael mountains. Named for Jacinto Damien Reyes, thirty-year forest ranger.

REYES POINT   Marin
   It is presumably the "Cabo de Pinos" discovered by Cabrillo, November 14, 1542. On January 6, 1603 Sebastian Vizcaino passed the point, the day of the "Three Holy Kings, or Wise Men" of the New Testament. The Spanish explorers named the bay "Puerto de los Reyes" and "Punta de los Reyes" for the Point. The Coast Survey used the present form since 1855.

POINT REYES
   Has replaced the former Olema Station, April 1, 1833. The Post Office was established in 1887.

REYES RANCHO, PUNTA DE LOS   Marin
   Land grant given to A. M. Osio, in 1843 for an area of eleven leagues. Named because of nearby Point Reyes.

RICARDO   Kern
   Spanish for Richard. Rudolf Hagen pioneer who owned Red Rock Canyon had a son named Richard of whom he was very fond. He nicknamed him Ricardo. His son died mysteriously and Hagen named the town after him. (From Hanna, p. 254.)

RIEGO   Sutter
   Spanish for irrigation. Named for the small streams which were used from time to time for irrigation.

RINCONADA   San Diego
   Occurs frequently as place name in California. The Spanish word means the inside angle formed by the junction of two walls or lines. This term is widely used in describing land grants and so occurs as widely as a name.

RINCON   Riverside
   A township platted in 1888 located on the Santa Ana River.

RINCON DEL ALISAL   Santa Clara
   In Spanish means corner of the alder grove. Land grant dated December 28, 1844. (Has disappeared from present toponymy).

RINCON DE LOS BUEYES   Los Angeles
   Spanish for oxen (Bueyes). Name applied to he land grant of December 7, 1821. Rincon meaning a nook, bend in a river, secluded place, inside corner is current in southwestern U.S.A. However, nowadays in Spanish geographical nomenclature "rincon" designates a small portion of land. We find "rincon" in about twenty land grants..

RINCON POINT

Previously called Santa Clara de Monte Falso, also known by Portola as El Bailarin. However, Anza on February 1776 mentions Rancheria del Rincon; as for Font he called it La Rinconada (the corner). Also Rincon Creek, Rincon Mountain (Ventura, Santa Barbara counties).

RINCON POINT   Santa Barbara

The surrounding area was known by the first Spanish travelers as "Santa Clara de Monte Falso", Portola's men called it "El Bailarin" presumably because one of the Indian chiefs who excelled in dancing. On February 24, 1776 Anza calls this region "Rancherias del Rincon" and later on, Font named it "La Rinconada". Rincon Point is recorded as such in 1862.

RINCON POINT   San Francisco

Named for the terminus of the Bay Bridge.

RINCON RANCHO , EL   Santa Barbara and Ventura

Land granted to Teodora Arellanes in 1835 for an area of one league.

RINCON RANCHO, EL   San Bernardino

Land granted to Juan Bandini in 1839 for an area of one league.

RIO

Spanish for river. A popular generic term found in several land grants; used in names of post offices and localities also.

RIO, EL   Ventura

Spanish for river. Founded by Simon Cohn in 1875 and known as New Jerusalem.

RIO BRAVO   Kern

For the previous name of Kern River. The name was given in the 1890's for the Pacific Railroad Station.

RIO DELL   Humboldt

Early called Eagle Prairie. The present name was given after 1890 when the post office was established.

RIONIDO   Sonoma

The post office was established in 1912. The name is a combination of Rio (river) and nido (nest) two pleasant Spanish sounds. The resort was founded in 1910.

RIOS (DOS)   Mendocino

Spanish for two rivers. Because two forks of the El River meet here.

RIO OSO   Sutter

Spanish "oso" means bear. The station of the Sacramento Northern was named in 1907 because of its location nearby the Bear (Oso) River.

RIO VISTA   Solano

The town called previously "Brazos del Rio" was founded in 1857 by Colonel N. H. Davis. It was Thus named because it was near the three arms of the Sacramento River. "Brazos" means "arms" in Spanish. The name changed to the present in 1860.

RITAS, PUNTAS DE LA   Santa Barbara

Spanish for point of the rites. Refers to some religious Indian ceremony held upon that spot that Spanish explorers witnessed.

RIVERA   Los Angeles

Spanish for river, brook, or stream. The name was given by the late senator R. F. del Valle in 1886 because floods of 1867-68 had caused San Gabriel River to divide from the Rio Hondo and placed the community between two water courses. The former name of the district was Maizaland because the chief crop of the region was corn. In 1886 when the Santa Fe reached the locality, the name was changed to the present.

ROBLA   Sacramento
Spanish for a fee, for pasturage, a permit. Named after the request from Mexican owners of the pasture for a fee to give permission to the cattle to graze.

ROBLE, ROBLAR
Spanish "deciduous oak", place where deciduous oaks grow. These terms were used for place naming in Spanish times, but they were less popular than "encina" (live oak). These terms are found in "Paso de Robles" (San Luis Obispo county) and "Roblar de 1a Miseria" (Sonoma county). In present times the terms have been preserved in, Santa Clara, Santa Barbara, San Luis Obispo, Sonoma, Los Angeles, Monterey, Tehama, Sacramento and Tulare counties.

RODEO
The word was used originally for an enclosure at a fair where cattle were sold. In Mexico it meant for the rounding up of cattle for counting and sale. It became the usual term for the American Cowboy contest. The place name is found in Contra Costa, San Mateo, San Francisco, Los Angeles, and Santa Cruz counties. The term applies to canyons, creeks, lagoons, etc.

RODEO   Contra Costa
Spanish for cattle roundup. Name given when it was planned to be a cattle slaughtering and meat packing center. These plans never developed and instead it became the site of an oil refining operation.

RODEO CREEK   Contra Costa
The town was founded in the early 1860's laid out on the Pinole Grant. The post office was listed in 1898.

RODEO RANCHO, ARROYO DEL   Santa Cruz
Land grant to Francisco Rodriguez in 1834 for an area of one and a quarter leagues.

RODEO DE LAS AGUAS   Los Angeles
Spanish for gathering of the waters. A name once given to the present "La Brea Rancho", for the nearby kind of amphitheatre which collects the greater portion of the water flowing from the neighboring mountains.

RODEO VALLEY   Contra Costa
It appears on a plat of the rancho in 1860.

ROMERO CREEK   Merced
Named for Jose Romero, an early settler who was killed by the Indians.

ROSA, DEL   San Bernardino
Barbaric Spanish for "of or by the rose." Correct usage would be de la Rosa. Named because of the profusion of wild roses.

ROSALES (LOS)   San Diego
Spanish for the rose-bushes. Nothing in the new land brought to the explorers sweeter memories of their distant home than "the roses of Castile" which grew so luxuriantly in this area. This spot is located two leagues from Santa Margarita and seventeen leagues from San Diego. As early as 1769 documents of the Spanish times mention "la cañada de los Rosales" (the glen of the rose bushes).

ROSE "ROSA CALIFORNICA"
Is responsible for 45 place names. Las Pulgas Canyon (the fleas canyon) in San Diego county was named "Canada de Santa Praxedis de los Rosales" because of the profusion of rosebushes.

RUBIO CANYON   Los Angeles
Spanish for red, reddish, blond. Two sources, one that it was named because of the reddish colors seen on the cliffs; the other named for Jesus Rubio, a Spaniard who became an American and settled at the mouth of the Canyon circa 1865.

SABLON   San Bernardino
 Spanish for coarse sand, gravel (sablón). Station named in 1912 because of the nature of the soil, basically of coarse sand.

SACATE   Santa Barbara
 Spanish for grass or hay. Name of the station of the Southern Pacific for the abundance of grass along the railroad tracks.

SACO   Kern
 Spanish for sack. Applied to Southern Pacific siding after 1900.

SACRAMENTO   Sacramento
 Spanish for holy sacrament. In the fall of 1848 John A. Sutter, Jr. and Sam Brennan laid out the town at embarcadero of Sutter's Fort and named it Sacramento after the river. Gabriel Moraga gave the name to river on October 8, 1808.

SACRAMENTO COUNTY
 Spanish for holy sacrament. Created February 18, 1850, for chap. 15. Area 985 sq. mi.

SACRAMENTO MOUNTAINS   San Bernardino
 Named for the Sacramento River by miners who worked there in the 1860's.

SACRAMENTO RIVER   Siskiyou, Shasta, Tehama, Glenn, Butte, Colusa, Sutter, Yolo, Sacramento and Solano counties.
 Spanish for holy sacrament. The name appears on early documents. Father Juan Crespi and Don Pedro Fages on March 30, 1772 saw the San Joaquin and Sacramento rivers for the first time. These two rivers were called the "Rio de San Francisco". On October 8, 1808 Gabriel Moraga explored the region and gave the name Sacramento River to the Feather River. In 1817 an expedition led by Father Ramon Abella and Narciso Duran recorded in their reports that they met the junction of the San Joaquin and the Sacramento. The trappers of the Hudson's Bay Company called this river the "Bonaventura", "Buenaventura" or the "Big River". The Wilkes expedition finally established the present name.

SACRAMENTO VALLEY   Shasta and Tehama counties and Glenn, Butte, Colusa, Sutter Yuba, Placer and Yolo counties, Delta, Sacramento and Solano counties.
 Was first explored by Fages and Crespi; then by Moraga (1808). Agriculture became important in the 1850's. The Central Valley Project increased in irrigation as acreage employed mounted to 1,000,000 acres in 1950. It also aided to control flood, and increased electrification in the valley.

SAGRA-DA FAMILIA RANCHO, LA   Contra Costa
 See Boca de la Canada del Pinole Rancho.

SAL, POINT   Santa Barbara
 Named by Vancouver for Hermenegildo Sal, Commandante at San Francisco (1792) in recognition for services rendered to the British Captain.

SALADA BEACH   San Mateo
 Takes its name from adjacent Laguna Salada or "salted lagoon".

SALADA LAGUNA   San Mateo
 See above.

SALADO ARROYO   Orange and Imperial
 "Salty brook". Because of the saline content of these streams.

SALIDA   Stanislaus
 Previously known as Murphy's Ferry. John Murphy operated the Ferry at this location. Donated land to Southern Pacific railroad for the right-of-way and the name changed to Salida. (exit or outskirts).

SALINAS (CITY)   Monterey

Named for the Salinas River. The name means salt marshes. Named because salt marshes do exist at its mouth. The town was founded in the late 1850's. The post office is listed in 1858.

SALINAS RANCHO, LAS   Monterey

Land grant to Gabriel Espinosa, in 1836 for an area of one league. It takes its name from the nearby Salinas River. Spanish for salt-marshes.

SALINAS RANCHO, RINCON DE LAS   Monterey

Land grant to Cristina Delgado in 1833 for an area of half a league. Spanish meaning "the inside corner of the salt marshes". Named after the Salinas River.

SALINAS Y POTRERO VIEJO, RINCON DE LAS   San Francisco and San Mateo counties

Land grant of October 10, 1839 and May 30, 1840 to Jose Cornelio Bernal for an area of one league. Spanish for "the corner of salt marshes and the old pasture".

SALINAS RIVER   San Luis Obispo, Monterey

The name of the river is derived from the Salinas (salt marshes) numerous near the river mouth. During Spanish times the river had several names: "Santa Delfina", "San Antonio", "Rio de Monterey", "Salines River", "Rio San Buenaventura", "Rio Salinas", and "Rio San Elizario".

SALSIPUEDES

Used in geographic nomenclature usually for narrow enclosures or canyons where terrain is very rough. Spanish meaning "get-out-if-you-can."

SALSIPUEDES RANCHO, CANADA DE   Santa Barbara

A land grant to Pedro Cordero of May 18, 1844 for an area of one and a half leagues. The stream is known under the name of "Arrollo de Salsipuedes" Spanish "get-out-if-you-can-glen ranch". Captain Arguello, in his diary of the expedition of 1821, refers to his struggles in getting out of a certain canyon in these terms: "on account of its difficult situation it was named "Montana de Maltrato y Arroyo de Sal si Puedes." (Mountain of ill-treatment and creek of get out if you can).

SALSIPUEDES RANCHO   Santa Cruz

Land grant to Manuel Jimeno Casarin, in 1834 and 1840 for an area of eight leagues. Spanish: (See above Salsipuedes)

SALUD, LA   Santa Clara

Spanish for health. This place is not far from the San Lorenzo River reached by the Portola expedition on October 22, 1769. The Spaniards suffered from scurvy during this journey. A terrible storm wetted all the men but instead of getting worse, the men recovered from their sickness. This was the reason for giving the canyon the name of "la Salud".

SAN ADRIANO, EL VALLE DE   San Luis Obispo

(See Morro Bay).

SAN ANDREAS   Calaveras

Mining camp of '49 rich in placer gold and quartz. Named by early Mexican miners for St. Andrew, brother of Simon Peter.

SAN ANDRES RANCHO   Santa Cruz

For a land grant of May 21, 1823 to Joaquin Castro for an area of two leagues. Land grant named after the Saint.

SAN ANDREAS VALLEY   San Mateo

It was named "Cañada de San Andres" as early as 1774, for St. Andrew because of the day of discovery.

SAN ANDREAS LAKE   San Mateo

This reservoir was built in 1875 and the mispelled name of the saint has been kept.

SAN ANDRES, ENSENADA DE   Los Angeles
    See San Pedro Bay.

SAN ANGELO   San Diego
    See Batequitos Lagoon.

SAN ANSELMO   Marin
    Honors St. Anselm (1033-1109 A.D.) distinguished 11th century church scholar. The name appears as early as 1840 and was applied to the North Pacific Coast Railroad in 1992.

SAN ANTONIO RANCHO   Alameda
    Three land grants, two of which were made to Luis Peralta in 1820. On their site stand now the cities of Alameda, Berkeley, Emeryville and Oakland.

SAN ANTONIO MOUNTAIN   Los Angeles
    According to some sources it was named for St. Antony of Padua. According to others it was for Antonio Maria Lugo, grantee of nearby Santa Ana del Chino Rancho in 1841. The Peak was nick-named "Old Baldy" for its barren summit.

SAN ANTONIO   Los Angeles
    Or Rodeo de las Aguas Rancho granted in 1831 to Maria Rita Valdez for an area of one league. It is the present site of the city of Beverly Hills.

SAN ANTONIO RANCHO   Los Angeles
    A land grant to Antonio Maria Lugo in 1838. Several cities have been founded on its original site, such as Bell, Downy, Lynwood, Maywood and Southgate.

SAN ANTONIO
    A very popular name during Spanish times, especially in mission days because Saint Anthony was the patron Saint of the Franciscan Order.

SAN ANTONIO RIVER   Monterey
    Named by Father Serra.

SAN ANTONIO CREEK   Monterey

SAN ANTONIO VALLEY   Monterey
    See above.

SAN ANTONIO DE PADUA MISSION   Monterey
    It was founded by the Franciscan Fathers July 14, 1771. The mission was dedicated to Saint Anthony of Padua who joined the Franciscan Order of Padua in 1221. He died in 1231. After its secularization in June 1835, the first owner was Mariano Soberanes. A post office was listed from 1867-1887.

SAN ANTONIO CREEK   San Bernardino
As early as 1774 the name of the arroyo called San Antonio is mentioned.

SAN ANTONIO CANYON   San Bernardino

SAN ANTONIO HEIGHTS   San Bernardino

SAN ANTONIO MOUNTAINS   San Bernardino

SAN ANTONIO PEAK   San Bernardino

SAN ANTONIO POST OFFICE   San Bernardino
    Listed 1892.

SAN ANTONIO, RIO DE   San Luis Obispo and Monterey
  See Salinas River.

SAN ANTONIO RANCHO   San Mateo
  Or Pescadero Rancho was granted in 1833 to Juan Jose Gonzalez. The city of Pescadero is located
  on the original site of the grant.

SAN ANTONIO CREEK   Santa Barbara
  The creek crosses "El Rancho Todos Santos y San Antonio".

SAN ANTONIO   Santa Clara
  A land grant dated 1830 to Juan Prado Mesa.

SAN ANTONIO RANCHO, LAGUNA DE   Sonoma and Marin
  A land grant dated November 25, 1845 to Bartolome Bojorgues for an area of six leagues. The creek
  is on the Laguna de San Antonio grant.

SAN ANTONIO CREEK   Ventura
  The name figures already as early as 1837 on a land grant.

SAN ARDO   Monterey
  Laid out in 1886 when Southern Pacific reached this place and was named San Bernardo. The post
  office objected because of the confusion with San Bernardino. M.J. Brandenstein created new name
  by dropping off "Bern".

SAN AGUSTIN   Santa Barbara
  The original name was "Isla de Baxos", then it became "San Agustin". There is some confusion as
  this site named presently Richardson Rock, was also mentioned as "Isla de Lobos" and "Farallon
  de Lobos" in the early 1750's. The Southern Pacific Station is a survivor of the Spanish times.

SAN AGUSTIN CREEK   Santa Cruz
  Named after the Bishop of Hippo, Saint Augustine to a land grant of November 23, 1833 and April
  21, 1841. The creek which crosses the land grant was mentioned as "Rio San Augustine".

SAN AUGUSTIN RANCHO   Santa Cruz
  Named after the creek. For a land grant of 1841 to Juan Jose Crisostomo Mayor, for an area of one
  league.

SAN BENANCIO GULCH   Monterey
  As early as 1834 it figures as "Canada de San Benancio". Named after Saint Venantius.

SAN BENITO COUNTY
  Named to honor Saint Benedict (480-543) named in turn for the San Benito River. Created Feb. 12,
  1874, chap. 87. Area 1,397 sq. mi.

SAN BENITO RIVER   San Benito
  Stems from San Benito river which was named by Father Juan Crespi who camped here on an expedition. It was the day of St. Benedict. (San Benito in Spanish), March 21, 1772.

SAN BENITO MOUNTAIN   San Benito

SAN BENITO VALLEY
  Was named before 1774, 'Canada de San Benito'. The present San Benito River was formerly San
  Juan River.

SAN BENITO RANCHO
  Land grant dated 1842 to Francisco Garcia for an area of one and a half leagues. Named for the San
  Benito River.

SAN BERNABE　　　　　　　　　　　　　　Monterey

Named for Saint Barnabas one of the original 12 disciples of Jesus of Nazareth. The valley was named by Font on April 15, 1776, "La Cañada de San Bernabe". A land grant dated March 10, 1841 and April 6, 1842 to Petronilos Rios for an area of three leagues.

SAN BERNARDINO COUNTY

Named for Saint Bernard of Sienna, the Franciscan preacher, named in turn for the valley. Created April 20, 1853, chap. 78. Area 20,131 sq. mil.

SAN BERNARDINO VALLEY　　　　　　　　San Bernardino

Father Francisco Dumetz seeking suitable sites for inland chain of missions stopped here on May 20, 1812, the day devoted to St. Bernardine of Siena and named the site.

SAN BERNARDINO MOUNTAIN

See above.

SAN BERNARDINO PEAK

See above.

SAN BERNARDINO NATIONAL FOREST

Was established in 1893 by order of President Harrison.

SAN BERNARDINO RANCHO　　　　　　　　San Bernardino

Land grant of 1843 to Ignacio Coronel for an area of two leagues. It was named after the Saint. The present cities of Colton, Loma Linda, Redlands and San Bernardino are located on the original site of the grant.

SAN BERNARDO RANCHO　　　　　　　　　Monterey

Named after one of the Saint Bernards probably Bernard de Clairvaux of France. (1090-1153). There were three grants of the name San Bernardo; one in Southern Monterey county; of 1841 to Mariano Soberanes for an area of three leagues. The present city of San Ardo is located on the site of the original grant. The second in San Luis Obispo county dated 1840 to Vicente Cane for an area of one league; the third is located in western San Diego county dated 1842 to Joseph Francisco Snook contains present Lake Hodges.

SAN BERNARDO CREEK　　　　　　　　　San Luis Obispo

The name derived from the land grant San Bernardo; the French saint, Bernard of Clairvaux who organized the Second Crusade in the 12th century.

SAN BONADVENTURE RIVER

See Sacramento River.

SAN BRUNO　　　　　　　　　　　　　　San Mateo

In honor of St. Bruno (1030-1101 A.D.) Founder of the order of Carthusian monks (famed for Chartreuse). The name was first applied by Palou in November 1774 to a creek located north of San Bruno Mountain. The town bears the name after the creek.

SAN BRUNO MOUNTAIN　　　　　　　　　San Mateo

Was called "Sierra de San Bruno" (1826), and as "Montes San Bruno" (1841); then as "San Bruno Mountains" (1844); Punta San Bruno (1851) which is the present San Bruno Point.

SAN BRUNO CANYON　　　　　　　　　　Santa Clara

Previously known as "Cañada de San Bruno" (1847).

SAN BUENAVENTURA　　　　　　　　　　Ventura

The portola expedition was to establish a mission at Santa Barbara Channel named San Buenaventura named for Saint Bonaventure (1221-1274) minister general of the Order of Friars Minor. They reached the site which was called "La Asuncion de Nuestra Señora" (The Assumption of Our Lady). The Mission was founded March 31, 1782 by Fathers Junipero Serra and Pedro Benito Cambon.

SAN BUENAVENTURA RANCHO   Shasta

Land grant dated 1844 to Pierson B. Reading for an area of six leagues. The present towns of Anderson and Redding are located on the original site.

SAN CARLOS   San Mateo

Honors one of the saints called Charles probably St. Charles Borromeo for whom San Carlos Borromeo mission was named.

SAN CARLOS BORROMEO DEL CARMELO MISSION   Monterey

It was first established on June 3, 1770 as San Carlos de Monterey; then the mission was moved to its present location in 1771. It was named for Saint Charles Borromeo (1538-1584), Archbishop of Milan. The mission was secularized in 1834 and belonged to Jose Antonio Romero.

SAN CARLOS PASS   Riverside

The Anza expedition crossed the mountains by this pass on March 16, 1774. Anza named it "El Puerto Real de San Carlos".

SAN CARLOS DE JONATA RANCHO   Santa Barbara

Land grant dated 1845 to Joaquin Carrillo for an area of six leagues. The present Buellton is located on the site of the original grant.

SAN CARLOS RANCHO, EL POTRERO DE   Monterey

From a land grant of October 9, 1837 to a certain Fruetuoso for an area of one league.

SAN CARLOS CANYON   Monterey

For name, see San Carlos Borromeo.

SAN CARLOS PEAK   San Benito

For name, see San Carlos Borromeo.

SAN CARPOFORO CREEK   Monterey

Was first visited by Portola expedition in September 1769. They went through the Canyon of this creek, called "Santa Humiliana" by Crespi. The creek takes its name from a rancho of Mission San Antonio for one Saint Carpophorus. The name changed to Saint Carpoforo (1841).

SAN CAYETANO RANCHO   Ventura

See Sespe Rancho.

SAN CAYETANO RANCHO, BOLSA DE   Monterey

Land grant of Oct. 12, 1822 to Ignacio Vallejo for an area of two leagues.

SAN CAYETANO MOUNTAIN   Ventura

Named after the San Cayetano (or Sespe) grant of November 22, 1833.

SANCHEZ RANCHO, PARAJE DE   Monterey

Named after the Indian fighter Jose Antonio Sanchez. From a land grant of October 16, 1806 and of June 8, 1839 to Francisco Lugo for an area of one and a half leagues. The grant was located on the west side of the Salinas River.

SANCITO RANCHO   Monterey

A corruption from "Saucito" (Little alder tree). From a land grant of 1833 to Graciano Manjares for an area of one and a half leagues.

SAN CLEMENTE (Town)   Orange

Seaside residential community developed in 1925 by Ole Hanson. Probably got the name from San Clemente Island. The town was known as "The Spanish Village".

SAN CLEMENTE BEACH STATE PARK   Orange

Named for San Clemente Island, it is a recreational area of 100 acres and beautiful beach. It was created as a park in 1931.

SAN CLEMENTE ISLAND   Los Angeles
On November 24, 1602 Sebastian Vizcaino reached Santa Catalina Island and noticed the existence of two other islands. He named one of them San Clemente because the 23 of November was St. Clement's day. St. Clement was in charge of the Church as Pope. He discovered through a miracle, a spring of water in a deserted island.

SANDIA   Imperial
The word means "watermelon" in Spanish. It was named because of the big production of watermelons in the region. When in 1924 the Southern Pacific Line was built, the station took this name.

SAN DIEGITO RANCHO   San Diego
From a land grant to the Silva family in 1831; then in 1840 to Juan Maria Osuna, for an area of two leagues. Several sources indicate the origin: 1) Diegito as the corruption of Dieguito, (St. James, the Lesser). 2) It is the Franciscan designation for St. Jacobus. 3) A diminutive used to distinguish from San Diego. In Font's documents of January 10, 1776 we find a place and a spring named "San Dieguillo". In 1778 a rancheria "San Dieguito" is mentioned under the jurisdiction of San Diego Mission.

SAN DIEGO BAY   San Diego
In 1542 Mendoza sent out Cabrillo and Ferelo to explore northward along the peninsula. They discovered a fine harbor which they named San Miguel. Later the name was changed to San Diego. It is also said that the bay was named by Vizcaino in honor of the Saint's day of San Diego de Alcala (1602). "On November 20, having taken on food and water, the party set sail, the Indians shouting a vociferous farewell from the beach." Then after 160 years of sleep, the Spaniards waked up and determined to establish a chain of missions along the California coast. Father Junipero Serra was appointed president of these missions, and the first one was founded by him at San Diego in 1769. The name was originally applied to the "Old Town", some distance from the present city.

SAN DIEGO   San Diego
Named after San Diego Bay. The city was incorporated March 27, 1850.

SAN DIEGO COUNTY
Named in honor of Saint Didacus who entered the order of Saint Francis. Died in 1207. The county was created February 18, 1850, chap. 15. Area 4,258 sq. mi.

SAN DIEGO DE ALCALA MISSION   San Diego
The mission of San Diego de Alcala was established on July 16, 1769 at the Indian rancheria of Cosoy, known today as "Old Town". It was founded by Father Junipero Serra. Five years later the mission was moved to Nipaguay, because of the lack of water at Cosoy. The mission takes its name from San Diego Bay.

SAN DIEGO RANCHO, ISLAND OR PENINSULA OF   San Diego
From a land grant of 1846 to Pedro C. Carrillo for an area of 4,185 acres. Coronado and North Island are located on the site of the original grant.

SAN DIMAS   Los Angeles
Named for St. Dismas, the good thief crucified with Jesus Christ. The name first applied to San Dimas canyon by Don Ignacio Polomares, owner of San Jose Rancho early in the 19th century because Serrano Indians made periodical forays on ranch to steal cattle and horses. (From Hanna, p. 271.)

SAN DOMINGO CREEK   Calaveras
Named for Santo Domingo (Saint Dominic) Spanish saint of the 13th century, founder of the Dominican Order.

SAN DOMINGO CREEK   Sacramento
See above for origin of name.

SAN ELIJO LAGOON   San Diego

First named San Alejo by POrtola' expedition July 16, 1769 to honor Saint Alexius because his feast day was the next day; the same year the Valley figures as "Cañada de San Alexos". The creek appears under the name of "San Elejo". "Elijo" is a mispelled form of "San Alejo".

SAN ELIZARIO, RIO DE   San Luis Obispo and Monterey

See Salinas River.

SAN EMIGDIO (OR EMIDIO) RANCHO   Kern

Named for a rancho of Mission Santa Barbara, named in turn for St. Emygdius who was consecrated bishop in Rome and was put to death under Emperor Diocletian A.D. 304. From a land grant of July 13, 1842 to José Antonio Dominguez for an area of four leagues.

SAN FELIPE

A popular place name in San Benito, Santa Clara and San Diego counties, for Saint Philip the apostle who was crucified in Asia Minor.

SAN FELIPE RANCHO, BOLSA DE   San Benito

A land grant of April 1, 1836 and Nov. 13, 1837 to Francisco Perez Pacheco for an area of three leagues. (For name see above.)

SAN FELIPE Y LAS ANIMAS RANCHO (CAÑADA DE) Santa Clara

For a land grant dated August 17, 1839 and August 1, 1844 to Thomas Bowen for an area of two leagues.

SAN FELIPE RANCHO, VALLE DE   San Diego

For a land grant of Feb. 21, 1846 to Felipe Castillo for an area of three leagues.

SAN FERNANDO   Los Angeles

Named from San Fernando Rey de España Mission founded September 8, 1797 which was named for St. Ferdinand III (1198-May 30, 1252). King of Leon and Castile and member of 3rd order of St. Francis. The city was founded in 1874. Portola called the site "El Valle de Santa Catalina de Bononía de los Encinos." San Fernando Valley was formerly owned by Eulogio Celis.

SAN FERNANDO, REY DE ESPANA MISSION Los Angeles

This mission was founded September 8, 1797 by Fathers Fermin Francisco Lasuen and Francisco Dumetz. (For name see San Fernando). In 1834 the mission like all other missions of California was secularized. Its first commissioner was Antonio del Valle.

SAN FRANCISCO   San Francisco

The saints named Francis have been among the most popular in place naming during the Spanish times.

SAN FRANCISCO BAY   San Francisco

Appears as early as 1590 on Dutch documents. Already "El Cabo de San Francisco" is known. Effectively on Nov. 6, 1595 Sebastian Rodriguez Cermeno, a Portuguese navigator, entered the harbor now known as Drakes Bay which he named "Bahia or Puerto de San Francisco" in honor of Saint Francis of Assisi. Of course the British kept on naming the bay "Drakes Bay". On Nov. 2, 1769 Jose Francisco Ortega, a sergeant with Portola expedition, discovered the present San Francisco Bay and the name was applied to the present area.

SAN FRANCISCO CITY   San Francisco

The city was founded on Sept. 17, 1776 when the presidio of San Francisco was under the command of Lieutenant Jose Joaquin Moraga. Fathers Francisco Palou and Tomas de la Peña gave their spiritual assistance. Yerba Buena is said to be the original site of the city. On July 9, 1846 the American forces under Captain John B. Montgomery took the town from the Mexicans. During the gold rush of 1849 it became an important trading and supply center and one of the chief ports of the Pacific Coast. The city was incorporated April 15, 1850.

SAN FRANCISCO, LA BOCA DEL PUERTO DE   Sa⁻ rancisco
Spanish for the mouth of the port of San Francisco. Was the name given by the Spanish-Californians to what is now the Golden Gate, the previous Chrysopylae of Frémont named after the harbor of Byzantium (Constantinople).

SAN FRANCISCO COUNTY
Named for Saint Francis of Assisi. Created Feb. 18, 1850, chap. 15.

SAN FRANCISCO DE ASIS MISSION   San Francisco
San Francisco de Asis Mission, better known as Mission Dolores, was founded by Fathers Tomas de la Pena, Francisco Palou, Pedro Benito Cambon and Jose Nocedal, on October 9, 1776. The mission derives its name from the presidio of San Francisco. Saint Francis was born in Assisi, Italy in 1182 and died in 1226. He was the founder of the Franciscan order or the Third Order of Friars Minor, and the patron saint of the origina' province of California. In September 1834 the mission was secularized and its commissioner was Joaquin Estudillo.

SAN FRANCISCO DE LAS LLAGAS RANCHO   Santa Clara
Spanish for St. Francis of the wounds. For a land grant dated 1834 to Carlos Castro for an area of six leagues.

SAN FRANCISCO RANCHO   Ventura and Los Angeles
A land grant dated 1839 and given to Antonio del Valle. The present towns of Newhall and Saugus are located on the site of the original grant.

SAN FRANCISCO
See Sacramento River.

SAN FRANCISCO SOLANO MISSION   Sonoma
The last Franciscan mission to be established in California (there were 21 altogether) was founed on July 4, 1823 in what is today the city of Sonoma. Father Jose Altimira established it. The mission was named f.r St. Francis Solano (1549-1610) a Franciscan friar who served many years in South America. Like the other twenty missions St. Francis Solano was secularized in November 1834. Its first commissioner was Mariano Guadalupe Vallejo.

SAN FRANCISQUITO
A diminutive as it was commonly applied to show that some geographic feature was smaller than another one previously named. It is an awkward situation when a geographic term is mixed with a diminutive name of a saint for instance Gudde cites, "Arroyo de San Francisquito might properly be translated as "Little San Francisco Creek" but it is not the Holy Francis who is little, but the creek."

SAN FRANCISQUITO CREEK   San Mateo, Santa Clara
At the time of Palou exploration to set missions in California he found this place suitable on November 28, 1774, nearby Palo Alto. He decided that this mission would be dedicated to Saint Francis of Assisi. Anza's papers mention an "Arroyo de San Francisco"; later on the stream became "Arroyo de San Francisquito".

SAN FRANCISQUITO RANCHO   Los Angeles
From a land grant of 1845 to Henry Dalton for an area of two leagues. The present Temple City is located on the site of the grant.

SAN FRANCISQUITO RANCHO   Monterey
From a land grant dated November 7, 1835 to Catalina M. deMunrás for an area of two leagues.

SAN FRANCISQUITO RANCHO   San Mateo
From a land grant dated May 1, 1839 to Antonio Buelna, on site of which is located Stanford University.

SAN FRANCISQUITO RANCHO, RINCON DE   Santa Clara
From a land grant of March 29, 1841 to José Peña for an area of undescribed extent. The town of

Mayfield is located on the site of the original grant.

SAN GABRIEL   Los Angeles
 The name is from San Gabriel Arcangel Mission. In Spanish California days the town was known as
San Miguel de los Temblores because of numerous earthquakes here.

SAN GABRIEL ARCANGEL MISSION   Los Angeles
 It was first established on the Rio Hondo September 8, 1771 by Fathers Pedro Benito Cambon and
Angel Somera and was named for the "Arcangel of the Incarnation and of Consolidation and of the
Power of God." It was also known as Mision de los Temblores because of the numerous earthquakes
here. The mission was secularized in November 1834; its first commissioner was Nicolas Gutierrez.

SAN GABRIEL MOUNTAINS   Los Angeles
 At the origin of the Spanish explorations the mountain chain was called "Sierra Madre". It is not before
1806 that a "Cierra de San Gabriel is mentioned.

SAN GABRIEL POST OFFICE   Los Angeles
 The post office was established in 1858.

SAN GABRIEL RIVER   Los Angeles
 On January 4, 1776 Font mentions "El Arroyo de San Gabriel". The river rises in the San Gabriel
Mountains and empties itself in the ocean near the Orange County boundary.

SAN GABRIEL VALLEY   Los Angeles
 It was discovered by the Portola expedition and named "San Miguel Arcangel" on July 30, 1769.

SAN GERONIMO RANCHO   Marin
 From a land grant dated Feb. 12, 1844, known as "Cañada de San Geronimo"; to Rafael Cacho for an
area of two leagues.

SAN GERONIMO CREEK   Marin
 Honors St. Jerome famous for his compilation of the Vulgate edition of the Bible and greatest scholar
of the 15th century. It takes its name from San Geronimo Rancho. The old name for the creek was
"Arroyo Nicasio".

SAN GERONIMO RANCHO   San Luis Obispo
 From a land grant dated July 24, 1842 to Rafael Villavicencio for an area of two acres. The present
town of Cayucos is located on the southern boundary of the original grant.

SAN GORGONIO MOUNTAIN   San Bernardino
 The name is from the rancho which in turn is named for St. Gorgonius, he is one of the obscure saints
in Roman Martyrology. All that is known of him is that he lived in Nicaea in the 3rd century and was
the victim of religious persecution. "San Gorgonio" was no more than a cattle ranch of Mission San
Gabriel in 1824.

SAN GORGONIO PASS   Riverside
 Is the only way to go between San Gorgonio and San Jacinto and connecting the San Bernardino Valley
with the Colorado desert. Captain Jose Romero was the first white man to cross the pass. It takes its
name from the San Gorgonio Ranch.

SAN GORGONIO (Town)   San Bernardino
 It is called Beaumont in modern times.

SAN GREGORIO CREEK   San Mateo
 Named after Gregory the Great, Benedictine saint, and Pope (590). "El Arroyo de San Gregario"
appears before 1839. The post office was listed in 1870.

SAN GREGORIO RANCHO   San Mateo
 From a land grant dated April 16, 1839 to Antonio Buelna for an area of four leagues.

SAN ISIDRO   San Benito, Santa Clara

Also spelled San Ysidro name given to a land grant to Ignacio Ortega in 1809 and in 1833.

SAN JACINTO MOUNTAIN   Riverside

(See San Jacinto River). The peak has an elevation of 10,805 ft.

SAN JACINTO NUEVO Y POTRERO RANCHO   Riverside

"The new San Jacinto and pasture rancho" from a land grant dated 1846 to Miguel Pedrorena. The present Eden and Lakeview are located on the site of the original grant.

SAN JACINTO RIVER   Riverside

Derives from original San Jacinto Rancho probably after St. Hyacinth of Silesia (1185-1231) who joined the Dominican order.

SAN JACINTO HOT SPRINGS   Riverside

The old name for Gilman Hot Springs, named for William Earl Gilman who bought this resort from Mr. Branch who had founded and named the resort of San Jacinto Hot Springs in 1880.

SAN JACINTO RANCHO, SOBRANTE DE   Riverside

Spanish for "the residue", "the overplus of San Jacinto Rancho", from a land grant of 1846 to Maria del Rosario Estudillo de Aguirre for an area of five leagues.

SAN JACINTO STATE PARK MOUNTAIN   Riverside

Named from Mt. San Jacinto. For name see San Jacinto River. The park has an area of 12,708 acres. It was established in 1933.

SAN JACINTO VIEJO RANCHO   Riverside

Spanish for "Old San Jacinto Ranch", from a land grant of 1842 to Jose Antonio Estudillo. The present Hemet and San Jacinto are located on the original site of the grant.

SAN JOAQUIN   Fresno

Settlement of the '50's named from the river which was named by Alferez Gabriel Moraga about 1806 during the expedition into Central Valley. The name honors St. Joachim (Father of the Virgin Mary).

SAN JOAQUIN CITY   San Joaquin

Takes its name from the San Joaquin River. The city was laid out in 1849.

SAN JOAQUIN COUNTY

Named in honor of Saint Joaquin named after the San Joaquin River. Created February 18, 1850, chap. 15. Area 1,410 sq. mi.

SAN JOAQUIN HILLS   Orange

From a land grant of May 13, 1842, known as "Bolsa de San Joaquin". The land grant consisted of an area of eleven leagues and was granted to José Sepulveda in 1837 and 1844. The present cities of Corona del Mar and Balboa are located on the site of the original grant.

SAN JOAQUIN PEAK   San Benito

From a lang grant of April 1, 1836, known as San Joaquin or Rosa Morada. The land grant was given to Cruz Cervantes for an area of two leagues.

SANJON DE LOS ALISOS   Alameda

Although the Spanish spelling is Zanjon, it was common to see this form. The Sanjon de los Alisos is one of the large drains through which Alameda Creek empties into San Francisco Bay.

SANJON RANCHO, RINCON DE   Monterey

Spanish for the inside corner of the channel. Land granted in 1840 to Eusebio Boronda for an area of one and a half leagues.

SAN JOSÉ

Of all the saints, San José (Saint Joseph) husband of the Virgin Mary is certainly the most popular for place names in Spanish-speaking countries. It does not escape to its popularity in California where it has been used as geographical name from the beginnings of colonization. In fact the first expedition to settle Alta California was placed under the protection of Saint Joseph the patron saint, and the ship which brought partially the Portola expedition was named "San José"; unfortunately the ship was lost at sea. We find the name "San José" in more than ten geographic features and at least fifteen land grants and claims; originally this number should be doubled.

SAN JOSÉ   Santa Clara

"Pueblo de San José de Guadalupe" was the first city to be founded in California. It was settled on November 29, 1777 by five colonists from Sonora, Mexico who named it after St. Joseph spouse of the Virgin Mary and for the river on which the town was located; the modern city is the oldest civic muncipality of the state. It became the first capital of the State of California when the legislature convened here on December 15, 1849. The city was incorporated March 27, 1850.

SAN JOSÉ MISSION   Alameda

Was founded on June 11, 1797 by Father Fermin Francisco Lasuén. It was named and dedicated to Saint Joseph. Like all other Californian missions it was secularized in 1837. Its first commissioner was Jesus Vallejo.

SAN JOSÉ MOUNTAIN   Shasta

Was discovered and named Mount San José by the Sacramento Valley expedition commanded by Captain Luis Arguello in 1821. The present name is Lassen Peak in honor of Peter Lassen.

SAN JOSÉ RANCHO   Los Angeles

Named after the San Jose land grant dated 1837 and October 3, 1840 to Ricardo Vejar and Ignacio Palomares. The present towns of La Verne, Pomona and San Dimas are located on the site of the original grant.

SAN JOSÉ RANCHO   Marin

Land grant dated 1840 to Ignacio Pacheco for an area of one and a half leagues.

SAN JOSÉ CREEK, THE

Flows through San Marin County and was named after San Jose land grant.

SAN JOSÉ RIVER   Santa Clara

Old maps represent "El Rio de San Jose" for "Guadalupe River".

SAN JOSÉ RANCHO, VALLE DE   San Diego

From a land grant dated April 16, 1836 to Silvestre de la Portilla.

SAN JOSÉ RANCHO, VALLE DE   Alameda

From a land grant dated 1839 to Antonio M. Pico. The present cities of Livermore, Sunol and Pleasanton are located on the site of the original grant.

SAN JOSÉ VALLEY   San Diego

It was named "San Jose in 1795 by the fathers of the San Diego Mission. In 1821 it was mentioned as "el valle de San José o Guadalupe". There were two adjoining ranchos with names similar to this in northern San Diego county. One was the Valle de San Jose Rancho and the other was the San Jose del Valle Rancho. The land grants dated April 16, 1836 and November 27, 1844. Juan Jose (Jonathan Trumbull) Warner bought both grants and they became known as the Warner Ranch.

SAN JOSÉ Y SUR CHIQUITO RANCHO   Monterey

From a land grant of 1839 to Marcelino Escobar for an area of two leagues.

SAN JUAN (NORTH)   Nevada

A miner who was also a veteran in the Mexican War, named Christian Kientz found a resemblance of the nearby hill to the Castle of San Juan de Ulloa, the fort defending Vera Cruz. He is responsible for the naming of it in 1853. When the post office was established in 1857, "North" was added to avoid confusion with the other San Juans.

SAN JUAN (POINT)   Orange
Known at one time as San Juan Point, today's Dana Point was named after Richard Henry Dana, author of *Two Years Before the Mast*. (1815-1882).

SAN JUAN Y LOS CARRISALITOS RANCHO, PANOCHE DE
                                                    Merced
Spanish "panoche" is a corruption of "panocha" (panicles). From a land grant dated 1844 to Julian Ursúa for an area of five leagues.

SAN JUAN RANCHO   Sacramento
From a land grant of 1844 to Joel P. Desmond for an area of four and a half leagues.

SAN JUAN BAUTISTA   San Benito
Takes its named from the 15th mission to be founded by Franciscans in Upper California by Fathers Fermin Francisco Lasuen, José Manuel Martiarena and Magín Catalá. Named for St. John the Baptist June 24 being St. John's day. The present San Benito Valley was called "Llano de San Juan" (1826); "San Juan Valley" (1849).

SAN JUAN RANGE   San Benito
Became Gabilan Range (1850).

SAN JUAN BAUTISTA, RIO DE
Old name of the San Joaquin River.

SAN JUAN BAUTISTA MISSION   San Benito
Was founded by the Franciscan Fathers in Upper California. (See San Juan Bautista).

SAN JUAN BAUTISTA RANCHO   Santa Clara
From a land grant dated March 30, 1844 to Jose Agustin Narvaez for an area of two leagues. Named for St. John the Baptist.

SAN JUAN DE SANTA ANA RANCHO   Orange
From a land grant dated 1837 to Juan P. Ontiveros. Present Anaheim, Fullerton, Placentia and Brea are located on the site of the original grant.

SAN JUAN CAPISTRANO   Orange
Named for San Juan Capistrano Mission. It was first named by Crespi, Santa Maria Magdalena to honor the saint's day July 22, 1769. It was so known until the foundation of the mission in 1776 when the present name was given.

SAN JUAN CAPISTRANO MISSION
It was named for St. John Capistran, (1385-Oct. 23, 1456) first General of the Observantive Franciscans. The mission was founded Nov. 1, 1776 by Fathers Junipero Serra and Gregorio Amurrio.

SAN JUAN CAPISTRANO RANCHO, POTREROS DE   Orange and Riverside
Spanish "the pasture of San Juan Capistrano Ranch" from a land grant dated 1845 to John Forster.

SAN JUAN GRADE   San Benito
Takes name from San Juan Bautista Mission.

SAN JUAN DE PERUCIA   San Luis Obispo
See Oso Flaco Lake.

SAN JUAN HOT SPRINGS   Orange
Several sulphural thermal springs located in San Juan Canyon. Both the Canyon and the Hot Springs derive their names from San Juan Capistrano Mission.

SAN JULIAN   Santa Barbara
For a land grant dated April 7, 1837 to George Rock. Named after St. Julian de Brioude, Roman soldier born at Vienne (France) martyred at Brioude in 304. His feast is August 28.

SAN JUSTO   San Benito
Named after St. Justin born at Flavia Neapolis (100-165) author of two *Apologies of the Christian Religion*; martyred at Rome. His feast is on April 13. For a land grant dated April 15, 1839 to Jose Castro for an area of four leagues. Present Hollister is located on the site of the original grant.

SAN LADISLAO   San Luis Obispo
The soldiers of the Portola expedition, on September 4, 1769 met a local chief who had an enormous goitre hanging from his neck; they nicknamed him "Buchon" ("Big Craw", "Big Pouch") and thus the site was called. But Father Crespi the diarist of the expedition gave a more dignified name, which was San Ladislo. The Christian name, however, has disappeared to be replaced by "Buchon Point".

SAN LEANDRO (Town)   Alameda
From the San Leandro Rancho which was granted in 1842 to Joaquin Estudillo. The name honors St. Leander, Archbishop of Seville who died in 186 A.D. The town was laid out in 1855 and the post office established in 1858.

SAN LEANDRO CREEK   Alameda
As early as 1828 the *Registro* mentions "Arroyo de San Leandro"; and in subsequent documents we notice a "Rio San Leandro". The name honors Saint Leander.

SAN LEANDRO RANCHO   Alameda
From a land grant dated Oct. 16, 1842 to Joaquin Estudillo, for an area of one league. The name commemorates St. Leander, Archbishop of Seville, known as "the Apostle of the Goths" who died in 596 A.D. The present town of San Leandro is located on the site of the original grant.

SAN LORENZO CREEK   Alameda
This stream was known under different names from the time of its discovery: on March 25, 1772, Crespi named it "Arroyo de San Salvador de Morta". It was also nicknamed "Arroyo de la Harina" (Creek of the flour). When it was named "San Lorenzo" it is not sure, however, we find in a San Lorenzo land grant a mention of a "San Lorenzo Creek" (1854). The creek is named after Saint Laurence.

SAN LORENZO CREEK   Monterey
From land grants named in turn after the St. Laurence.

SAN LORENZO RANCHO   Alameda
Two land grants, one for a land grant dated on October 10, 1842 and in 1844 to Francisco Soto for an area of one and a half leagues. The other the easternmost in 1841 and 1843 to Guillermo Castro for an area of one league and 600 varas. The present towns of Hayward, San Lorenzo and Mt. Eden are located on the site of the original grants.

SAN LORENZO RANCHO   Monterey
From a land grant dated August 9, 1841 to Feliciano Soberanes for an area of five leagues. For another land grant dated Nov. 16, 1842 to Francisco Rico for an area of five leagues.

SAN LORENZO RANCHO   San Benito
From a land grant dated 1846 to Rafael Sanchez for an area of eleven leagues.

SAN LORENZO RIVER   Santa Cruz
It was named for St. Laurence by the Portola expedition on Oct. 17, 1769. In 1843 the name appears in the title of a grant "Cañada del Rincon en el Rio San Lorenzo". Circa 1850 the name was Americanized in "San Lorenzo River".

SAN LORENZO (TOWN)   Alameda
From one of the San Lorenzo ranches; it honors one of the many St. Lawrences, probably third century St. Laurence of Rome who was roasted to death by the emperor Valerian in 258 A.D. The feast day is

August 10.

SAN LUCAS   Monterey
Name is from San Lucas Rancho granted May 9, 1842 to Rafael Estrada for an area of two leagues. It honors St. Luke fellow apostle of St. Paul and author of the *Third Gospel* and *Acts of the Apostles*. The post office was established in 1892.

SAN LUCAS (ISLAS DE)   Santa Barbara
See Miguel Island.

SAN LUCAS CREEK   Santa Barbara
A tributary of Santa Ynez River, named after Saint Luke the Evangelist.

SAN LUCAS   Santa Barbara
See Santa Rosa Island.

SAN LUCAS RANCHO   Monterey
From a land grant dated May 9, 1842 to Rafael Estrada for an area of two leagues. The name commemorates St. Luke.

SAN LUIS CREEK   Merced
On Jun 21, 1805 an expedition sent from the presidio of San Francisco, camped on the banks of the creek and gave the name of San Luis Gonzaga because it was the day of St. Aloysius Gonzaga (1568-1591) an Italian priest who distinguished himself during the pestilence stricken Rome.

SAN LUIS HILL
See above.

SAN LUIS GONZAGA RANCHO   Merced and Santa Clara
For a land grant of October 3, 1843 to Francisco Rivera for an area of 48,821 acres. The name honors St. Aloysius Gonzaga. (See above).

SAN LUISITO CREEK   San Luis Obispo
Spanish diminutive for nearby San Luis Obispo, it was named for the San Luisito grant.

SAN LUISITO RANCHO   San Luis Obispo
Named after the land grant of August 6, 1841, to Guadalupe Cantua, called "San Luisito grant".

SAN LUIS OBISPO COUNTY
Named in honor of Saint Louis, Bishop of Toulouse. Created February 18, 1850, chap. 15. Area 3,326 sq. mi.

SAN LUIS OBISPO   San Luis Obispo
Named by Father Juan Crespi. The local legend says it was named because of the shape of hills to the north of the settlement which resembled the bishop's mitre. On August 21, 1769 Crespi named it because the day was the saint's day of St. Louis of Toulouse. The present city was founded August 25, 1850.

SAN LUIS OBISPO DE TOLOSA MISSION   San Luis Obispo
This fifth Californian mission was founded Sept. 1, 1772 by Fathers Junipero Serra and José Cavaller. The mission was named after St. Louis Bishop of Toulouse (France) son of the king of Naples and Sicily (1274-1297) and great nephew of Saint Louis IX, King of France.

SAN LUIS OBISPO RANCHO, POTRERO DE   San Luis Obispo
From a land grant of Nov. 8, 1842 to Concepcion Boronda for an area of one league.

SAN LUIS, PORT   San Luis Obispo
The port was named after San Luis Obispo; it is located on San Luis Obispo Bay. It was known as Port Harford for Captain John Harford who was very active in 1872-1873 in the development of piers

and in short line railroads hereabouts.

SAN LUIS REY   Santa Barbara
The Portolá expedition of 1769 camped on the site of a rancheria. Crespi called the place "San Luis Rey" because it was the eve of the saint's day of Louis IX, King of France. But the soldiers observing a seagull nesting on the spot, called it "La gaviota" (Spanish name for seagull). San Luis Rey disappeared and Gaviota was retained. St. Louis, King of France was born at Poissy in 1215 the son of Louis VIII and Blanche de Castille, he became noted for his saintliness, and twice led an army of crusaders in the "holy war."

SAN LUIS REY MISSION   San Diego
Fathers Fermin Francisco Lasuén, Antonio Peyri and Juan José Norberto Santiago, founded this eighteenth mission on June 13, 1798. Its original name was: "San Luis Rey de Francia" after St. Louis IX (April 25, 1215 - August 25, 1270), King of France. It was some confusion with the naming of it because Father Crespi the diarist of the Portola expedition who camped there July 18, 1769 had given the name of "San Juan Capistrano". But the mission of this name was located at a different place. Like all other missions, the Mexican government secularized it in November 1834 and its first commissioner was Pablo Portilla.

SAN MARCOS   San Diego
Named from the valley known as Los Vallecitos de San Marcos. A grant to San Luis Rey Mission, "the little valleys of St. Mark", named after St. Mark the Evangelist.

SAN MARCOS CREEK   San Luis Obispo
Appears on early maps as "El Arroyo de San Marcos" (1795). Named after Saint Mark.

SAN MARCOS PASS   Santa Barbara
From the San Marcos Ranch; in 1846 Lieutenant Colonel John C. Fremont avoided an ambush by the Spanish-Californians by using the route over the San Marcos. The name of the pass appears also in 1855 as "Marcos Pass".

SAN MARCOS RANCHO   Santa Barbara
From a land grant dated June 8, 1846 to Nicolas A. Den.

SAN MARCOS RANCHO, LOS VALLECITOS DE   San Diego
From a land grant dated April 22, 1840 to Jose M. Alvarado (Spanish for the little valleys of St. Mark.)

SAN MARTIN   Santa Clara
Father Francisco Palou reached the area Nov. 25, 1772, named it "Las Llagas de Nuestro Padre San Francisco". Later an Irish man acquired the ranch and built a chapel to St. Martin. The settlement that grew up took the name.

SAN MARTIN, CAPE   Monterey
The name is in relation with Juan Rodriguez Cabrillo's voyage. The original name was "Punta Gorda", which became "Point Gorda". Named for St. Martin Bishop of Tours (France) 316-397. He is known for his great charity.

SAN MARTIN, ISLAS DE   San Diego
Juan Rodriguez Cabrillo was the first white man to see the islands "Los Cuatros Martires Coronados" (the four crowned martyrs) from which was named Coronado, on September 17, 1542. He called them "Islas Desiertas" (the deserted islands). On November 8, 1602 Vizcaino explored them and called them Islas de San Martin but it was Father Antonio de la Ascension who named them "Los Cuatros Martires Coronados", because they were sighted on the saint's day of the four martyres.

SAN MARTIN, SIERRAS DE   San Luis Obispo
Was originally named in November 1542 "Las Sierras de San Martin" by Juan Rodriguez Cabrillo. When Sebastian Vizcaino sighted the mountains on December 14, 1602 he named them for St. Lucy born in Syracuse (circa 283-304) because of the Saint's day Dec. 13, which was the day before.

SAN MATEO (City)   San Mateo

Derives its name from a station of San Francisco de Asis Mission before 1827. The name was for one of the saint Matthews, the one who was chosen instead of Judas. The city of San Mateo was known as Baywood.

SAN MATEO COUNTY

In honor of Saint Matthew, disciple of Jesus Christ (died in 64); one of the 12 apostles he was chosen instead of Judas. Feast day February 24. Created April 19, 1856. Chap. 125. Area 454 sq. mi.

SAN MATEO CANYON AND CREEK   San Diego

From Arroyo de San Mateo existed already in the State Papers of March 1778. There was a "Rio San Mateo" on a diseno (plat of Spanish and Mexican land grants) of 1845.

SAN MATEO CREEK   San Mateo

Anza and Font mention "El Arroyo de San Mateo" as early as 1776. Mission Dolores had a sheep ranch named "San Mateo". In 1810 we find on documents "Esteros de San Mateo" and "Punta de San Mateo" (Provincial State Papers, XIX, 280).

SAN MATEO POINT   San Diego and Orange

It is located at the confluence of "Los Cristianos Canyon" and "San Mateo Creek". It was named for St. Matthew (see above).

SAN MATEO RANCHO   San Mateo

Land grant dated May 6, 1846 to Cayetano Arenas for an area of two leagues. It was named for St. Matthew (see above). The present cities of Burlingame and of San Mateo are located on the site of the original grant.

SAN MIGUEL

A favorite among the nomenclature of place names during the Spanish times, it is still in existence in a dozen of geographic places. They all concern the archangel.

SAN MIGUEL ISLAND   Santa Barbara

On October 18, 1542, Juan Rodriguez Cabrillo discovered San Miguel Island. He named this island as well as Santa Rosa "Islas de San Lucas". But the name in the following years changed to "Isla de la Posesion", "Juan Rodriguez", "La Capitana". According to Henry R. Wagner ". . . the name San Miguel was first applied by Miguel Castanso in his map of 1770 to what is now Santa Rosa. As the island to the east of it had been named Santa Cruz in 1769 it is very likely that Costanso gave his own name, Miguel to the middle island, when he made the map in Mexico. In this position the name appears on most of the later maps but it was finally transferred to the island which now bears that name."

SAN MIGUEL   San Luis Obispo

This town was named for San Miguel Arcangel Mission established on July 25, 1797 (see below). The post office was established in 1887. In November 1886 the Southern Pacific had reached the site and the name was applied to the station.

SAN MIGUEL   San Diego

See San Diego Bay.

SAN MIGUEL ARCANGEL MISSION   San Luis Obispo

The mission was established on July 25, 1797 by Fathers Fermin Francisco Lasuen and Buenaventura Sitjar. Upon the suggestion of the Marquis de Branciforte, Viceroy of Mexico, the mission was named "San Miguel Arcangel" (St. Michael Archangel). The mission was secularized by the Mexican government in 1836 and its first commissioners were Inocente Garcia and Ignacio Coronel.

SAN MIGUEL CANYON   Monterey

The real name was "Bolsa de los Escarpines" from a grant dated Oct. 7, 1837. However, on the plat of the grant appears "Cañada de San Miguel."

SAN MIGUEL HILLS San Francisco

    The old San Miguel Hills, which is today Mount Davidson, still figures under its previous name because it is on the San Miguel land grant of Dec. 23, 1845.

SAN MIGUEL RANCHO San Francisco

    From a land grant of Dec. 23, 1845, to José de Jesus NOé. Named for San Michael.

SAN MIGUEL RANCHO Sonoma

    From a land grant of Nov. 2, 1840 and 1844 to Mark West, for an area of six leagues. The name commemorates Saint Michael.

SAN MIGUEL RANCHO Ventura

    From a land grant of July 6, 1841 to Raimundo Olivas for an undescribed area. Named for St. Michael.

SAN MIGUEL DE LOS TEMBLORES Los Angeles

    See San Gabriel.

SAN MIGUELITO RANCHO Monterey

    From a land grant of September 25, 1839 to Rafael Gonzalez for an area of five leagues. The diminutive concerns the place name San Miguel.

SAN MIGUELITO RANCHO San Luis Obispo

    From a land grant of 1842 to Miguel Avila, for an area of two leagues. The towns of Avila and Port San Luis are located on the site of the original grant.

SAN MIGUEL (RIO) Tulare

    The Indians call it "Kaqeah" and its meaning is not known although some scholars have said it means "I sit down". The river was discovered by Gabriel Moraga October 20, 1806. He named the two branches "Rio San Miguel" and "Rio San Gabriel".

SAN NICOLAS ISLAND Ventura

    On December 6, 1602 the crew of Vizcaino's launch "Los Tres Reyes" named the island for the saint's day of St. Nicholas. This saint is the patron saint of children; he was Archbishop of Myra.

SAN ONOFRE San Diego

    Stems from San Onofre Rancho. The name honors St. Onuphrius, an Egyptian hermit who lived alone for 60 years in the desert of Thebais in the fourth century.

SAN ONOFRE Y SANTA MARGARITA RANCHO San Diego

    See Santa Margarita y Las Flores Rancho.

SAN ONOFRE, CANADA Santa Barbara

    A valley on early documents of 1795 named for St. Onuphrius.

SAN PABLO POINT Contra Costa

    Father Ramon Abella member of the San Francisco de Asis Mission named the two opposite points in San Pablo Bay: San Pablo Point and San Pedro Point. San Pablo Point (Punta de San Pablo) or (Saint Paul Point) was named on Oct. 16, 1811. The early name of this point was Point Huchones.

SAN PABLO Contra Costa

    Named after San Pablo Point. The town was founded in the early 1850's. The post office was established in 1858.

SAN PABLO RANCHO Contra Costa

    From a land grant of April 23, 1823 to Francisco Castro for an area of four leagues. The rancho takes its name from the "Punta de San Pablo". The towns of Giant, Richmond and San Pablo are located on the site of the original grant.

SAN PASCUAL RANCHO   Los Angeles
There were two grants in the same county: one granted September 24, 1840 to Enrique Sepulveda and José Perez for an area of three leagues. The second of July 10, 1843 to Manuel Garfias for an undescribed area. The cities of Altadena and Pasadena are located on the site of the first grant. These grants were named for St. Paschal, a Franciscan of the 16th century.

SAN PASQUAL   San Diego
This pueblo was under the jurisdiction of San Diego Mission before 1841. The name commemorates St. Paschal Babylon, a 16th century Franciscan lay brother. This site was the witness of a bloody battle between the troops of General Kearny and Captain Andres Piso's Spanish Californian troops.

SAN PEDRO
One of the most popular saint's place names in Spanish times. It was given in land grants, titles and geographic features. Today more than twenty place-names bear the name of the apostle and the other saints named Peter.

SAN PEDRO BAY   Los Angeles
Juan Rodriguez Cabrillo first sighted it on October 8, 1542. He called it La Bahia de los Fumos y Fuegos (Bay of the smokes and fires). Vizcaino saw it next in 1602 and got saints mixed up and called it Ensenada de San Andres (the bight of St. Andrew). Cabrera Bueno mapped Vizcaino's report and found his error and designated the bay San Pedro on Nov. 26. This was the feast day of St. Peter, Bishop of Alexandria who was beheaded by order of African pro-consul, Galerius Maximus, during the persecution of the Christians. San Pedro was annexed to Los Angeles August 28, 1909. (From Hanna, p. 284).

SAN PEDRO, BAHIA DE   Monterey
See Monterey Bay.

SAN PEDRO DE ALCANTARA   Santa Cruz
See Scott Creek.

SAN PEDRO DE REGLADO RANCHO, POTRERO Y RINCON DE
                                                         Santa Cruz
From a land grant of 1838 to Jose R. Buelna for an undescribed area.

SAN PEDRO DE SACRO TERRATO   San Luis Obispo
See Oso Flaco Lake.

SAN PEDRO, POINT   Marin
As early as 1807 and 1811 we find on documents: "Rancheria San Pedro" and "Punta de San Pedro" "Puntas San Pablo y San Pedro" (1831). The point was named "Punta San Pedro" by Father Ramon Abella, attached to San Francisco de Asis Mission, on Oct. 16, 1811, in honor of St. Peter, first Bishop of Rome (died 64 A.D.). His feast is celebrated June 29.

SAN PEDRO, POINT   San Mateo
On Oct. 30, 1769 Father Juan Crespi, the diarist of the Portola expedition named the site "Punta del Angel Custodio" (point of the guardian angel). The soldiers who found there a great quantity of mussels, called it "Punta de las Almejas" (mussels point). Named from a land grant San Pedro as a rancho of Mission Dolores.

SAN PEDRO RANCHO   Los Angeles
From a land grant dated circa Nov. 20, 1784 to Juan Jose Dominguez for an undescribed area. In 1822 it was regranted to Cristobal Dominguez as a land grant of an area of ten leagues. Several localities were founded on the site of the original grant: Compton, Gardenas, Los Angeles, Redondo Beach, Torrance . . .

SAN PEDRO RANCHO   San Mateo
From a land grant dated 1839 to Francisco Sanchez for an area of two leagues. Rockaway Beach and Salada Beach are located on the site of this original grant.

SAN PEDRO, RIO DE   Tulare
    See Tule River.

SAN PEDRO, SANTA MARGARITA Y LAS GALLINAS RANCHO
                                            Marin
    Spanish (the ranch of St. Peter, St. Margaret and the hen chickens).   From a land grant dated Nov.
    18, 1840 and Feb. 12, 1844 for an area of five leagues.

SAN PEDRO Y SAN PABLO DE BICUNER MISSION
    See Purisima Concepcion de Maria Santisima Mission.

SAN QUENTIN, POINT   Marin
    See Quintin.

SAN RAFAEL   Marin
    Derives from San Rafael Arcangel Mission, which was founded as an "asistencia" of Mission Dolores on
    December 14, 1817 and was named "San Rafael Arcangel".   The town sprung around the house of
    Timoteo Murphy (1841). The post office was listed on November 6, 1851.

SAN RAFAEL ARCANGEL MISSION   Marin
    It was founded by Fathers Luis Gil y Taboada, Ramon Abella, Vicente Francisco Sarria and Narciso
    Duran on December 14, 1817.   This was the twentieth Franciscan mission established in California.
    The mission honors St. Raphael, Archangel.   The mission was secularized by the Mexican government
    in Oct. 1834 and its first commissioner was Ignacio Martinez.

SAN RAFAEL RANCHO   Los Angeles
    From one of the oldest land grants dated Oct. 20, 1784 and January 12, 1798 to Jose Maria Verdugo
    for an area of eight leagues.   The original name was "Hahaounuput" or "Arroyo Hondo" or "Zanja"
    and finally "San Rafael".   The present communities of Burbank, Glendale, Montrose and Verdugo City
    are located on the site of the original grants.

SAN RAFAEL MOUNTAINS   Santa Barbara
    It is designated as "Sierra de San Rafael" (1846).

SAN RAMON   Contra Costa
    First known as Lynchville then as Limerick because of many Irish settlers.   The present name applied
    April 22, 1860 when the residents dedicated the Catholic church to San Ramon.   There are three St.
    Raymunds in Roman martyrology, which one the town is named for is a mystery.   According to other
    sources the name did not honor a saint, but for a sort of Sheepherder named Ramon attached to the
    Mission San José.   The name of the creek "San Ramon" gave the name to the town.   The creek was
    also called "Arroyo del Injerto" (The creek of the Graft).

SAN RAMON RANCHO   Contra Costa
    For a land grant dated June 5, 1833 to Rafaela Soto de Pacheco for an area of two leagues.   A second
    land grant dated 1834 to Jose M. Amador for an area of one league.   A third land grant dated 1834
    to Jose Maria Amador for an area of four leagues.

SAN ROQUE   Santa Barbara
    See Carpinteria.

SAN ROQUE CANYON

SAN ROQUE CREEK   Santa Barbara
    Named after the French Carmelite Saint Roque (Saint Roch) 1295-1327, who distinguished himself
    for his devotion to pestilence-stricken people.   His feast is August 16.   Documents of 1824 mention
    "un paraje llamado San Roque (A place called Saint Roque).   The rancheria nearby was named "San
    Roque" by Juan Crespi Aug. 17, 1769.

SAN SALVADOR   Los Angeles

See Agua Mansa Rancho also Santa Catalina Island.

SAN SEBASTIAN   Imperial

See Harpers Well.

SAN SEBASTIAN, RIO GRANDE DE   Marin

See Tomales Bay.

SAN SIMEON   San Luis Obispo

Originally a coastal ranch attached to San Miguel Mission. Many St. Simeons but it is reasonable to assume it was named after St. Simeon Stylites, a fifth century Syrian who died 459 A.D. His feast day is Feb. 18.

SAN SIMEON BAY AND CREEK   San Luis Obispo

Stemmed from "El Rancho de San Simeon". "El Arroyo de San Simeon" appears on a plat of the Santa Rosa Grant (1841).

SAN SIMEON CREEK BEACH STATE PARK   San Luis Obispo

At the mouth of San Simeon Creek stand the recreational area of 42.24 acres on two miles of ocean frontage. It was made a State Park in 1932. (For origin of name see above.)

SAN SIMEON RANCHO   San Luis Obispo

From a land grant dated Oct. 1, 1842 to Ramon Estrada for an area of one league. It was named after St. Simeon (see above).

SAN SIMON LIPNICA   San Diego

See Agua Hedionda Creek.

SANTA ANA

The name of St. Anne has been used often in Spanish times. It honors the mother of the Virgin Mary; her feast is July 26.

SANTA ANA (Town)   Orange

The Portola expedition camped on the banks of the river on July 28, 1769 and the following name was given: "El dulcísimo nombre de Jesus de los Temblores" (the most sweet name of Jesus of the Earthquakes), because that day they experienced an earthquake. The soldiers knew the river as "El Rio de Santa Ana". On July 27 Portola had camp on a site near the river, to which the name of "Santiago" patron of the Spains". Santiago (St. James the Greater), a brother of St. John, was an apostle, his feast is July 25. The name of Santa Ana derives from the "Santiago de Santa Ana Rancho". The present city located on the site of the original grant of the Santiago de Santa Ana Rancho was founded by W. H. Spurgeon in October 1869.

SANTA ANA CANYON   Orange

See Santa Ana.

SANTA ANA MOUNTAINS   Orange

See Santa Ana.

SANTA ANA DEL CHINO RANCHO   San Bernardino

Spanish chino meaning Chinese or curly. From two land grants dated 1841 and 1845 to Antonio Maria Lugo for an area of five and three leagues. The present Chino is located on the northern part of the original grant.

SANTA ANA RANCHO   Ventura

From a land grant of April 14, 1837 to Grisogono Ayala for an undescribed area. Named in honor of St. Anne, the mother of the Virgin Mary.

SANTA ANA RANCHO, CAÑON DE   Orange
From a land grant dated 1834 to Bernardo Yorba on the north side of the Santa Ana River, for an area of three leagues. Named after St. Anne.

SANTA ANA RIVER   San Bernardino, Riverside and Orange
See Santa Ana.

SANTA ANY Y QUIEN SABE RANCHO   San Benito
Spanish meaning Saint Anne and who knows? ranch. From a land grant of April 8, 1839 to Manuel Larios and Juan Maria Anzar for an area of seven leagues. Present Tres Pinos is located on the original grant.

SANTA ANITA RANCHO   Los Angeles
A diminutive of the place name Santa Ana. From a land grant of Apirl 16, 1841 and March 31, 1845 to Hugo Reid for an area of three leagues. The present Sierra Madre, Arcadia and Santa Anita Race Track are located on the site of the original grant.

SANTA BARBARA ISLAND   Los Angeles
This island was named by Vizcaino when he entered the channel on Dec. 4 (St. Barbara's feast day) 1602. St. Barbara was beheaded by her father because she had become a Christian (third century A.D.)

SANTA BARBARA VIRGEN Y MARTIR MISSION
The mission was founded Dec. 4, 1786 by Fathers Fermin Francisco Lasuen, Antonio Paterna and Cristobal Oramas. It was the tenth of the Franciscan Missions in California. The mission was named for Saint Barbara, who was the daughter of a rich merchant of Heliopolis (Egypt) in the 3rd century. When the father learned that she had become a Christian he beheaded her. After her death he was struck by lightning and died. She is the patron saint in time of thunderstorms, fire and the protector of firemen, artillerymen and miners. The mission was secularized by the Mexican government in Sept. 1834.

SANTA CATALINA DE BONONIA DE LOS ENCINOS, EL VALLE DE
                     Los Angeles
See San Fernando.

SANTA BARBARA COUNTY
Vizcaino entered the channel on St. Barbara's day in 1603. The county is named for the mission. Created Feb. 18, 1850, Chap. 15. Area 2,745 sq. mi.

SANTA BARBARA   Santa Barbara
It was originally a Chumash Indian village named Yammonalit, the name of their chief. The Spaniards named it "San Joaquin de la Laguna". On Dec. 3, 1602 Vizcaino reached here, which was the first vespers of St. Barbara and he remained there on her feast day, December 4. The present city was founded with the presidio on April 21, 1782 and incorporated April 9, 1850.

SANTA CATALINA ISLAND   Los Angeles
The island was discovered by Juan Rodriguez Cabrillo on October 7, 1542. At first he thought there were two islands which he named "San Salvador" and "La Vitoria" after his two ships. On November 24, 1602 Vizcaino sighted the island on the eve of St. Catharine's feast, thus he named the island to commemorate Catharine of Alexandria who was martyred in 310 A.D.

SANTA CATALINA ISLAND RANCHO   Los Angeles
From a land grant dated 1846 to Thomas M. Robbins for an area of 45,825 acres representing the whole island off the shore of Los Angeles county. For name see Santa Catalina Island.

SANTA CLARA   Santa Clara
Takes its name from Santa Clara Mission. The city grew up by the infiltration of gold miners who took up ranching and residence there. In 1970 the population was 87,717.

SANTA CLARA COUNTY
In honor of St. Claire, abbess who founded an order outside Assisi. Created Feb. 18, 1850, chap. 15. 439 sq. mi.

SANTA CLARA DEL NORTE RANCHO   Ventura
Spanish for St. Clare of the North Ranch. From a land grant dated May 18, 1837 to Juan Sanchez for an undescribed area.

SANTA CLARA DE MONTE FALCO   Santa Barbara
See Rincon Point.

SANTA CLARA, EMBARCADERO DE   Santa Clara
See Alviso.

SANTA CLARA MISSION   Santa Clara
This mission was founded January 12, 1777 by Father Tomas de la Pena. It was the eighth of the Franciscan missions in California. It commemorates St. Clare of Assisi (July 16, 1194-August 11, 1253) co-founder of the Order of Poor Ladies (or Clares), and first Abbess of San Damiano. In 1837 the Mexican Government secularized the mission and Ramon Estrada became its first commissioner.

SANTA CLARA RANCHO, EL POTRERO DE   Santa Clara
Spanish for the pasture of Santa Clara. From a land grant dated February 29, 1844 to James Alexander Forbes for an area of one league. The present city of Santa Clara is on the site of the original southern part of the ranch. The name derives from the Santa Clara Mission.

SANTA CLARA RANCHO, RIO DE   Ventura
From a land grant dated May 22, 1837 to Valentin Cota for an undescribed area. The present Hueneme and Oxnard are located on the original site of the grant.

SANTA CLARA RIVER   Los Angeles and Ventura
It rises in the mountains near the Antelope Valley and empties into the Pacific Ocean south of the city of Ventura. The valley gave its name to the river which flows into it. It was named "Cañada de Santa Clara" by Portola expedition in honor of St. Clare, on August 12, 1769 because it was the feast day of St. Clare. St. Clare was the first woman to embrace the Franciscan Order and who founded "The Poor Clares". Father Crespi named the river "Rio de los Santos Martires Hipolito y Casiano."

SANTA CRUZ
Spanish for Holy Cross. It was the first name applied to California by its discoverer Ortuno Ximenez who landed in lower California by the Bahia of La Paz in 1533; he thought the peninsula was an island and named it "Isla de Santa Cruz". "Triunfo de la Santa Cruz". Santa Cruz is frequently used as a place name in Spanish-speaking countries. It was a very popular place name in Spanish times.

SANTA CRUZ   Santa Cruz
The site of this town was discovered and named by Portola expedition on Oct. 18, 1769. The name derives after Santa Cruz Mission. The city was chartered in 1866. Its population in 1970 was 32,076.

SANTA CRUZ COUNTY
"Holy Cross" in Spanish. One of the first names of the State of California, a place near San Elijo Lagoon (San Diego county) was named by the Portola expedition: "Triunfo de la Santa Cruz". Created Feb. 18, 1850, chap. 15. 439 sq. mi.

SANTA CRUZ CREEK   Santa Barbara
The plats of the Tequepis grant of 1845 and of the San Marcos grant (1846) bear "Canada de Santa Cruz" and "Arroyo de Santa Cruz".

SANTA CRUZ ISLAND   Santa Barbara
Juan Rodriguez Cabrillo discovered a group of islands in 1542 that he named "Islas de San Lucas"; among them was the present Santa Cruz island. In January 20, 1543 another Spanish explorer Ferrer renamed it San Sebastian. In 1602 during Sebastian Vizcaino exploration of the same islands, it was

said that this particular island was inhabited by men wearing beards. Consequently the explorer named it "Isla de Gente Barbudo" (Island of bearded people). In April 1769, the "San Antonio", a ship commanded by Juan Perez was in the vicinity of the island. Some sailors landed on the island accompanied by a friar who left a staff with a cross on it; that seems to be the origin of the naming of the place.

SANTA CRUZ MISSION   Santa Cruz
(The Mission of the Holy Cross). Portola expedition crossed a creek which was named "Arroyo de Santa Cruz" on October 18, 1769. The mission later on was founded on this site September 25, 1791 by Fathers Alonso Salazar and Baldomero Lopez. The mission was secularized August 24, 1834 and its first commissioner was Ignacio Del Valle. The Mission is situated in modern Santa Cruz.

SANTA CRUZ RANCHO, ISLAND OF   Santa Cruz
(Holy Cross). From a land grant dated 1839 to Andres Castillero, of an undescribed area, comprising the whole of the Santa Barbara Channel island of Santa Cruz.

SANTA CRUZ MOUNTAINS   Santa Cruz
They are mentioned in 1838 as "Cierra Madre de Santa Cruz" on a plat of the San Antonio Grant. Hecker Pass is a major east-west route through the mountains.

SANTA DELFINA, RIO DE   San Luis Obispo and Monterey
See Salinas River.

SANTA FE
(Holy Faith). The Spanish name, except for the New Mexico city, has not been as popular with place names as the other saints, such as John, Joseph, et.c.

SANTA FE RANCHO   San Diego
From a land grant, a part of the San Diego Rancho was developed as a modern exclusive country estate in 1922.

SANTA FE SPRINGS   Los Angeles
This location was formerly known as Fulton Sulphur Springs and Health Resort from its founder J. E. Fulton. It was founded in 1973. When the Santa Fe Railway reached this site they purchased the resort (1886) and renamed it Santa Fe Springs.

SANTA GERTRUDES RANCHO   Los Angeles
Named for St. Gertrude (626-659) patron saint of travelers, feast March 17. For two land grants of the same name dated 1834 to Joseph Cota, the widow of Antonio Maria Nieto, for an area of five leagues; and of July 27, 1833 to Antonio Maria Nieto for an area which is undescribed. Present Downey and Los Nietos are located on the site of the original grants. The right spelling of the name should be Gertrudis.

SANTA GERTRUDIS CREEK   Riverside
Is mentioned as "un ojo de agua llamado Santa Gertrudis" (A spring of water named St. Gertrude) in documents of the 1820's. The name commemorates St. Gertrude Abbess of Nivelle (Brabant) daughter of Pepin of Landen, patron saint of the travelers. The feast is March 17.

SANTA INEZ   Santa Barbara
See Santa Ynez.

SANTA ISABEL   San Diego
See Santa Ysabel.

SANTA LUCIA CANYON   Santa Barbara
The plat of the Jesus Maria grant (1837) bears "La Cañada de Santa Lucia" (The canyon of St. Lucy).

SANTA LUCIA RANGE   San Luis Obispo
See Sierras de San Martin.

SANTA MANUELA RANCHO   San Luis Obispo
From a land grant dated April 6, 1837 to Francis Ziba Branch for an undescribed area. It honors the Santa Manuela (feast day June 24).

SANTA MARGARITA   San Luis Obispo
This town was named for St. Margaret of Cortona unless it was for St. Margaret of Antioch in Asia Minor. The site and river are mentioned by Anza in 1776.

SANTA MARGARITA   Santa Barbara
See Santa Rosa Island.

SANTA MARGARITA RANCHO   San Luis Obispo
From a land grant dated Sept. 27, 1841 to Joaquin Estrada for an area of four leagues. Apparently the origin of the name stems from "El rancho de Santa Margarita de Cortona". The present town developed in the 1870's and is located on the site of the original land grant. The name honors St. Margaret.

SANTA MARGARITA Y LAS FLORES RANCHO   San Diego
(St. Margaret and the flowers Ranch.) From a land grant of Feb. 23, 1836 and May 10, 1841, to Pio and Andres Pico for an area of 133,000 acres. At the times where the ranch belonged to San Luis Rey Mission, it was known as "El San Onofre y Santa Margarita Rancho". It was Portola who named the "Rio Santa Margarita" in 1769.

SANTA MARGARITA RIVER   San Diego
On July 20, 1769 the Portola expedition camped on the banks of the "Rio San Margarita". As July 20 was the day of the saint they named it hence the river.

SANTA MARGARITA VALLEY   Marin
Named after 1844 for the land grant of "San Pedro, Santa Margarita y las Gallinas" (St. Peter, St. Margaret and the hen chickens.)

SANTA MARIA
A favorite place name in Spanish times it has survived and appears in several California counties, Kern, Santa Barbara, San Diego, San Luis Obispo.

SANTA MARIA (city)   Santa Barbara
For Santa Maria Valley founded in 1867 by B. Wiley on government land and is said to be the only major city in Santa Barbara county not located on land that once comprised a ranch grant. The community, first known as Central City, was laid out in 1875. The change to the present name occurred in the early eighties. (From Hanna, p. 291). Nearby oil discoveries and Vandenberg Air Force Missile Base have brought great increases in population which in 1970 was 32,749.

SANTA MARIA MAGDALENA   Orange
See San Juan Capistrano.

SANTA MARIA RIVER   San Luis Obispo
From a land grant Santa Maria dated April 6, 1837.

SANTA MARIA VALLEY   San Diego
It appears on a land grant of November 21, 1843 under the name of "Valle de Pamo" "Valle de Santa Maria".

SANTA MONICA   San Diego
During many years this name was used as the alternate name for "El Cajon de San Diego" grant, September 23, 1845.

SANTA MONICA BAY   Los Angeles
Was named after the mountains. See below.

SANTA MONICA (City)   Los Angeles
Named from San Vicente y Santa Monica Rancho. The city was founded by Co. R. S. Baker and Senator
John P. Jones in July 1875. The post office was established in 1880. The city was incorporated in 1886.
The city early became a residential and resort area with a popular amusement park. In the 1920's the
Douglas Aircraft Co., and then Rand Corp. established themselves there. The 1970 population was
88,289.

SANTA MONICA CREEK   Santa Barbara
Named after the mountains. See below.

SANTA MONICA MOUNTAINS   Los Angeles
On May 4, 1770, the feast day of Santa Monica (Mother of Saint Augustine) the Portola expedition sighted the mountains and named them thus. As early as 1822 official documents record, "Sierra de Santa Monica" and ". . . paraje de Santa Monica", Sierra de Santa Monica and finally "Santa Monica Mountains"
(1881).

SANTA MONICA RANCHO, BOCA DE   Los Angeles
The name was used for two grants: one dated June 19, 1839 to Francisco Marquez for an area of one and a
half acres. The present Palisades is located on the original land grant.

SANTA MONICA, SAN VINCENTE Y   Los Angeles
A second grant dated Dec. 20, 1839 and June 8, 1846 for an area of undescribed extent.

SANTA PAULA (City)   Ventura
The name stems from Santa Paula y Saticoy Rancho. In 1872 the community started when N.W. Blanchard bought a portion of the rancho and became a prominent citrus grower of the region. It became also
an oil refinery center. In 1970 it had a population of 18,001.

SANTA PAULA MINERAL SPRINGS   Ventura
Named after Sant Paula y Saticoy Rancho. Santa Paula a Roman who became a disciple of Saint Jerome.

SANTA PAULA Y SATICOY RANCHO   Ventura
From a land grant dated July 31, 1834 and April 28, 1840 to Manuel Jimeno Casarin for an area of
four leagues. Saticoy stems from the Chumash Indian word "sati-koy", the name of an Indian settlement.
The present town of Saticoy is located on the site of the original grant.

SANTA RITA
A very popular Saint's name used in Spanish times that has survived in modern times. The name commemorates St. Rita, a 15th century Italian Saint who professed the rule of St. Augustine at Cassia (Italy)
who worked several miracles. The feast day is May 22.

SANTA RITA
Was named after a land grant dated September 30, 1837 located on "Los Gatos" or "Santa Rita" grant.
The town was laid out in 1867.

SANTA RITA (Town)   Alameda
Named for Santa Rita Rancho of DoloresPacheco. From a land grant of April 10, 1839.

SANTA RITA PEAK   San Benito
Located Southeast of New Idria. Named after the saint of the 15th century Santa Rita de Cassis, an
Augustinina. Her feast day is May 22.

SANTA RITA PEAK   San Bernardino
Named after Santa Rita (see above).

SANTA RITA RANCHO   Santa Barbara
From a land grant dated 1845 to José Ramon Malo for an area of three leagues.

SANTA RITA RANCHO, SANJON DE   Merced
Spanish "sanjon" (ditch). From a land grant dated September 7, 1841 to Francisco Soberanes for an
area of eleven leagues.

SANTA RITA SLOUGH   Merced
Apparently this site was discovered by Gabriel Moraga during his expedition of 1806 or his previous
one. "Arroyo de Santa Rita" is represented in several maps after 1809.

SANTA ROSA   Sonoma
Named for Cabeza de Santa Rosa Rancho which in turn took its name from Santa Rosa Creek. Father
Juan Amoros baptized an Indian squaw here on the saint's day of St. Rose of Lima on August 30, 1820.
The modern city was laid out in 1853 and became the county seat of Sonoma county in 1854. In the

101

1960's the city grew enormously as a residential suburb. Wineries and fruit processing plants are located there. In 1970 its population was 50,006.

SANTA ROSA CREEK Sonoma
Named by a Father of Sonoma mission who baptized an Indian girl in this particular creek. The priest gave the girl the name of Santa Rosa which was the saint of the day.

SANTA ROSA ISLAND Santa Barbara
Juan Rodriguez Cabrillo discovered the island October 18, 1542 and named it "San Lucas" for the saint of the day. In 1602 Vizcaino named it "San Ambrosio" to honor that saint. In 1774 Juan Perez is apparently the first one to mention the present name in his journal for what is now San Miguel Island because to him, the name of Santa Rosa was Santa Margarita. (According to Henry R. Wagner).

SANTA ROSA DE LAS LAJAS, POZAS DE
Spanish for the wells of Santa Rosa's flat rocks. See Yuha Plain.

SANTA ROSA RANCHO Riverside
From a land grant dated January 30, 1846 to Juan Moreno for an area of three leagues. These three grants were named for Santa Rosa a 17th century member of the Third Order of St. Dominic.

SANTA ROSA RANCHO San Luis Obispo
One of the three grants with this name granted to Julian Estrada in 1841 for an area of three leagues. Present Cambria is located on the site of the original grant. See Santa Rosa Rancho.

SANTA ROSA RANCHO Santa Barbara
From a land grant dated July 30, 1839 to Francisco Cota for an area of three and a half leagues. See Santa Rosa Rancho.

SANTA ROSA RANCHO, CABEZA DE Sonoma
Spanish for the head of St. Rose. From a land grant dated 1841 to Maria Ignacia Lopez of an undescribed area.

SANTA ROSA RANCHO, ISLAND OF Santa Barbara
From a land grant of the entire island of Santa Rosa granted in 1843 to Jose Antonio and Carlos Carrillo, for an undescribed area. Named after St. Rose.

SANTA ROSA RANCHO, LLANO DE Sonoma
Spanish, Plain of St. Rose. From a land grant dated January 8, 1831 to Rafael Gomez for an undescribed area. The present city of Sebastopol is located on the site of the grant.

SANTA SINFOROSA San Diego
See Buena Vista Creek.

SANTA SUSANA Ventura
Honors St. Susanna, third century Roman maiden who is said to have been a niece of Pope St. Caius who upon her refusal to marry a pagan relative of Emperor Diocletian (about 190 A.D.) was put to death as a Christian. (From Hanna, p. 293).

SANTA SUSANA MOUNTAINS Los Angeles
As early as 1804 we find documents "El camino de Santa Susana y Simi" (St. Susanna and Simi's road); in 1834 "una gran cuesta conocida por Santa Susana" (A large hill known as St. Susanna); in 1837 a plat bears "Sierra de Santa Susana". Finally the present names appear in the Statutes of 1850. The mountains were named to honor St. Susanna.

SANTA TERESA RANCHO Santa Clara
From a land grant dated July 11, 1834 to Joaquin Bernal for an area of one league. It was after Santa Teresa de Avila, born in 1515 who died at Alba in 1582. She devoted her life to the Carmelite Order and founded thirty two convents. The feast day is October 15.

SANTA YNEZ   Santa Barbara
The town was founded in 1882 as a trading center for the great College Ranch of 35,000 acres. Named from Santa Ynez Mission.

SANTA YNEZ MOUNTAINS   Santa Barbara
The Spanish name "Sierra de Santa Ines" was officially used and kept on most of the maps. Before 1865, however, the name took the present form through the Whitney Survey. "Santa Inez Mountains". Finally the Geographic Board decided for the spelling of Santa Ynez.

SANTA YNEZ RIVER   Ventura and Santa Barbara
Named after the Santa Ynez Virgen y Martir Mission it rises in the mountains of western Ventura county and empties into the Pacific Ocean. Portola expedition called the river "Santa Rosa" and "San Bernardo"; then in 1817 we find the stream "Rio de Calaguasa", name of the mission (Indian name given to the site of the mission). It is circa 1835 that we find "Rio de Santa Ynes o La Purisima."

SANTA YNEZ VIRGEN Y MARTIR MISSION   Santa Barbara
The mission was founded on Sept. 17, 1804 by Fathers Estevan Tapis, Jose Antonio Calzada, Romualdo Gutierrez and Marcelino Cipres. This was the nineteenth Franciscan mission in California. It was named for Santa Ines (St. Agnes). The mission was secularized June 23, 1836.

SANTA YSABEL   San Diego
An asistencia of San Diego Mission named for St. Isabel, daughter of King Louis VIII who, *The Book of Saints* records "refused to give her hand to Emperor of Germany, eldest son and heir in order to consecrate her virginity to God." The feast day is July 8.

SANTA YSABEL RANCHO   San Diego
From a land grant dated November 8, 1844 to Jose Joaquin Ortega for an area of four leagues. The name honors St. Elisabeth. The present Santa Ysabel is located on the site of the original grant.

SANTA YSABEL RANCHO   San Luis Obispo
From a land grant dated May 12, 1844 to Francisco C. Arce for an area of four leagues. The name is also spelled "Isabel" and commemorates St. Elisabeth.

SANTIAGO   Santiago
"St. James", the apostle and patron of the Spains has unfortunately survived only in few place names in Orange and Kern counties.

SANTIAGO CREEK   Orange
On July 27, 1769 Portola expedition camped on the banks of the creek, two days after Santiago's feast day. The creek was named "Arroyo de Santiago".

SANTIAGO CREEK   Kern
One of the few survivors of the name "Santiago" in Kern county.

SANTIAGO DE SANTA ANA RANCHO   Orange
From a land grant of July 1st, 1810, to Antonio Yorba for an area of eleven leagues. Portola expedition camped on the site of the present grant on July 27, 1769. Since the first camping in the area several cities have sprung: El Modeno, Olive, Santa Ana, Orange and Newport Beach.

SANTIAGO PEAK   Orange and Riverside
The mountain known as "Old Saddleback" was named Santiago Peak by the Geological Survey of 1894. In the old Spanish times it was known as "Pico de Trabuco" (blunderbuss peak) and later as Temescal peak.

SANTIAGO, POINT
See Point Bonita and Bonita Point.

SANTIAGO, SIERRA DE   Orange
See Santa Ana Mountains.

SANTOS MARTIRES HIPOLITO Y CASIANO   Los Angeles and Ventura
    See Santa Clara River.

SANTOS REYES, RIO DE LOS   Fresno and Kings
    See Kings River.

SAN TIMOTEO CREEK   San Bernardino
    Named after a land grant dated Dec. 31, 1830. The name commemorates Timothy, a disciple of Paul who died Bishop of Ephesus in 97 A.D. Feast day is January 24.

SAN TOMAS AQUINAS CREEK   Santa Clara
    The streams appear on the plats of several land grants as "Arroyo de San Tomas Aquinas" (1850). The name honors the famous theologian Saint Thomas Aquinas "the Angelic Doctor" (1225-1274).

SAN VINCENTE
    A very popular name among the saints and the place names of Spanish times. It has survived in California at least in six localities.

SAN VICENTE CREEK   Santa Cruz
    The "Arroyo de San Vicente" is on the land grant of April 16, 1839. The name commemorates St. Vincent de Paul, French Roman Catholic noted for his work to aid the poor, 1576-1660.

SAN VICENTE CREEK AND VALLEY   San Diego
    Are on the land grant of January 25, 1846 named "Canada de San Vicente y Mesa del Padre Barona".

SAN VICENTE MOUNTAIN   Los Angeles
    One finds on several documents of the early 1800's "Paraje San Vicente". The mountain was named after a land grant of 1828 and December 20, 1839.

SAN VICENTE RANCHO   Santa Clara
    From a land grant dated August 1, 1842 to José R. Berreyesa for an area of one league. It is uncertain for whose saint it is named. Apparently the name honors St. Vincent de Paul, French Roman Catholic noted for his work to aid the poor, 1576-1660. Another source mentions St. Vincent Ferrer, a 15th century Spanish Dominican who had the gift of prophecy and worked several miracles.

SAN VICENTE RANCHO   Santa Cruz
    From a land grant dated April 16, 1839 to Antonio Rodriguez for an area of two leagues. For name see above.

SAN VICENTE RANCHO   Monterey
    From a land grant dated September 20, 1836, to Francisco Soto and Estevan Munras for an area of two leagues. For name see San Vicente Rancho, Santa Clara.

SAN VICENTE Y MESA DEL PADRE BARONA RANCHO, CAÑADA DE
     San Diego
    Spanish "the stream of St. Vincent and the plateau of Father Barona". From a land grant dated January 25, 1846 to Juan Lopez for an area of three leagues. Father Barona was a Franciscan attached to the missions at San Juan Capistrano and San Diego. (1764-1827).

SAN VICENTE Y SANTA MONICA RANCHO   Los Angeles
    From a land grant dated December 20, 1839 and June 8, 1846 to Francisco Sepulveda for an area of 31,000 acres. The name commemorates St. Vincent and St. Monica (Mother of St. Augustine). Her tears converted her pagan son to christianity.

SAN YSIDRO (City)   San Diego
    Was named for St. Isidore the "plowman", who became Bishop of Seville 600 A.D. It was established by the presidio of San Diego in the early 1820's as a "county seat" called in Spanish a "sitio". The feast day is May 10.

SAN YSIDRO MOUNTAINS   San Diego
Named for a rancho "San Ysidro" that belonged to the San Diego Mission. The ranch in turn was named after the Spanish St. Isidore.

SAUSAL REDONDO (City)   Los Angeles
Spanish for round willow grove. From a land grant dated March 15, 1822 and May 20, 1837 to Antonio Ignacio Avila for an area of five leagues. The present cities of El Segundo, Manhattan and Hermosa beaches and Lawndale are located on the site of the original grant. Although Redondo Beach takes its name from the land grant it is not located on it but on the adjoining San Pedro Rancho.

SAUSALITO   Marin
Meaning little willow thicket. The name first appears on a map of 1831 by English navigator Captain Frederick William Beechey. From a land grant dated 1835 to Jose Antonio Galindo for an area of three leagues. February 11, 1838 the land owner sold it to Captain William A. Richardson. The present localities of Sausalito, Muir Woods and Stinson Beach are established on the site of the original grant. The spelling of the name has experienced the capricious ears and tongues of the Americans: Saucelito, Saucilito, Saucilita, Sausolita, Sausaulito, Sausolito, Sauselito, Sousoulito, Sauceletou, etc. The present town was laid out in 1868, the post office "Saucelito" was established December 12, 1870.

SAUCOS RANCHO   Tehama
"Alder trees". From a land grant dated December 20, 1844 to Robert H. Thomas for an area of five leagues. The present city of Tehama is located on the site of the original grant.

SCOTT CREEK   Santa Cruz
It was originally named San Pedro de Alcantara by Father Juan Crespi of the Portola expedition, on October 19, 1769, because of the saint's day. However, the soldiers of the expedition named it "El Alto de Junin" (the highland of Junin). The naming of the present feature is a mystery.

SEBASTIAN, CABO BLANCO DE   Del Norte
See Point St. George.

SEBASTIAN, RIO GRANDE DE   Marin
See Tomales Bay.

SECOND GAROTTE   Tuolumne
See Groveland.

SEGUNDA RANCHO, CAÑADA DE LA   Monterey
Spanish "Canyon of the second". Origin of the name is unknown. From a land grant dated April 4, 1839 to Lazaro Soto for an area of one league. "Canyon Secundo" is found on the Monterey Atlas sheet.

SEGUNDO, EL   Los Angeles
Named by officials of the Santa Fe Railroad shortly before the establishment of the Standard Oil Company's refinery here in April 1911. The word is Spanish meaning the second because it was the second oil company located in the state and the first in Richmond. It is a community near Santa Monica Bay, south of Los Angeles International Airport.

SEPULVEDA   Los Angeles
Commemorates Francisco Sepulveda, a settler of the 1815's whose adobe was at the foot of the Verdugo Mountains and who became acting mayor in 1825. He was granted the San Vicente y Santa Monica grant in 1839. In 1873 the railroad from Los Angeles to San Fernando and the station was named after Francisco Sepulveda.

SEPULVEDA CANYON   Los Angeles
Named after Francisco Sepulveda. See above.

SERENA, LA   Santa Barbara
Spanish for the serene. Was an ambitious project in October 1888 for Santa Barbara county. This

dream never materialized; it became one more project overshadowed by the fast pace of growing California.

SERRA   Orange

This railroad station by the name of "San Juan by the Sea" was changed to the present in 1910 to honor the first president of Spanish missions in California, Father Junipero Serra.

SERRANO   San Luis Obispo

In 1828 Miguel Serrano, a native from Mexico settled on the site where the Southern Pacific Station was established in 1893. After a series of negotiations the Serrano family sold the right of way to the railroad company.

SESPE CREEK   Ventura

From a land grant "Sespe" or "San Cayetano" dated November 22, 1833. See below.

SESPE HOT SPRINGS   Ventura

Take their name from the Sespe Rancho.

SESPE OIL FIELD

An oil development named after the Sespe Rancho.

SESPE RANCHO   Ventura

From a land grant of November 22, 1833 to Carlos Antonio Carrillo for an area of six leagues. The ranch takes its name from the Chumash Indian rancheria Secpe (Sespe) or San Cayetano. The present town of Sespe is located on the site of the grant.

SEVILLE   Tulare

Apparently named for Seville, Spain, a citrus country as is the Californian Seville. It was named in 1913 by The Santa Fe Railroad Company.

SIERRA

The descriptive term for "mountain range" ridge of mountains and craggy rocks from "saw" was a very popular term in Spanish speaking countries. Although it is not considered as a generic, it has been used as such in many instances (Sierra Azul, Sierra Morena, etc.)

SIERRA AZUL   Santa Cruz

Named after the mountain range "Sierra Madre".

SIERRA BUTTES   Sierra

A gold mining site of the 1850's. It is said to have produced gold valuing $7,000,000.00 over 30 years. It is located north of Sierra City.

SIERRA CITY   Sierra

Named because of its location in the northern Sierra. The small town was destroyed by an avalanche in 1852. With the discovery of the "monumental nugget" in 1868, the town was revived.

SIERRA COUNTY

Spanish for mountain range. Named for its location near the Sierra Nevada. Created April 16, 1852, chap. 145. Area 6,313 sq. mi.

SIERRA MADRE   Los Angeles

Spanish for mother mountains. Sierra Madre Villa was the nucleus of the present community which is one of the earliest resorts in Los Angeles county built in the 1870's. "Sierra Madre de California" were the various ranges in Kern, Los Angeles, Riverside and San Bernardino counties. The Fathers who accompanied explorations and missions used to refer to them as "Sierra Madre."

SIERRA MORENA   San Mateo

See Sierra Azul.

SIERRA NATIONAL FOREST   Fresno, Madera, and Mariposa

It is one of five national forests created on February 14, 1893. In 1907 the names of all forest reserves were changed to national forests by Act of Congress. In 1908 the area was of 6,660,000 acres, but some transfers were made and the present area is 1,343,184 acres.

SIERRA NEVADA

A common descriptive Spanish term for a mountain range covered with snow. It is one of the highest mountain ranges in the U.S.A. In November 1542 Juan Rodriguez Cabrillo applied the name to the Santa Lucia Mountains. In 1776 Father Font named the present range. The Sierra Nevada is a single range of mountains and should be used in the singular. People have a tendency to use the plural "Sierras Nevadas" or "Sierra Nevadas" or "Sierra Nevada Mountains".

SIERRA PELONA   Los Angeles

Spanish for bald mountain range. Named because of the summit devoid of trees.

SIERRA POINT   Yosemite National Park

It was discovered by Charles A. Bailey, Warren Cheney, W. E. Dennison, and Walter E. Magee. On June 14, 1897 it was named to honor the "Sierra Club".

SIERRA RANCHO, LA   Riverside

From two land grants of June 15, 1846 to Bernardo Yorba for an area of four leagues; and to Diego Sepulveda. The present Norco is located on the site of one of the ranchos.

SIERRA DE SALINAS   Monterey

Named after the Salinas River.

SIERRAS NEVADAS   San Luis Obispo

See Santa Lucia Range and Sierras de San Martin.

SIGNAL HILL   Los Angeles

This geographic nomenclature was known in Spanish times as "Los Cerritos" (the small mountains). With the erection of a signal on the hill (1889-1890) it became known as Signal Hill. The post office was established in 1926. The missionary fathers of San Gabriel used it as warning elevation and observation point to warn against Indian depredation. Later on the owners of the surrounding ranchos used it as elevation point to watch their cattle and sheep.

SIMI HILLS   Ventura

From the land grant of 1795. See Simi Rancho. "Un Valle que se llama Simi".

SIMI PEAK

See above.

SIMI TOWN

See above.

SIMI RANCHO   Ventura

From a land grant of 1795 and March 8, 1821 and April 25, 1842 granted originally by Governor Diego de Borica to Javier, Patricio and Miguel Pico, to a grant recorded as "San José de Gracia de Simi" for an Indian village.

SITIO

A measure for one square league; also a "place" or a "station" meaning in the Spanish "paraje" for location.

SOBERANES CREEK   Monterey

For the ancestor José María Soberanes of the Soberanes family, prominent in the political life of the Monterey district during the Mexican regime. The Soberanes were grantees of several important land grants. The creek was named after the family, not for José María Soberanes who came with the Portola expedition in 1769.

SOBERANES POINT   Monterey
    See Soberanes Creek.

SOBRANTE
    Spanish for "residue" "overplus" "rich". This Spanish generic term was mostly used with land grants in reference to surplus land of an area after "the granted land had been measured and separated from the public domain."

SOBRANTE, EL   Contra Costa
    From the name of a land grant of 1841. Name of the Central Pacific Station.

SOBRANTE RANCHO, EL   Contra Costa
    Spanish meaning the surplus. From a land grant dated April 23, 1841, to Juan Jose Castro for an area of eleven leagues. The post office was established in 1945.

SOBRANTE RIDGE   Contra Costa
    See El Sobrante Rancho.

SOLANA BEACH   San Diego
    Meaning "sunny place". Named by Ed Fletcher, community developer when he subdivided this site in 1923.

SOLANO COUNTY
    Named after the apostle of South America Saint Francis Solano (16th century) and his namesake Francisco Solano, chief of the Suisun Indians. On November 25, 1795, Padre Antonio Danti, on a site called "San Francisco Solano", raised a cross where Mission San Jose was later set up. The county was created February 18, 1850.

SOLEDAD   Monterey
    Named by Father Pedro Font Franciscan missionary diarist. He named it thus because when he asked an Indian the name of the area, he replied what sounded like "Soledad". However, the other version for the naming is that Soledad stands for "solitude" but refers for the shortening of "Nuestra Senora de la Soledad" (Our Lady of Solitude).

SOLEDAD PASS   Los Angeles
    Was named "New Pass" by its discoverer Williamson; then Blake renamed it "Williamson's pass." The land office has "La Soledad Pass" on maps.

SOLEDAD VALLEY   San Diego
    On June 15, 1769 the Portola expedition crossed this valley and named it Santa Isabel, in honor of Elisabeth (Queen of Portugal), a saint of the 14th century. Anza's diary mentions the Indian Rancheria of the valley, under the name of "La Soledad" (January 10, 1776). We find the name under a grant dated April 13, 1838.

SOLYO RANCH   Stanislaus
    Solyo corruption of the Spanish word "Sollo" (pike), a possible translation of the owner's name. The ranch has an area of 4,400 acres. Grains, grapes and cattle make the riches of this ranch. It was established by Roy Melville Pike in 1918.

SONORA   Tuolumne
    A corruption of Señora from a State in Mexico by the expedition of Francisco Vasquez de Coronado in 1540. In 1848 mining camps were founded by groups of Mexican miners from the state of Sonora who did most of the diggings. The discovery of gold nuggets in the area attracted a crowd in the 1850's. The city before 1850 was known as Stewart; however, in May 1851 it was incorporated as Sonora.

SONORA PASS   Tuolumne
    Was renowned as a control point on the wagon road from the San Joaquin Valley via this pass to the Esmeralda mines. The Sonora Pass has an elevation of 9,264 ft.; in the early 1860's it became a widely used Sierra Crossing. (From Hanna, p. 311).

SOTOYOME RANCHO   Sonoma

From the Spanish "soto" and the Indian "yo-me" meaning "the place of Soto". On March 28, 1836 we find in the *Vallejo Documents*, III, 347 "Rio de Satiyome". On a plat of the Molino Grant, September 28, 1841 and November 12, 1844 there is a "Rio Sotoyome". The land grant was given to Henry D. Fitch for an area of eight leagues. The present communities of Healdsburg and Lytton are located on the site of the original grant.

SOUTH DOS PALOS   Merced

The post office was established in 1907. It was named after Dos Palos. See Dos Palos.

SOUTH LAGUNA   Orange

This resort was founded in 1926. The post office was established in 1933 and was at this time named "Three Arches" because of the nearby shape of rocks. In 1934 the name was changed to the present. The town is located just south of the famous "Laguna Beach".

SOUTH PASADENA   Los Angeles

The city was laid out in 1885 on the old San Pasqual Rancho. The city was incorporated in 1888. The post office was named Hermosa after the famous Hermosa Vista Hotel.

SOUTH RIVERSIDE   Riverside

See Corona.

SOUTH SAN DIEGO   San Diego

See Imperial Beach.

SOUTH SAN FRANCISCO   San Mateo

In 1849 an attempt was made to establish a sub-division on what is now Hunters Point; unfortunately it did not materialize. Then the Railroad station south of San Bruno Mountain was established and given the name of Baden. In 1908 the city was incorporated and the name of South San Francisco was accepted.

SPANISH

It appears in about thirty place names in the state of California, most of them as a remembrance of the gold rush where Spanish-speaking workers would flock the mining camps. The name is still preserved in the following counties: Fresno, Butte, Plumas, San Mateo.

SPANISH BAR

In 1848 a gold rush attracted a group of Mormons on the south side of the middle fork of the American River. They were lucky when they found gold.

SPANISH DRY DIGGINGS   El Dorado

In 1848 this site was one of the luckiest of the region by the richness of its gold quartz. The place was called Dutchtown. However, Spanish Dry Diggings kept its colorful name.

SPANISH FLAT   El Dorado

From the two "Spanish Flats" there is one which has survived. It is located in the northwest part of Coloma. It was a gold mining site that produced its share of gold in the early 1850's.

SPANISH TOWN   Butte

See Yankee Hill, Butte county.

SPANISHTOWN   San Mateo

See Half Moon Bay.

ST. GEORGE, POINT   Del Norte

It is believed this geographic feature is the "Cabo Blanco de Sebastian" discovered by the Vizcaino expedition of 1602-03. It was named by Vancouver "Point St. George" April 23, 1792 for the hero who fought and conquered the legendary dragon.

STOCKTON   San Joaquin

Its original name when it was founded in 1847 was Tuleburg (the town of tules "rushes"). But the name lasted only one year. In 1848 it was renamed for Commodor Field Stockton. The city was incorporated July 23, 1850.

SUISUN BAY   Contra Costa

As early as August 1775 the bay was explored by Juan Manuel de Ayala, he named Suisun Bay "Junta de los cuatro Evangelistas" (The meeting place of the four Evangelists.) Later on, upon the report of the explorers the bay was known as "Puerto Dulce" (Freshwater port). Suisun is the name of an Indian village on the north shore. On May 13, 1817 Arguello mentions "la Bahilla de Suysun". The present spelling is related to the land grant of January 28, 1842.

SUISUN RANCHO   Solano

From a land grant dated January 28, 1842 to Francisco Solano for an area of four leagues. The present towns of Fairfield and Suisun are located on the original site of the land grant. See Suisun Bay.

SUNOL   Alameda

The town, as well as the surrounding area comprising the valley and several hills were named for Antonio Sunol, a native of Spain who came to California on board of "Le Bordelais", a French ship in 1818. Sunol was far away to be a seaman, he dreamed of immense and open space: he deserted ship and settled in San Jose where he became later owner of the "Rancho El Valle de San Jose". He acquired San Rafael mission when it was secularized by the Mexican government. When he died in 1865 he left an impressive fortune and estate to his heirs. One of his daughters married the French vintner Pierre Sansevain, nephew of Jean-Louis Vignes.

SUR   Monterey

Spanish for south. Was the name of a land grant dated July 30, 1834 to Juan B. Alvarado. The nearby cape the "Morro de la Trompa" or "Punta que Parece Isla" the Coast Survey gave the name "Point Sur". The post office of 1892 became "Big Sur".

SUR, DEL   Los Angeles

"Of the south". Known because of the organization here of the first school district. Named as an opposite to Del Norte.

SUR RANCHO, EL   Monterey

"The South Rancho". From a land grant dated July 30, 1834 to Juan B. Alvarado for an area of two leagues.

SUTIL ISLAND   Los Angeles

As a remembrance to the "Sutil", a ship of the Galiano expedition of 1792. The island was formerly known as "Gull Island". The geographic Board changed its name in 1939.

TACHE RANCHO, LAGUNA DE   Fresno and King

From a land grant dated December 12, 1843 to Manuel Castro for an area of eleven leagues. The Spanish meaning is "the lagoon of the Tache".

TAJIGUAS   Santa Barbara

Hispanicization of the name of a former Chumash Indian village "Tahijuas". It is derived from a Chumash village "El rancho del Refugio en Tajiguas". This village gave the name to the creek which in turn gave the name to the Southern Pacific Station (1910).

TAMBO   Yuba

Spanish American word for "hotel" or "inn' applied to Western Pacific station when line was built in 1907.

TARRAGONA   Santa Barbara

Named after the picturesque Spanish city.

TASSAJARA   Contra Costa
    A corruption of the Spanish "Tasajera" (a place where meat is cut in strips and hung in the sun to cure). The origin of the naming is because the mixed population of Spanish-speaking and Anglo-Saxons, used to dry their beef in the sun in this small locality.

TASSAJARA CREEK   Alameda
    See Tassajara, Contra Costa county.

TASSAJARA CREEK   Monterey
    See Tassajara, Contra Costa county.

TASSAJARA HOT SPRINGS   Monterey
    See Tassajara, Contra Costa county.

TASSAJARA VALLEY   Contra Costa
    See Tassajara.

TEJON CANYON   Kern
    In 1806 the expedition of Lieutenant Francisco Ruiz crossed this canyon and found a dead badger, hence they named the place "Cañada del Tejon" (Valley of the badger). The name of the canyon was applied to a land grant.

TEJON FORT   Kern
    Was founded August 10, 1854 to control marauding Indians. But by 1864 the fort was abandoned.

TEJON PASS   Los Angeles
    This pass was visited by Pedro Fages in 1772 and he named it "El Paso de la Buena Vista" (The pass of the fine view). When Francisco Ruiz led his expedition from Santa Barbara Mission to the San Joaquin Valley in July 1806, he gave it the present name (see Tejon Canyon).

TEJON RANCHO, EL   Kern
    From a land grant dated November 24, 1843 to Jose Antonio Aguirre and Ignacio del Valle for an area of 22 leagues. (For name see Tejon Canyon).

TEMBLADERA   Monterey
    Apparently a Spanish word corrupted from "Tremedal" (Guagmire, or boggy ground) naming these hundreds of acres covered by a dense vegetation.

TEMBLOR
    Spanish for earthquake, a common name applied in Spanish times in California. We find among the surviving "Temblor" names: Temblor Range, Kern and San Luis Obispo counties; Rio de los Temblores, Kern, Orange, Riverside counties. See Santana, Orange county.

TERRA BELLA   Tulare
    A combination of a Latin word "terra" (land) and a Spanish word "bella" (beautiful) applied by the Southern Pacific when it was built in 1889. The community developed around 1900. It is said the name was chosen because in the spring the countryside was covered with flowers.

TERRA BUENA   Sutter
    A combination of the Latin "terra" (land) and the Spanish "buena" (good) because of the richness of the soil. The town was laid out in the early 1900's.

THARPS ROCK   Tulare
    See Alta Peak.

TIA JUANA   San Diego
    It is certainly a name of Indian origin which has been corrupted in its Spanish form of "Tia Juana" (Aunt Jane). The initial name was "Tijuana". The name appears as early as 1829 as "Tiajuan".

TIBURON   Marin

Spanish meaning shark. First appeared on a map of San Francisco Bay by Captain Frederick William Beechey who mapped the bay in 1826. In José Sanchez' diary on July 6, 1823 "Punta de Tiburon" (point of the shark) is mentioned. The post office was established in 1886. The locality was known to Spanish-speaking people as "Rinconada del Tiburon".

TICO   Ventura

Named for Fernando Tico, owner of the Ojai Rancho who also was mayor (alcalde) at Santa Barbara in 1837.

TIERRA

Spanish for "earth" or "land" is a commonly used word in Spanish place names. There were three grants with the name of "Corral de Tierra". (Earth Corral). One grant in Monterey County dated April 10, 1836 to Guadalupe Figueroa for an undescribed area. Recorded as "Corral de Tierra Rancho".

TIERRA RANCHO, CORRAL DE   San Mateo

One grant from the land grant of the same name dated October 5, 1839 to Francisco Palomares for an area of one league. The present town of Moss Beach is located on the site of the original land grant. Another grant on the same county from the same original land grant dated October 16, 1839 to Tiburcio Vasquez for an area of one league.

TIERRA ALTA   Santa Clara

Highland, descriptive name.

TIERRA BLANCA MOUNTAINS   San Diego

Named after the white side of the mountain devoid of trees.

TIERRA BUENA   Colusa

Spanish for "good earth". Hence the name for the fecondity of its soil.

TIERRA REDONDA MOUNTAIN   San Luis Obispo

"Round earth mountain" because of the shape as a balloon of its summit.

TIJERA RANCHO, CIENEGA O PASO DE LA   Los Angeles

"The swamp of pass of the scissors". From a land grant dated February 23, 1823 and May 12, 1843 to Vicente Sanchez for an area of about two leagues.

TIZON, RIO DEL

See Colorado River.

TODOS SANTOS   Contra Costa

See Concord.

TODOS SANTOS Y SAN ANTONIO   Santa Barbara

"All Saints and San Anthony". Name of a land grant dated August 28, 1841. "Una cañada nombrada todos santos (valley called All Saints) is mentioned on documents as early as 1834. The grant for an area of five leagues was given to William E. P. Hartnell.

TOMALES BAY   Marin

Sebastian Vizcaino explored this bay in January 1603. He named it "Rio Grande de Sebastian". It is assumed for St. Sebastian whose feast day is January 28. Another Spanish explorer, Juan B. Matute, reached the bay in 1793 and named it as "Bahia Don Juan Francisco" in honor of Juan Francisco de Bodega y Cuadra. The name was changed to its present form after 1850 for the Coast Miwok Indian tribe of Tamalinos, which stems from "Tamal" (bay in Miwok).

TOMALES Y BAULINES RANCHO   Marin

From two ranchos which joined together; they originated from three land grants dated March 17, 1836 and June 8, 1839 (Punta de los Reyes, or Cañada de Tamales); March 18, 1839 (Tomales y Baulened); June 12, 1846 (Bolsa de Tomales) granted to Rafael Garcia for an undescribed area.

TOPO CREEK   Monterey and San Benito

Spanish for mole or gopher. The creek was named thus because of the great number of moles living on its banks.

TORO

Spanish "bull". A frequent word used with place names during Spanish times.

TORO, EL   Orange

The first name applied by explorers was "La Cañada de los Alisos", also known as "Aliso" which at times was confused with the nearby "Alviso". Meanwhile a bull fell and drowned into a well, thus the changing of Aliso to El Toro.

TORO RANCHO, EL   Monterey

From a land grant dated 1835 to Ramon Estrada for an area of one and a half leagues. Named after "El Arroyo del Toro" (the present Toro Creek).

TORTUGA   Imperial

Desert turtles are found here in great numbers. Spanish name means tortoise. The name was applied before 1900 to the Southern Pacific station on the Yuman division because of the slow speed of the trains.

TORTUGA, CAÑADA   Santa Barbara

Because of the great number of tortoises in this area, the Spanish settlers named it "Cañada Tortuga".

TRABUCO CANYON   Orange

Spanish "blunderbuss". The Portola expedition of July 1769 is responsible for the naming because a soldier lost his blunderbuss (trabuco) in the arroyo. Also creek named after the site.

TRABUCO PEAK   Orange and Riverside

See Santiago peak.

TRABUCO RANCHO   Orange

"Blunderbuss". From a land grant dated July 31, 1841 to Santiago Arguello for an area of five leagues.

TRABUCO, SIERRA DE   Orange

See Santa Ana Mountains.

TRAMPA CANYON   Contra Costa

See Las Trampas.

TRANCA

Spanish for "bar". In the old Spanish times it was a bar across a door or a window used for protection. The Vallejo family was well known for "Las Trancas", the barrier erected at the head of the tidewater on Napa River to prevent the cattle to cross. A land grant dated September 21, 1838 bears the name "Trancas y Jalapa". There were many grants bearing the name of Las Trancas. The name appears also as "Los Trancos" and "Strancos". The name is found in Los Angeles, Napa, Santa Cruz, and Santa Clara counties.

TRANQUILLON MOUNTAIN   Santa Barbara

Spanish for "mixed grain", "Meslin". Named for the profusion of mixed grain growing wild in this particular area. That was the name chosen by the Geological Survey of 1904 when the Guadalupe Quadrangle was mapped.

TRES OJOS DE AGUA RANCHO   Santa Cruz

Is an area of 1,500 varas bordering the ocean in Santa Cruz county. Granted March 18, 1844 to Nicolas Dodero meaning "three springs of water rancho."

TRES PINOS   San Benito

Spanish for "three pine-trees". The name is simply a transfer from a nearby locality. The post office was established in 1880. There is a creek bearing the same name, however, in maps anterior to 1890 it was recorded as "Arroyo del Puerto del Rosario" as well as "Arroyo del Rosario".

TRINIDAD   Humboldt
Named for Trinidad Head founded April 8, 1850 as a supply point for mines. Its first name was Warnersville, to commemorate R. V. Warner, one of the first settlers.

TRINIDAD HEAD   Humboldt
On June 11, 1775, Bruno Heceta, the Spanish explorer discovered the point and named it "Puerto de la Trinidad", the feast of the "Santisima Trinidad" (the most holy Trinity). He had entered the bay the day before.

TRINITY COUNTY
Named in honor of the Trinity Sunday when the Spaniards visited this region. Created February 18, 1850, chap. 15. Area 3,191 sq. mi.

TRINITY RIVER   Trinity
Was given the name of Trinidad Bay (Trinity Bay) because it was believed that the river emptied into the bay of same name. When the gold rush of Reading's Bar (1848) happened nobody thought of changing the name of the river. Trinity Mountains take their name after the river.

TRIUNFO   Los Angeles
Spanish "triumph". There are two sources. First possibly named for Jose Miguel Triunfo, one of the grantees of nearby ranch. Second, when the Portola expedition camped on January 13, 1770 on this site the diarist of the expedition named it: "El Triunfo del Dulcisimo Nombre de Jesus" (The triumph of the very sweet name of Jesus). Later on the name was abbreviated under "El Triunfo". The settlement dates from the early 1840's.

TRUCHAS, RIO DE LAS   San Luis Obispo and Monterey
See Nacimiento River.

TULARE   Tulare
Named for Tulare Lake and Valley, named in turn after "Tule" (rushes). The town was founded in 1872 as a division headquarters and repair center of the Southern Pacific Railroad.

TULARE COUNTY
Takes its name from Tulare Lake, named for "Los Tules", a plant with blade-like leaves (scirpus acutus). The word is taken from the Aztec "tullin" (rushes or reeds). Created April 20, 1852, chap. 153. 4,845 sq. mi.

TULARE LAKE   Kings
Pedro Fages, the Governor of California (1782-91) had discovered the lake in 1773 in the course of an expedition. Fages hispanicized "Tulare" as "Los Tules". When Captain Gabriel Moraga visited the place in 1806 he called the canyon "Valle de los Tules".

TULEBURG   San Joaquin
See Stockton.

TULE LAKE   Siskiyou
Was named in 1846 by Fremont, Rhett Lake, until 1900. Tule Lake post office was established in 1900.

TULE RIVER   Tulare and Kings
Rises in the mountains of Tulare county and empties into Lake basin, in Kings county. Named for the profusion of tules growing on its banks. Gabriel Moraga discovered the river October 26, 1806 and named it "Rio de San Pedro". In 1850 we find "Tule River" on Derby's map.

TULARCITOS CREEK AND VALLEY Monterey

As early as 1822 we find records of "Cañada de los Tularcitos". A land grant was named "Tularcitos", apparently deriving from several small ponds invaded with rushes nearby the Tularcitos Creek.

TUNITAS CREEK San Mateo

Spanish diminutive of tuna (prickly Indian fig, or prickly pear cactus). As early as 1839 we find on the plats of the San Gregorio and Cañada Verde grants "Arroyo de las Tunitas", thus named because of the profusion of prickly pears.

UVAS CREEK Santa Clara

Spanish for "grapes". The word was very well used in Spanish times for the sites were wild grapes would grow. The Uvas Creek takes its name from a land grant "Canada de las Uvas" dated June 14, 1842.

UVAS RANCHO, LAS Santa Clara

Spanish for "grapes". Named after a land grant dated June 14, 1842 to Lorenzo Pineda for an area of three leagues. Present city of Zayante is located on the site of the original grant.

VACA CANYON Contra Costa

Named after the Vaca Creek (Cow Creek) which appears on a plat of Rancho Pinole grant of 1865.

VACA STATION Solano

See Elmira.

VACAVILLE Solano

Named for Manuel Vaca born in New Mexico who settled in California in 1841. He was granted 'Las Putas Rancho" in 1843. The town was laid out in 1850 and the township was created November 1, 1852. It was named Vacaville.

VALLECITO

Spanish "little valley" was used as a generic term in Spanish times and was very popular in the names of numerous land grants and titles, as well as geographic places. However, in modern times the name is barely found in California toponymy, as a generic term of "valley" (Valle) but we still find it under its diminutive form "Vallecito".

VALLECITO Calaveras

"Little Valley". The town was the center of a number of mining camps of the 1850's. The name was misspelled "Vallecitas" but it was corrected by all official agencies.

VALLECITO San Diego

In 1846 the troops of General Stephen W. Kearny camped on the site that was known to them as "Bayo Cita", "Bayou Cita", "Vallo Citron" or "Bayeau Chitoes". It was not long before some connoisseurs of the Spanish language would use his ears and interpret "Vallecito". However, the proper spelling, that is "Vallecito" appears on documents in 1848. From 1858 to 1861 Vallecito was an important stage station of the Butterfield Overland stage line.

VALLECITO MOUNTAINS San Diego

Named after the Butterfield Overland stageline station of "Vallecito".

VALLECITOS CREEK San Benito

Named after Vallecitos Canyon.

VALLECITOS DE SAN MARCOS San Diego

Name of a land grant dated April 22, 1840. It is located forty five miles west of the Vallecito Station of the Butterfield Overland Stage Line.

VALLE, DEL Los Angeles

For the Del Valle family. First of which was Antonio del Valle who arrived in 1819. He was granted San Francisco Rancho in 1839.

VALLE DE SAN JOSE Alameda

Is the name of a land grant dated February 23, 1839. (Valle de San José Rancho, Alameda County).

VALLEJO (CITY) Solano

Named for General Mariano Guadalupe Vallejo who founded the present city April 3, 1850. In October 1850 a general state election designated Vallejo as the State Capital. But in 1852 all archives were moved to Sacramento.

VALYERMO Los Angeles

Named by W. C. Petchner, proprietor of the Valyermo Ranch. The name is a coinage of "val" (valley) and "yermo" (desert) 1909. The post office was established in 1912.

VAQUERO

Spanish "cowboy". Commonly used in California place names.

VAQUEROS RANCHO, CAÑADA DE LOS Contra Costa

From a land grant dated February 29, 1844 to Francisco Alviso for an undescribed area.

VASQUEZ ROCKS Los Angeles

In the 1870's a notorious bandit, Tiburcio Vasquez had his hideouts among the rocks and caverns of "Robbers Roost". He was captured and hanged in San Jose in 1875. The Cañon and rocks were named after him.

VEGA Monterey

Spanish for plain or a level ground. The name is derived from the land grant's name "Vega del Rio del Pajaro" (plain of the bird's river), dated April 17, 1820 and June 14, 1833. It was a Southern Pacific Station named when the line reached this place November 27, 1871.

VENADO Colusa and Sonoma

Spanish "deer". The origin of the name of these two localities was given because of the profusion of deer in these areas. The post office for Venado in Colusa county was established in 1890. The post office of Venado in Sonoma county was established in 1921.

VENTANA CONE Monterey

A volcanis cone so called because of an opening in the hills which resembles a "ventana" (window).

VENTURA Ventura

Shortened for San Buenaventura. The first mention of the name is in a letter from Don Jose de Galvez to Father Junipero Serra on September 15, 1768 in which he called the town San Buenaventura. The Portola expedition camped on the site on August 14, 1769 and the diarist named it "La Asuncion de Nuestra Senora" because the following day was the feast of the Virgin Mary. Padre Serra was directed by José de Galvez to name a mission between San Diego and Monterey to commemorate San Buenaventura, a learned prelate of the 13th century. The town was incorporated in 1866.

VENTURA COUNTY

From the Spanish Buenaventura, the name of a mission established on March 31, 1782. (See Ventura, above). Created March 22, 1872, chap. 151.

VENTURA RIVER Shasta and Tehama

See Buenaventura. The name of the river appears in its abbreviated form after 1895.

VERANO, EL Sonoma

Spanish "summer". So named because of the nice climate that surprised the first settlers for its lasting summer.

VERDE

Spanish "green". Was a popular adjective during Spanish times. It has survived in several counties. Loma Verde (Los Angeles); Verde Canyon (Marin). It is found in coinage such as: Anaverde Valley (Los Angeles); Valverde (Riverside); Verdemonte (Verdemont, San Bernardino); etc.

VERDE Y ARROYO DE LA PURISIMA RANCHO, CAÑADA DE
San Mateo
From a land grant dated March 25, 1838 and June 10, 1839 to José M. Alviso for an area of two leagues.

VERDUGO Los Angeles
See Glendale.

VERDUGO CANYON Los Angeles
The name honors José Maria Verdugo who was granted a land on October 20, 1784 and January 12, 1798. He came to California in 1772 as a Spanish soldier; he became a corporal at the San Diego presidio. When he died in 1831 he had become a very prominent ranchero in the area. The mountains "Sierra de los Verdugos", "La Cañada de los Verdugos" are named after the Verdugo family.

VERDUGO CITY Los Angeles
For origin and naming see Verdugo Canyon. Verdugo City was laid out by Harry Fowler in 1925; now it is a part of the city of Glendale (see Glendale).

VERGELES RANCHO, LOS Monterey
Spanish for orchards. From a land grant dated August 2, 1834 and August 28, 1835 to José Joaquin Gomez for an area of two leagues.

VERNAL FALL Yosemite National Park
Spanish "pertaining to spring". Was applied by Dr. L. H. Bunnell of the Mariposa Battalion because of the constant feeling of spring time.

VIBORAS CREEK San Benito
Spanish for vipers. The name derived from "Arroyo de las Viboras", name given to the creek in Mexican times.

VICENTE POINT Los Angeles
Named November 24, 1793 by English explorer Captain Vancouver in honor of Father Vicente Santa Maria, chaplain on the "San Carlos" in 1776. Padre Vicente served at San Francisco, San Antonio and Santa Clara. He was responsible for the founding of Mission San Buenaventura March 31, 1782. It was also spelled Vincente.

LA VIDA SPRINGS Orange
Spanish "life". So named because of the believed special virtues of longevity given by the springs to the area, hence the name "la Vida" (life).

VIEJA, MISSION Los Angeles
This was the old side of the Mission San Gabriel after the mission was built on its present place, five miles away.

VIEJAS VALLEY San Diego
Spanish "old women". From an old plat designated as "Valle de las Viejas" (1845); because when an early Spanish expedition approached the Indian village, all men and young maiden fled leaving only the old women in the place. The Spanish soldiers called the village "The Valley of the old women": The creek, the Indian Reservation and the mountains of this area take their name after the "Valley".

VINA, LA Tahama
Spanish "vineyard". Was the name of the Ranch of Leland Stanford; it was the largest vineyard in the world with an area of 55,000 acres. In November 11, 1885 he conveyed the ranch to Stanford University. The post office was listed in 1880.

VIRGENES RANCHO, LAS Los Angeles
Spanish "the Virgins". From a land grant dated April 6, 1837 to José Maria Dominguez for an area of two leagues. Named after the spring water which was as pure as "virgins".

VISTA

Spanish "view" or "sight". Was used as place name in Spanish times; however, most of the components of the original "vista" are modern applications. Many counties still have "vista" among the generic or specific part of place namings: Vista Robles (Butte), Valle Vista (Contra Costa), Vista del Mar, Vista del Valle (Los Angeles), Sierra Vista (Merced), Valle Vista (Riverside, Vista (San Diego), Chula Vista, Monte Vista, Sunny Vista (San Diego), Vista Grande (San Mateo), Alta Vista (Sonoma). What surprises the most is the combination of the Spanish and American such as for instance: "Sunny Vista" where one can call the "Spanglish."

VISTA   San Diego

"View" or "sight". Named after the Buena Vista Rancho on which the community is located.

VISTA, RIO   Solano

Spanish "river view". The former name for this community was "Brazos del Rio" (Arms of the River). The town was laid out and founded by Colonel N. H. Davis in 1857 on a low point of the Sacremento River. In 1867 a terrible flood destroyed the town and the new town was relocated at its present site.

VITORIA, LA   Los Angeles

See Santa Catalina Island.

VIVORAS, LAS   San Benito

See Oso Flaco Lake and Las Viboras.

VIZCAINO, CAPE   Mendocino

Named after Sebastian Vizcaino (1550-1628) explorer of the North west coast of America. From 1602 to 1603 he was ordered by the Viceroy of Mexico to explore the Gulf of California to find ports for the galleons to find a safe shelter. He reached San Diego Bay on November 10, 1602. He discovered Catalina Island, San Diego and Monterey and named them.

YANKEE HILL   Butte

When the gold rush was at its peak in 1850 a great deal of Mexican and Chilean invaded the site known then as Rich Gulch. Because of the great number of Spanish-speaking miners the town became known as Spanishtown. A decade later when Anglo-Saxons outnumbered the other nationalities the present name was adopted.

YBARRA CANYON   Los Angeles

Named for the Ibarra (Ybarra) family who settled in the Los Angeles area as early as 1814 and was active in community affairs.

YEGUAS

Spanish "mares". A favorite during the Spanish times it has survived in several counties and has been more used than "Caballos, cavallos" (horses). Isla Plana for instance, was called "Isla de la Yegua" (Isle of the mare). As for "cavallo" besides the "Cavallo Point" of Marin county and "Ojo de Caballo" (Contra Costa) we do not find names containing the Spanish word "Caballo".

YERBA BUENA   San Francisco

Spanish "good herb". For the "Micromeria chamissonis". Font was one of the first persons to find this herb in the surroundings of Mountain Lake in San Francisco (March 1776), and later the name was applied to the present city of San Francisco, and kept the old name until March 10, 1847.

YERBA BUENA ISLAND   San Francisco

Spanish "good herb". Island off the northwest tip of the peninsula of San Francisco. Named because it is adjacent to Yerba Buena, the old name for San Francisco. The island was renamed Goat Island but the original name was restored on May 15, 1931.

YERBA BUENA RANCHO   Santa Clara

From a land grant dated November 25, 1833 and February 24, 1840 to Antonio Chabolla for an undescribed area.

YERMO   San Bernardino

Spanish for desert or wilderness. The post office was established in 1908 and adopted the present name. The town was called at that time Otis, changed its name to the present one. The town had previously been named Otis by the San Pedro, Los Angeles and Salt Lake Railroad built its station there.

YGNACIO VALLEY   Contra Costa

Was named for Ygnacio Martinez (Ignacio) "comandante" at the "Presidio de San Francisco" (1822-1827). (Also see Martinez and Pinole).

YORBA LINDA   Orange

It was originally known as San Antonio named after one of the oldest pioneers of California Antonio Yorba. Later on it was changed to "Yorba" and finally in more recent times to "Yorba Linda" for promotional purposes. Antonio Yorba was one of Fages' Catalonian volunteers in 1769. The site is on a land grant of the "Cañon de Santa Ana".

YSIDORA   San Diego

It honors Yisdora Maria Ygnacio Pico, younger sister of Pio Pico and later wife of Juan Forster, the owner of the rancho is 1864. It was named by the railroad company which built the line through this area in 1882.

YUHA PLAIN   Imperial

Was originally called "Pozas de Santa Rosa de las Lajas" (the wells of Santa Rosa's flat rocks" by Juan Bautista de Anza in 1774.

ZACA   Santa Barbara

Spanish "first authorized registry of a sale". Probably comes from La Zaca rancho.

ZACA RANCHO, LA   Santa Barbara

From a land grant of 1838 to Cesareo Lataillade for an undescribed area. The sources as for its meaning differ: 1) It was an Indian drink. 2) The name of a Nahua Chief. 3) The first authorized registry of a sale. 4) Sack. 5) Peace. There is also a Zaca Creek.

ZAMORA   Yolo

Apparently it was named after the name of a province and city in Spain. The former name was "Blacks". The name was changed to Zamora in 1910.

ZANJA, ZANJON

Spanish "ditch, trench, drain, a deep ditch, a large drain, a channel," a term often used in Spanish times. The name appears on land grants and titles; it is also spelled "Sanjon". The terms appear in the following counties: Alameda, Fresno, Los Angeles, Merced, Monterey, San Bernardino, Santa Barbara.

ZANJA, LA   Los Angeles

The San Rafael grant was first called La Zanja.

ZANJA COTA CREEK   Santa Barbara

As early as 1795 we find in documents "La Zanja que llaman de Cota" (PSP, XIII, 28) (the deep ditch or channel which is called Cota's). It is named after the Cota family. The name is mispelled as Santa Cora, and appears also as Santa Cota.

ZANJA CREEK   San Bernardino

It was the Mission Indian in 1819 who dug the big ditch which runs through Redlands, to divert water from Mill Creek. It was named "La Zanja".

ZANJA PEAK   San Bernardino

Was named after the creek.

ZANJONES RANCHO   Monterey
  From a land grant of 1839 to Gabriel de la Torre for an area of one and a half leagues.

ZUNIGA SHOAL   San Diego
  As early as 1782 we find on documents "Barros de Zúñiga" for the shoal outside San Diego Harbor.
  It was named after Jose Zúñiga, an officer of the San Diego Company from 1781 to 1793.

ZUNIGA POINT
  See above.

CHRONOLOGICAL INDEX OF SPANISH INFLUENCE IN CALIFORNIA ONOMASTICS

1510   California is mentioned for the first time as a fictitious place in Montalvo's *Las Sergas de Esplandian.*

1533   The pilot Fortuno Ximenes (Jimenez) discovers an island, Baja California (Lower California) west of Mexico. He is killed while trying to land.

1535   On May 5 Cortes lands where Jimenez was killed. He visits the region and calls it "Santa Cruz". He names the country California.

1539   While surveying the shores of the Gulf of California (known as "Sea of Cortes) Francisco Ulloa misses the mouth of the Colorado River. At the end of his exploration he finds out that "Baja California" is not an island but a peninsula.

1540   Hernando de Alarcon discovers the Colorado River. In the same time Melchior Diaz crosses Arizona and Colorado River, near Yuma. They were the first white men to set foot in "Alta California".

1541   Bolanos explores "Baja California".

1542   Juan Rodriguez Cabrillo enters San Diego Bay, September 28, he names it "San Miguel". He discovers the islands off California, Santa Monica, Point Concepcion, and Monterey Bay.

1543   Death of Cabrillo. He is buried on a California island. Ferrelo is sent to explore northernmost California.

1579   Francis Drake enters a California Bay (Drake's Bay) to career the "Golden Hind", June 15. He takes the land for Queen Elizabeth and claims "Nova Albion".

1587   Unamuno visits Morro Bay.

1595   Cermeno enters Drake's Bay.

1602   Sebastian Vizcaino visits San Miguel Bay, November 10 and renames it San Diego de Alcala. He surveys San Pedro and on December 16 anchors in Monterey Bay.

1613   Torquemada continues to assert in *Monarquia Indiana* that California is an island.

1697   The first Spanish mission is established by a Jesuit, Father Juan Maria Salvatierra, at Loreta. This is considered as the first white permanent colony in Baja California.

1701   Father Eusebio Francisco Kino crosses Colorado River (November 21) into California and demonstrates thus that California is a peninsula.

1713   Birth of Junipero Serra.

1721   Birth of Juan Crespi.

1722   Birth of Francisco Palou.

1723   Birth of Gaspar de Portola.

1728   Birth of Felipe de Neve.

1730   Birth of Pedro Fages.

1735   Birth of Anza.

1738   Birth of Francisco Garces.

1746   Another explorer Consag proves that California is not an island.

1747	Birth of Felipe de Goycoechea.
1750	Birth of Jose Joaquin de Arrillaga.
1754	Birth of Jose Dario Arguello.
1757	Venegas publishes *Noticia de la California*.
1761	Birth of Pablo Vicente de Sola.
1765	Birth of Galvez, Visitador-General.
1765	Birth of Gabriel Moraga.
1767	King Carlos III, of Spain, issues decree banishing Jesuits from all Spanish colonies.
1768	Father Junipero Serra arrives at Loredo with 16 Franciscan monks; they take over the Jesuit missions in Baja California.
1769	Two Spanish ships arrive at San Diego Bay with supplies for the colony (April). A group of settlers and soldiers under Governor Gaspar de Portola, Captain Fernando de Rivera y Moncada and Father Junipero Serra, come overland from Baja California (May-June). The first mission, "Mision San Diego de Alcala" is founded by Father Serra (July 16). Portola visits Los Angeles area (August 2), he travels northward. On November 2, Jose Artego arrives at San Francisco Bay.
1770	"La Mission San Carlos de Monterey" is founded by Father Junipero Serra (June 3). This mission will be renamed "San Carlos Borromeo de Carmelo in 1771 after being removed to another site.
1770	Pedro Fages, "Comandante militar" of Alta California (1770-74).
1771	Foundation of "Mision San Antonio de Padua" and "Mision San Gabriel Arcangel". Felipe de Barri, governor of the Californias (1771-74).
1772	Captain Pedro Fages leaves Monterey to explore San Francisco Bay (March 20). He discovers the Tejon Pass. Fages and his companions are the first white men to see San Joaquin and Sacramento Valleys. Father Junipero Serra founds the "Mision San Luis Obispo de Tolosa" September 1.
1773	Viceroy Bucareli's "Reglamento" for California. Father Francisco Palou marks with a cross the Baja and Alta California boundary thirty miles south of the present Mexican border (August 19).
1774	Juan Bautista de Anza's first expedition to reach San Gabriel Mission from Sonora by overland route. Rivera y Moncada, "comandante militar" of Alta California (1774-77).
1775	Juan Manuel de Ayala on board of the ship "San Carlos" is the first white man to enter San Francisco Bay, August 1. Monterey becomes capital of California by royal decree (August 16). San Diego Mission is attacked by 800 Indians, Father Luis Jaume is killed (November 4). While en route from Sonora to San Francisco with Anza's colonists a woman gives birth to her son, Salvator Ignacio Linares who will be the first white child born in California (December 24). Heceta and Don Juan de la Bodega y Quadra explore the coastline. Felipe de Neve, Governor of the Californias (1775-82).
1776	On March 28, Anza and his colonists reach the site of San Francisco. On September 17 the Presidio of San Francisco is founded. The missions of San Francisco de Asis (Dolores) and San Juan Capistrano are founded. Escalante and Dominguez open the trail from Santa Fe to the Colorado River. Birth of Narciso Duran.
1777	"La Mision Santa Clara" is founded, January 12. "San José de Guadalupe", first pueblo in California is founded November 29. Monterey made capital of the Californias by Felipe de Neve.
1778	Birth of Alexander Forbes.

1779	Governor Felipe de Neve issues "El Reglamento", (regulations for government) for California, June 1. The site of Santa Clara log mission moved. Birth of Jean Louis Vignes.
1780	The Mission San Diego is rebuilt following an Indian attack. The non-Indian population reaches 600.
1781	Los Angeles is founded, September 4.
1782	"La Mision San Buenaventura" is founded, March 31. Pedro Fages, governor of California (1782-91). The presidio of Santa Barbara is established.
1783	Birth of Carlos Antonio Carrillo (1783-1852). Completion of the Mission San Diego Quadrangle.
1784	Father Junipero Serra dies (August 28) and is buried at San Carlos Borromeo Mission. Father Palou is named head of Alta California mission. Birth of Luis Antonio Arguello (1784-1830).
1785	Father Lasuen named head of Alta California missions (1785-1803). Birth of Garcia Diego y Moreno (1785-1846).
1786	Foundation of "La Mision Santa Clara". Jean Francois Galaup de la Perouse visits Monterey.
1787	Father Fermin Francisco de Lasuen founds four missions: Santa Barbara, La Purisima Concepcion, Santa Cruz, and La Soledad (1786-91). La Pérouse's *Voyage* . . . is published. Palou's *Life of Serra* . . . is published.
1790	Death of Palou.
1790	Constanso journal published in English.
1791	Romeu, governor (1791-92). Birth of Concepcion Arguello (1791-1857). Malaspina visits Monterey. John Graham (Groeham) first American to reach Monterey, dies the same day (Sept. 13).
1792	Captain George Vancouver of the RN, on board of his sloop "Discovery" reaches San Francisco (November 14). Arrillaga, governor of California (1792-94). Birth of Jose Figueroa (1792-1835).
1793	The pueblo of Branciforte is founded on the site of Santa Cruz. The Missions San Carlos (Carmel) and Santa Cruz are begun. Vancouver's second visit to California.
1794	Vancouver's third and final visit to California. Birth of George Yount (1794-1865). Borica, governor of California (1794-1800). The Castillo de San Joaquin fort is built in San Francisco. The Royal Presidio Chapel of Monterey is built.
1795	The mission of Santa Cruz quadrangle is completed.
1796	The Yankee skipper, Ebenezer Dorr, brings his ship, the "Otter" into Monterey Bay; it was the first U.S. vessel to anchor in California.
1797	Foundation of the Missions San Jose, San Juan Bautista, San Miguel Arcangel, San Fernando Rey de Francia (1797-1798).
1798	Vancouver published *A Voyage of Discovery*. Birth of James P. Beckwourth (1798-1867). Birth of Augustin Zamorano (1798-1842).
1799	Birth of Henry Delano Fitch (1799-1849); of John Marsh (1799-1856); of Jean Jacques Vioget (1799-1855).
1800	Arrillaga, governor of California (1800-14). Birth of Juan Bautista Alvarado (1800-82); of Juan Bandini (1800-59); of Peter Lassen (1800-59). The non-Indian population of Los Angeles is 140.
1801	Birth of Pio Pico (1801-94). The first de la Guerra settles in Santa Barbara.

1802	Birth of Alonzo Delano (1802-74).

1803   Father de Lasuen dies at Mision San Carlos (June 26). Tapis is named head of California missions. La Mision San Diego is destroyed by an earthquake.

1804   California is divided into Baja California and Alta California. Monterey is made capital of Alta California. Arrillaga is first governor of Alta California. Mission Santa Ines (Ynez) is founded.

1805   Completion of the Mission San Gabriel. Gabriel Moraga begins his explorations.

1806   Completion of the missions San Juan Capistrano and San Fernando. Moraga names the Merced River. Boscana's missionary career (1806-31). Nikolai Petrovich Rezanof visits San Francisco to buy supplies for the Russian trading post at Sitka.

1807   Langsdorff makes drawings of the bay area.

1808   Shaler's "Journal", on California is published in the U.S.A. Birth of Mariano Guadalupe Vallejo (1808-90).

1809   Completion of Mission San Jose de Guadalupe. The Russians settle Bodega Bay. Birth of Kit Carson (1809-68).

1810   Birth of Jose Castro (1810-60); Mexican revolts against Spain.

1811   San Joaquin and Sacramento rivers are explored for the first time by water (October 15). Kuskov begins Russian settlement.

1812   Fort Ross Russian trading post is established less than 100 miles north of San Francisco. Missions Santa Barbara, La Purisma Concepcion, San Buenaventura, and San Juan Capistrano destroyed by earthquake. Mission San Juan Bautista is dedicated.

1813   Mission San Antonio de Padua completed; Mission San Diego is built. Birth of John C. Fremont (1813-90); Jose Vallejo (1813-76).

1814   Arguello, governor (1814-15); John Gilroy becomes California's first non-Hispanic settler. Birth of Jose Sadock Alemany (1814-88).

1815   Dedication of mission San Luis Rey; San Antonio de Pala "asistencia" is established; de Sola, governor (1815-22).

1816   Thomas Doak lands from the "Albatross" near Santa Barbara and becomes the first American settler of California. Kotzebue starts his expedition.

1817   La Mision San Rafael Arcangel is founded, December 14. La Mision Santa Ines is dedicated; birth of Domingo Ghirardelli (1817-94).

1818   Completion of La Mision San Miguel; building of la Mision San Rafael and Santa Ysabela "asistencia". Birth of Lola Montez (1818-61). The French privateer Hippolyte de Bouchard with two of his ships of war enters Monterey Bay and captures the city, and sacks it, November 22. He continues to attack other coast towns, but resisted at San Diego he sails away.

1819   Birth of Francisco Arce (1819-78); Louise Amelia Knapp Smith, "Dame Shirley" (1819-1906).

1820   The non-Indian population of Alta California is 3,270. The population of Los Angeles is 650. The population of missions 20,500 Neophytes (Indian slaves). Birth of George Hearst (1820-91).

1821   Augustin Iturbide leads rebel army into Mexico City. He becomes the ruler. Mexico achieves independence from Spain. Luis Arguello makes his first extensive exploration of Sacramento Valley (October).

1822   Iturbide is proclaimed Emperor of Mexico (1822-23); California formally proclaimed province of Empire of Mexico (September 26). First provincial legislature elected and meets in Monterey. Luis Antonio Arguello, first native-born California governor elected (1822-25).

1823   Mission San Francisco Solano (Sonoma), the 21st and last of Alta California missions founded.

1824   Abdication of Emperor Iturbide and establishment of the Republic of Mexico (January 7). Birth of Jessie Fremont (1824-1902).

1825   California formally becomes a territory of the Mexican Republic (March 26). Mission Santa Clara finally completed. Echeandia, governor (1825-31). Duran named head of California missions (1825-27).

1826   Captain Frederick W. Beechey explores San Francisco Bay aboard the "Blossom", November 6. Jedediah S. Smith, with trappers, arrives at Mision San Gabriel: they are the first Americans to make an overland trip to California (November 27). Zamorano prints wood blocks without a press.

1828   Jedediah Smith discovers the Yuba River.

1829   Revolt of Joaquin Solis.

1830   Population of California non-Indians 4,256.

1831   Victoria, governor (January 31, December 6); Pio Pico, Juan Bandini and Jose Antonio Carrillo lead a revolt against Governor Manuel Victoria, forcing his resignation. Battle at Cahuenga Pass. Echeandia, governor, (1831-33).

1832   Pio Pico, governor (Jan-Feb); Zamorano, de facto governor in north (Feb. 1832 - Jan. 1833).

1833   Figueroa, governor (1833-35). Mexican Congress decrees secularization of missions, (completed in 1837). Joseph Walker and Zenas Leonard lead first white men westward through the Sierra Nevada.

1834   September 1, two hundred Mexican colonists arrive at San Diego from San Blas. Hijar and Padres colonizing plan. Zamorano acquires the first printing press in California.

1835   Jose Castro, governor (Oct. 1835-Jan. 1836); Figueroa "Manifiesto". William A. Richardson settles in Yerba Buena. Los Angeles becomes a city (May 23). Algerez Mariano G. Vallejo founds the presidio and pueblo at Mision San Francisco Solano. The settlement is named "Sonoma". The Mexican government receives an offer from the United States to buy California.

1836   Gutierez, governor (Jan. 2-May 1); Mariano Chic, governor (May 1-July 30); Guttierez, governor (July 30-December 9); Alvarado, governor (1836-42). Alvarado and "La deputacion" declare California a "Free and sovereign State" (the new "country" will remain free state for eight months). Belcher leads a naval expedition into California. Dana leaves California.

1837   Carlos Antonio Carrillo is appointed governor but he is unable to assume his office. La Place visits California.

1838   The first child born in San Francisco is Rosalia Leese.

1839   Jean Auguste (John Augustus) Sutter, a Swiss, lands in San Francisco. He is a prosperous businessman. In 1840 he acquires eleven square leagues of land, comprising New Helvetia, and builds Sutter's Fort. In 1841 he acquires Fort Ross, ending Russian encroachment in California. Vioget surveys San Francisco.

1840   The "Tribunal de Justicia" (First Supreme Court of California) is formed, March 10. Arrest of Isaac Graham, American trapper settled in California (April 7), is followed by imprisonment of all "foreigners" not married to California women. Graham is finally acquitted of treason and released, June 1841. The non-Indian population of California is 6,000. The mission San Francisco Solano (Sonoma) is built as a parish chapel.

1841   The first U.S. scientific expedition under the leadership of Wilkes arrives in San Francisco (August 14, 1841). The first reports confirms the discovery of gold found in the American River. The first overland immigrants train (Bidwell-Bartleson party), from midwestern U.S. arrives in California. Leidesdorff lands in San Francisco.

1842	Micheltorena, governor (1842-45). Discovery of gold in Santa Feliciana (Placerita Canyon), March 9, by Francisco Lopez, sheepherder. Twenty ounces of god dust are sent to Philadelphia mint, November 22, by Abel Stearns and Alfred Robinson. Commodore Thomas Catesby Jones, U.S.N., seizes Monterey and raises the American flag, Oct. 19. He departs two days later.

1843   Thomas Larkin becomes the first U.S. consul appointed to California. (1843-46).

1844   Captain John Charles Fremont, U.S. Army, arrives at Sutter's Fort (March 8). Fremont discovers Lake Tahoe. Duflot de Mofras publishes *Exploration*. Californians revolt forces Governor Micheltorena's abdication. (November 14). First wagon train over Truckee and Donner Lake route reaches Sutter's Fort.

1845   Further immigration of Americans to California is forbidden by the Mexican Government. Marshall arrives in California. Mary Peterson and James Williams, both from Missouri are the first Americans to be wed in California. Pio Pico, governor (1845-46).

1846   Flores, governor (October 31, 1846-Jan. 11, 1847). March 6, Fremont raises the American flag on Gabilan Peak, near Monterey. He retreats to Sutter's Fort. May 13, War between U.S. and Mexico declared. June 3, Colonel Stephen W. Kearny is ordered to march to California from Santa Fe and take command of U.S. forces there. Fremont takes command of Bear Flag revolt on July 5, declaring California's independence. June 10-July 9, the Bear Flag of "California Republic" is raised at Sonoma. July 9 - U.S. flag is raised in Yerba Buena and Sonoma. July 29, 1846 - January 1847 - Stockton, military governor. July 31 - Mormon colonist led by Brannan arrive in Yerba Buena. August 13 - Stockton and Fremont seize Los Angeles. August 15 - The *"California"*, the first California newspaper is published in Monterey, September 2 - Fremont appointed military commander of California. September 23 - The American garrison at Los Angeles is attacked by rebellious Californians. A general uprising led by Captain Jose Maria Flores follows. Ride of Juan Flaco Brown (September 24-28). Battle of San Pasqual (Dec. 6); Pauma Massacre. Fremont names the Golden Gate. Washington A. Bartlett, first American "alcalde" of San Francisco. The Donner party of immigrants halted by heavy snows at Donner Lake; 39 of them died.

1847   Last battle of rebellion won by U.S. forces at "La Mesa", January 9. Cahuenga Capitulation Treaty signed January 13. Yerba Buena is renamed San Francisco in January. John C. Fremont becomes the first American governor of California (Jan. 19 - March 1); he is replaced by Kearny (March 1 - May 31), who is replaced in turn by Mason (May 31, 1847) - Feb. 28, 1849).

1848   James Wilson Marshall while building a sawmill for Sutter on the American River, discovers gold (jan. 24). This is the beginning of the California "gold-rush". The Treaty of Guadalupe Hidalgo is signed, Feb. 2, ending the war with Mexico. The United States acquires California, New Mexico, Nevada, Utah, most of Arizona and part of Colorado. Sutter's son founds the town of Sacramento (Oct. 14). The first U.S. post office in California is established in San Francisco (Nov. 9). The white population of California reaches 15,000. Bryant publishes *What I Saw in California*. Fremont writes his *Geographical Memoir*. February 28 - the "California" first steamer to bring "gold-rush-passengers" enters San Francisco with 365 passengers.

1849   Persifor Smith, military governor (Feb. 28 - April 12); replaced by Bennet Riley (April 12 - Dec. 20). First civil governor (Dec. 20, 1849 - January 9, 1851). Constitutional Convention (Sept. - Nov.); state government activated prior to admission to Union (1850). San Jose is made capital of California. First great fire of San Francisco which destroyed fifty houses, December 24.

1850   The immigrant party of Jayhawkers reach San Francisquito Ranch after a great ordeal in Death Valley (Feb. 4). Creation of original 27 counties (Feb. 18). A law to protect the Indians is passed by the Legislature (April 22). Sacramento squatters' riot (August 14). President Fillmore signs act of Congress admitting California as the 31st state of the union (Sept. 9). California population (U.S. Census) 92,597.

1851   Capital moved to Vallejo. Nevada and Placer counties founded. Garra Revolt. Santa Clara University founded.

1852   State population: 255,000. Sierra County founded.

1853	Benicia becomes state capital. Alameda and San Bernardino counties founded. San Quentin prison opened. David Belasco (1853-1931).
1854	Sacramento made capital of the state, Feb. 25. Plumas County founded. Fort Tejon founded. Ridge writes *Joaquin Murieta.*
1855	Merced County founded.
1856	San Mateo County founded.
1857	Del Norte County founded.
1861	Mono County founded.
1872	Ventura County founded.
1874	San Benito County founded. Tiburcio Vasquez is captured.
1875	Pacheco, governor (Feb. 27-Dec. 9).
1893	Madera County founded.
1926	Mission Santa Clara burned down.
1931	High Sierra Wilderness Area established. Goat Island is renamed Yerba Buena.
1950	Population of State, 10,586,223; Los Angeles 1,970,358; San Francisco 775,357.
1963	Alcatraz prison closed.
1964	Bracero program ended.
1966	Chavez forms United Farm Workers Organizing Committee.
1968	San Onofre Nuclear Generating Station opened.
1970	Population: State 19,953,134; Los Angeles 2,809,813; San Francisco 715,674.
1980	Population: State 23,668,562; Los Angeles 2,966,763; San Francisco 678,974.

GLOSSARY OF SPANISH AND MEXICAN WORDS

ALCALDE

Leading civil officer of local government in a Spanish (and later Mexican) municipality. He was a combination of a mayor and justice of the peace. The office was established in California by the "Reglamento" (1779) of Governor Felipe de Neve.

ARROBA

A Spanish measure of weight equal to 25.37 pounds; a liquid measure equal to 4.26 gallons.

ASISTENCIA

Outlying branch of a mission but without a resident priest. The five establishments created by the Spanish served the missions of San Luis Obispo, San Luis Rey, San Deigo, Los Angeles, and San Francisco.

AUDIENCIA

In colonial epoch, Mexico supreme court was called an "Audiencia". The chief administrative authority comprehended a "presidente" and four justices, in the absence of the viceroy. In California a similar judicial body held a comparable executive power.

AYUNTAMIENTO

Was created as a colonial measure by the "Reglamento" (1779) of Governor Felipe de Neve. (1728-1784). It was a board of municipal officers including the "alcalde" and two "regidores" appointed by the governor. Later on the number was increased to twelve elected members. Their jurisdiction was restricted to the "pueblo" and dealt with schools, hospitals, sanitations, streets and prisons. The "Comissionado", the governor's military representative was supervising them.

BARRIO

"City Ward" or "District". Most recently it referred to urban areas considered to be ghettos of Spanish-speaking people.

BRACEROS

Spanish meaning strong-armed ones. Migratory workers who were the principal source of agricultural labor in the state until 1964. They were Mexican workers brought to the U.S. under Public Law 78 of the U.S. Congress (1951).

CALIFORNIOS

Persons of Spanish or Mexican heritage born in California or resident of California. This term was mostly used from 1830-1846.

DIPUTACION

In 1836 the first Mexican Constitution created the local legislature called Diputacion. The elected members were merely advisers to the governor; they did not have the power of independent legislators.

DISENO

Topographic sketch to define the boundaries of a "rancho" requested as a grant by an applicant. This document was presented to the Mexican governor of California.

DON

Spanish title derived from Latin "Dominus" for "Lord" was generously applied during the period of Mexican rule to any gentleman in California, of important standing such as landowners or "Rancheros".

EJIDO

A tract of public land belonging to a pueblo and intended for the use of its residents.

ENCOMIENDA

In New Spain colonies the soldiers who came there were given a grant of Indian labor bestowed in return for the aid of the grantee (encomendero) for conversion of the Indians. In Spain it was a grant from the Crown giving manorial rights over land seized from the Moors to Knights who had helped wrest those lands for Spain.

ESTANCIA
There were eleven "estancias" founded between 1785 and 1840. An "estancia" was a ranch for livestock operated by the missions at some distance from their settlement. Several of them included chapels.

FANEGA
A Spanish measure of grain equal to 1.58 U.S. bushels; a Mexican land measure equal to 8.81 acres. A "fanega" contained 12 almuds".

GABRIELENO
Indians of Shoshonean stock whose Spanish name derives from the fact that they were neophytes of Mission San Gabriel.

GACHUPIN
Nickname given by the Mexicans for men born in Spain. The term is used pejoratively to suggest smug superiority.

GENTE DE RAZON
Spanish term for colonials who were not Indians; they included "mestizos' and "mulattoes".

HACIENDA
Spanish for "landed property" commonly used in Mexico but rarely in California where the usual term was "rancho" indicating a farm on which one raised livestock rather than an estate on which one grew crops.

JUANENO
Indians of Shoshonean stock who derive their name from Mission San Juan Capistrano.

LUISENO
Indians who lived in present Riverside County and derived their name from Mission San Luis Rey. On their Rincon, La Jolla and Pauma reservations, they have preserved some of the old customs. They are notorious for their Pauma Massacre (1846).

MATANZA
Spanish word for "slaughter", the killing of cattle. The animals were killed by "vaqueros" riding through the herds and slitting the beasts' throats.

PACHUCO
Pejorative applied in the 1940's to young Mexican men accused of gang activities in Los Angeles and other urban areas.

PADRES
"Fathers" applied to men in religious orders who, in early California, were Franciscans, the founder of the missions.

POBLADOR
Word for founder or settler of a pueblo.

PRESIDIOS
There were four of them: San Diego (1769), Monterey (1770), San Francisco (1776), and Santa Barbara (1782). Each had a chapel, and 400 soldiers. They were military fortifications in charge of the protection of missions and neighboring pueblos.

PROVINCIAS INTERNAS
A frontier region that included Mexico, Texas, and the Californias. Felipe de Neve became Comandante General de las Provincias Internas in 1782.

PUEBLOS
During Spanish times in California, "pueblos" were the earliest towns with civil governments. The towns attracted "pobladores" (settlers) by granting them land and supplies. Each town was governed by a civil officer, an "alcalde" and a board, an "ayuntamiento".

RANCHERIA
Special settlement for Indians sponsored by a mission but lying some distance from it. It served as a kind

of Indian reservation with a church but did not include (necessarily) cultivated land. The term is still used for Indian reservations in California.

RANCHOS
Were large landholdings granted to individuals during Spanish and Mexican rule. They were presented as a reward for loyal service or as a means of attracting settlers to underdeveloped areas.

REGIDOR
Councilman in the Spanish system of local government; he served with the leading civil officer, the "alcalde", on the municipal board, the "Ayuntamiento".

SERRANO
Shoshonean Indians of several groups; one named Tejon, another called Serrano, meaning "sierrans" or "mountaineers". They lived in and south of present Kern County.

VARA
Spanish measurement equal approximately to 33 inches, used in description of land in California.

VISITADOR-GENERAL
Title of an officer appointed by the King or Queen of Spain to conduct a formal inspection of a province, and thus oversee a viceroy.

WAPPO
Indian tribe whose area centered on the Napa Valley.

WASHO
Indians of the Hokan linguistic family whose territory centered on Lake Tahoe. They were excellent basket makers.

WETBACKS
Pejorative term for Mexican nationals who illegally enter the U.S., so called because many of them swam across the Rio Grande. They are to be distinguished from the "braceros" whose entry and work have been legally arranged by an American employer.

BIBLIOGRAPHY

Adams, Ramon F.,: A Dictionary of the Range, Cow Camp and Trail. (University of Oklahoma Press, Norman, (Oklahoma), 1944.)

Bancroft, Hubert Howe: Chronicles of the Builders of the Commonwealth. 8 volumes. (The History Company, San Francisco, 1891-1892.)

Bancroft, Hubert Howe: History of California. 7 volumes. (A. L. Bancroft and Co., San Francisco, California, 1884.)

Bancroft, Hubert Howe: History of the North Mexican States and Texas. 2 volumes. (A. L. Bancroft & Company, San Francisco, Vol. I, 1884; Vol. 2, 1889.)

Bancroft, Hubert Howe: History of the Northwest Coast. 2 volumes. (A. L. Bancroft & Company, San Francisco, 1884.)

Bartlett, John Russell, United States Commissioner: Personal Narrative of Explorations and Incidents in Texas, New Mexico, California, Sonora and Chihuahua, Connected with the United States and Mexican Boundary Commission, During the Years 1850, '51, '52, '53. 2 volumes. (D. Appleton & Company, New York; Le Count & Strong, San Francisco, 1854.)

Beechey, Frederick William: Narrative of a Voyage to the Pacific and Beering's Strait, Etc., etc., etc. 2 volumes. (Henry Colburn and Richard Bentley, London, 1831.)

Book of Saints. Compiled by the Benedictine Monks of St. Augustine's Abbey, Ramsgate. (A. & C. Black, Ltd., London, 1921.)

Brewer, William H.: Up and Down California in 1860-1864: The Journal of William H. Brewer, Professor of Agriculture in the Sheffield Scientific School from 1864 to 1903. Edited by Francis P. Farquhar, with a preface by Russell H. Chittenden. (Yale University Press, New Haven, 1930.)

Brown, John Jr., and Boyd, James: History of San Bernardino and Riverside Counties. 3 volumes. (The Western Historical Association, the Lewes Publishing Company, Chicago, Illinois, 1922.)

Brown, Thomas P.: California Names: Their History and Meaning. (American Trust Company, San Francisco, 1934.)

Caballeria, Juan, Rev. Father: History of San Bernardino Valley from the Padres to the Pioneers, 1810-1851. (Times-Index Press, San Bernardino, Cal., 1902.)

California: A Guide to the Golden State: Compiled and written by the Federal Writers' Project of the Works Progress Administration for the State of California. American Guide Series. (Hastings House, New York, 1939.)

Chapman, Charles E.: A History of California: The Spanish Period. (The MacMillan Company, New York, 1925.)

Coues, Elliott: On the Trail of a Spanish Pioneer: The Diary and Itinerary of Francisco Garces. 2 volumes. (Francis P. Harper, New York, 1900.)

Cowan, Robert Ernest: A Bibliography of the History of California and the Pacific West, 1510-1906. (The Book Club of California, San Francisco, 1914.)

Coy, Owen C.: California County Boundaries. (California Historical Survey Commission, Berkeley, California, 1923.)

Curry, C. F.: California Blue Book or State Roster: 1907. (State Printing Office, Sacramento.)

Dictionary of American Biography. Published under the auspices of American Council of Learned Societies. Edited by Allen Johnson. 20 volumes. (Charles Scribner's Sons, New York, 1943.)

Drake, C. M.: California Names and Their Literal Meanings. (Jones Book and Printing Co., Los Angeles, Cal., 1893.)

Duarte, Feliz I.: Diccionario de Mejicanismos. Segunda edicion. (Herrero Hermanos, Editores, Mejico, 1898.)

Farquhar, Francis P.: Place Names of the High Sierra. (Sierra Club, San Francisco, 1926.)

Forbes, A. S. C., Mrs.: California Missions and Landmarks: El Camino Real. Eighth edition. (Mrs. A. S. C. Forbes, Los Angeles, California, 1925.)

Frenchman in the Gold Rush, A. The journal of Ernest de Massey, Argonaut of 1849. Translated by Marguerite Eyer Wilbur. (California Historical Society, San Francisco, 1927.)

Gannett, Henry: The Origin of Certain Place Names in the United States. U. S. Geological Survey Department, Bulletin 258. (Government Printing Office, Washington, D.C., 1905.)

Gazeteer of the Mountains of the State of California. (Compiled by Edward M. Douglas, Map Information Service, Federal Board of Surveys and Maps, Washington, 1929.)

Gidney, C. M.; Brooks, Benjamin; and Sheridan, Edwin M.: History of Santa Barbara, San Luis Obispo and Ventura Counties, California. 2 volumes. (The Lewis Publishing Company, Chicago, 1917.)

Glasscock, C. B.: Gold in Them Hills. (The Bobbs-Merrill Company, Indianapolis, 1932.)

Glimpses of Our National Monuments. United States Department of the Interior, National Park Service. (Government Printing Office, Washington, D.C., 1932.)

Gregory, Tom: History of Solano and Napa Counties, California. (Historic Record Company, Los Angeles, California, 1912.)

Gregory, Tom: History of Yolo County, California. (Historic Record Company, Los Angeles, 1913.)

Gudde, Erwin G.: California Place Names: A Geographical Dictionary. University of California Press, Berkeley and Los Angeles, 1949.)

Guinn, J. M.: Historical and Biographical Record of Southern California. (The Chapman Publishing Company, Chicago, 1902.)

Guinn, J. M.: History and Biographical Record of Monterey and San Benito Counties. (Historic Record Company, Los Angeles, 1910.)

Guinn, J. M.: A History of California and an Extended History of its Southern Coast Counties; Also Containing Biographies of Well-Known Citizens of the Past and Present. (Historic Record Company, Los Angeles, California, 1907.)

Guinn, J. M.: History of the State of California and Biographical Record of San Joaquin Valley. (The Chapman Publishing Company, Chicago, 1905.)

Handbook of American Indians North of Mexico. Edited by Frederick Webb Hodge. Smithsonian Institution, Bureau of American Ethnology, Bulletin 30. (Government Printing Office, Washington, D.C., 1912.)

Hanna, Phil Townsend: California Through Four Centuries: A Handbook of Memorable Historical Dates. (Farrar & Rinehart, Inc., New York, 1935.)

Hart, James D.: The Oxford Companion to American Literature. (Oxford University Press, New York, 1941.)

Hill, Robert T.: Southern California Geology and Los Angeles Earthquakes. (Southern California Academy of Sciences, Los Angeles, 1928.)

History of Contra Costa County, California. (W. A. Slocum & Co., San Francisco, 1882.)

History of Humboldt County, California. (Wallace W. Elliott & Co., San Francisco, 1881.)

History of Marin County, California. (Alley, Bowen & Co., San Francisco, Cal., 1880.)

History of Mendocino County, California. (Alley, Bowen & Co., San Francisco, Cal., 1880.)

History of Merced County, California. (Elliott and Moore, San Francisco, 1881.)

History of Napa and Lake Counties, California. (Slocum, Bowen & Co., San Francisco, Cal., 1881.)

History of Nevada. (Thompson & West, Oakland, 1881.)

History of Sacramento County, California. Edited by G. Walter Reed. (Historic Record Company, Los Angeles, California, 1923.)

History of San Mateo County, California. (B. F. Alley, San Francisco, 1883.)

History of Solano County. (Wood, Alley & Co., East Oakland, San Francisco, Ca., 1897.)

History of Sonoma County, Including its Geology, Topography, Mountains, Valleys, and Streams. (Alley, Bowen & Co., San Francisco, 1880.)

History of Sutter County, California. (Thompson & West, Oakland, 1879.)

Hoffman, Ogden: Reports of Land Cases Determined in the United States District Court for the Northern District of California. June Term, 1853 to June 1858, Inclusive. (Numa Hubert, San Francisco, 1862.)

Hoover, Mildred Brooke: Historic Spots in California: Counties of the Coast Range. (Stanford University Press, Stanford University, California, 1937.)

Johnson, Philip: Lost and Living Cities of the California Gold Rush. (Automobile Club of Southern California, Los Angeles, 1948.)

King, Elmer R.: Handbook of Historical Landmarks of California. (Elmer R. King, Los Angeles, Ca., 1938.)

Knowlton, Charles S.: Post Offices of Orange County, California, Past and Present. (Fullerton, Calif., 1947.)

Kroeber, A. L.: California Place Names of Indian Origin. University of California Publications in American Archaeology and Ethnology, Vol. 12, No. 2, June 15, 1916. (University of California Press, Berkeley, California, 1916.)

Kroeber, A. L.: Handbook of the Indians of California. Smithsonian Institution, Bureau of American Ethnology Bulletin 78. (Government Printing Office, Washington, 1925.)

Lardner, W. B. and Brock, M. J.: History of Placer and Nevada Counties, California. (Historic Record Company, Los Angeles, California, 1924.)

Lee, Bourke: Death Valley Men. (The MacMillan Company, New York, 1932.)

Lloyd, Elwood, IV: Californalogy (Knowledge of California). A compilation of more than 1,500 Spanish, Indian and unusual names found on the maps of California, together with information concerning their meaning, pronunciation, and history. (Hartwell Publishing Corp., Hollywood, Calif., 1930.)

McArthur, Lewis A.: Oregon Geographic Names. (Oregon Historical Society, Portland, 1944.)

McComish, Charles Davis and Lambert, Rebecca T., Mrs.: History of Colusa and Glenn Counties, California. (Historic Record Company, Los Angeles, 1918.)

McNary, Laura Kelly: California Spanish and Indian Place Names: Their Pronunciation, Meaning and Location. (Wetzel Publishing Co., Inc., Los Angeles, Calif., 1931.)

Mansfield, George C.: History of Butte County, California. (Historic Record Company, Los Angeles, 1918.)

Martin, Edward: History of Santa Cruz County, California. (Historic Record Company, Los Angeles, 1911.)

Maslin, Prentiss: Origin and Meaning of the Names of the Counties of California. In California Blue Book, pp. 338-344. (State Printing Office, Sacramento, 1909.)

Memorial and Biographical History of Northern California. (The Lewis Publishing Company, Chicago, 1891.)

Memorial and Biographical History of the Counties of Merced, Stanislaus, Calaveras, Tuolumne and Mariposa, California. (The Lewis Publishing Company, Chicago, 1892.)

Menefee, C. A.: Historical and Descriptive Sketch Book of Napa, Sonoma, Lake and Mendocino, Comprising Sketches of Their Topography, Productions, History, Scenery, and Peculiar Attractions. Reporter Publishing House, Napa City, 1873.)

Moreno, H. M.: Moreno's Dictionary of Spanish-Named California Cities and Towns. (n.p., 1916)

Morgan, Wallace M.: History of Kern County, California. (Historic Record Company, Los Angeles, California, 1914.)

Mott, Gertrude: A Handbook for Californiacs. A key to the meaning and pronunciation of Spanish and Indian place names. (Harr Wagner Publishing Co., San Francisco, 1926.)

Nevins, J. Allan: Fremont, the West's Greatest Adventurer. Being a biography from certain hitherto unpublished sources of General John C. Fremont, together with his wife Jessie Benton Fremont, and some account of the period of expansion which found a brilliant leader in The Pathfinder. 2 volumes. (Harper and Brothers, New York and London, 1928.)

PALOU, Francisco, Fray, O.F.M.: Historical Memoirs of New California. Edited by Herbert Eugene Bolton, 4 volumes. (University of California Press, Berkeley, California, 1926.)

PAUL, Rodman W.: California Gold: The Beginning of Mining in the Far West. (Harvard University Press, Cambridge, Mass., 1947.)

Pigne-Dupuytren, Dr. J. B.: Petit Dictionnaire Géographique de la Californie. In Almanach Français Pour 1860 à l'usage de la Population Française de la Californie. (Henry Payot, Libraire-Editeur; L. Albin, imprimeur. San Francisco, (n.d.).

Phillips, Michael James: History of Santa Barbara County, California. (The S. J. Clarke Publishing Col., Chicago, San Francisco, Los Angeles, 1927.)

Powers, Stephen: Tribes of California. In Contributions to North American Ethnology, Vol. 3. (Washington, 1877.)

Radcliffe, Corwin: History of Merced County. (A. H. Cawston, Merced, 1940.)

Raup, H. F.: Place Names of the California Gold Rush. Reprinted from the Geographical Review, Vol. XXXV, No. 4, pp. 653-658. (American Geographical Society, New York City.)

Reid, Hiram A.: History of Pasadena. (Pasadena History Company, Pasadena, 1895.)

Riesenberg, Felix: The Pacific Ocean. (McGraw-Hill Book Co., New York, 1940.)

Sabin, Edwin L.: Building the Pacific Railway. (J. B. Lippincott Company, Philadelphia and London, 1919.)

Salvator, Ludwig Louis: Los Angeles in the Sunny Seventies: A Flower From the Golden Land. (Bruce McCallister, Jake Zeitlin, Los Angeles, Ca., 1929.)

San Diego, A California City. Prepared by The San Diego Federal Writers' Project Works Progress Administration, State of California. American Guide Series. (The San Diego Historical Society, San Diego, Ca., 1937.)

Sanchez, Nellie Van De Grift: Spanish and Indian Place Names of California: Their Meaning and Their Romance. (A. M. Robertson, San Francisco, 1922.)

Scherer, James A. B.: The First Forty-niner, and the Story of the Golden Tea-caddy. (Minton, Balch & Company, New York, 1925.)

Shinn, Charles Howard: Mining Camps: A Study in American Frontier Government. (Charles Scribner's Sons, New York, 1885.)

Sixth Report of the United States Geographic Board: 1890 to 1932. (Government Printing Office, Washington, 1933.)

Small, Kathleen Edwards: History of Tulare County, California. (The S. J. Clarke Publishing Co., Chicago, 1926.)

133

Smythe, William E.: History of San Diego, 1542-1908. (The History Company, San Diego, California, 1908.)

Spanish Exploration in the Southwest, 1542-1706. Edited by Herbert Eugene Bolton. (Charles Scribner's Sons, New York, 1925.)

Steger, Gertrude A.: Place Names of Shasta County. (Redding Printing Co., Redding, California, 1945.)

Stewart, George R.: Names on the Land. (Random House, New York, 1945.)

Storke, Yda Addis, Mrs.: A Memorial and Biographical History of the Counties of Santa Barbara, San Luis Obispo, and Ventura, California. (The Lewis Publishing Company, Chicago, 1891.)

Tinkham, George H.: History of San Joaquin County, California. (Historic Recrod Company, Los Angeles, 1923.)

Tuomey, Honoria: History of Sonoma County, California. (The S. J. Clarke Publishing Co., Chicago, 1926.)

Underhill, Reuben L.: From Cowhides to Golden Fleece, A Narrative of California, 1832-1858, Based Upon Unpublished Correspondence of Thomas Oliver Larkin, etc. (Stanford University Press, Stanford University, California, 1939.)

Vancouver, George: A Voyage of Discovery to the North Pacific Ocean and Round the World, Etc., etc., etc. 3 volumes. G. G. and J. Robinson, Paternoster-row; and J. Edwards, Pall-Mall, London, 1798.)

Vallejo, Mariano G.: Report on the Derivation and Definition of the Names of the Several Counties of California. (H. H. Robinson, State Printer, San Jose, 1850.)

Wagner, Henry R.: Cartography of the Northwest Coast of America to the Year 1800. (University of California Press, Berkeley, California, 1937.)

Wagner, Henry R.: The Plains and the Rockies: A Bibliography of Original Narratives of Travel and Adventure, 1800-1865. Revised and extended by Charles L. Camp. (The Grabhorn Press, San Francisco, 1937.)

Wagner, Henry R.: Sir Francis Drake's Voyage Around the World: Its Aims and Achievements. (John Howell, San Francisco, California, 1926.)

Wagner, Henry R.: Some Imaginary California Geography. Reprinted from the Proceedings of the American Antiquarian Society for April, 1926. (American Antiquarian Society, Worcester, Massachusetts, 1926.)

Wagner, Henry R.: Spanish Voyages to the Northwest Coast of America in the Sixteenth Century. (California Historical Society, San Francisco, California, 1929.)

Waring, Gerald A.: Springs of California. (Government Printing Office, Washington, D.C., 1915.)

Watkins, Rolin G., Major, and Hoyle, M. F.: History of Monterey, Santa Cruz and San Benito Counties, California. (The S. J. Clarke Publishing Co., Chicago, 1925.)

Wheat, Carl I.: The Maps of the California Gold Region: 1848-1857: A Biblio-Cartography of an Important Decade. (The Grabhorn Press, San Francisco, 1942.)

Wheat, Carl I.: Trailing the Forty-Niners Through Death Valley. (Carl I. Wheat, San Francisco, 1939.)

Wheat, Carl I.: Books of the Gold Rush. (The Colt Press, San Francisco, 1949.)

Wheat, Carl I.: The Forty-Niners in Death Valley. A Tentative Census. Reprinted from the Quarterly, December, 1939, of the Historical Society of Southern California. (Los Angeles.)

Wheat, Carl I: Twenty-Five California Maps. (The Grabhorn Press, San Francisco, 1948.) Separate reprint of a chapter from Essays for Henry R. Wagner. (Grabhorn Press, San Francisco, 1948.)

Who's Who in California. Edited by Russell Holmes Fletcher. Vol. I. (Who's Who Publications Company, Los Angeles, 1941.)

Wilkes, Charles, U.S.N.: Narrative of the United States Exploring Expedition During the Years 1838, 1839, 1840, 1841, 1842. 5 volumes and atlas. (Lea and Blanchard, Philadelphia, 1845.)

Wyatt, Roscoe D.,: Names and Places of Interest in San Mateo County. (San Mateo County Title Company, Redwood City, California, 1936.)

Wyatt, Roscoe D. and Arbuckle, Clyde: Historic Names, Persons and Places in Santa Clara County. (San Jose Chamber of Commerce, San Jose, Ca., 1948.)

Zollinger, James Peter: Sutter: The Man and His Empire. (Oxford University Press, New York, 1939.)